Highest Courts and the Internationalisation of Law

Challenges and Changes

HAGUE COLLOQUIUM ON FUNDAMENTAL PRINCIPLES OF LAW

HIGHEST COURTS AND THE INTERNATIONALISATION OF LAW

Challenges and Changes

Edited by

Sam Muller and Marc Loth

Assistant Editor

Jantine de Goei

Hague Academic Press

An Imprint of T·M·C·ASSER PRESS

Published by Hague Academic Press, an imprint of T·M·C·Asser press
P.O.Box 16163, 2500 BD The Hague, The Netherlands

<www.asserpress.nl>

Hague Academic Press' English language books are distributed exclusively by:

Cambridge University Press, The Edinburgh Building, Shaftesbury Road,
Cambridge CB2 2RU, UK,
or
for customers in the USA, Canada and Mexico:
Cambridge University Press, 100 Brook Hill Drive, West Nyack, NY 10994-2133, USA

<www.cambridge.org>

The *Hague Colloquium on Fundamental Principles of Law* Series is based on the results of the bi-annual HCFPL Colloquium, which is an integral part of the Hague Prize for International Law. Held in honour of the Laureate its topic is selected by the Laureate and covers a fundamental principle of law. The Hague Colloquia are designed as high level expert workshops guided by multi-disciplinarity, where practice and academia meet.

ISBN 978-90-6704-288-8
ISSN 1877-279X

PREFACE

On 30 June and 1 July 2006 the *Hague Institute for the Internationalisation of Law* (HiiL) organized a Colloquium of sitting and former judges from highest courts and leading academics devoted to the changing role of highest courts in a world where law and society in general is internationalising. The Colloquium was part of the *Hague Colloquium on Fundamental Principles of Law* series, linked to the bi-annual Hague Prize.

This publication contains the reflection of the exchanges of views that were held. The rich discussions have not only resulted in this book, but have also formed the basis for a Conference that was held on the same topic in the Peace Palace on 23 and 24 October 2008. The proceedings of that Conference will build on the thoughts that were developed in this book. The 2006 meeting also became the platform on which a research project on the theme of *highest courts in a changing internationalised world* is being set up by HiiL.

The publication of this book would not have been possible without the help of many people. Besides the authors of the various contributions, the editors would in particular, like to thank Jantine de Goei and Elena Sabeva for the excellent editorial work they did. The team of T.M.C.ASSER PRESS deserves a special thank you for their enduring patience and coaching.

December 2008 Sam MULLER & Marc LOTH

TABLE OF CONTENTS

ABBREVIATIONS

All ER	All England Law Reports
BCLR	British Columbia Law Reports
BVerfGE	Bundesverfassungsgerichtsentscheidungen
CCP	Common Commercial Policy
CFI	Court of First Instance
CFSP	Common Foreign and Security Policy
CML Rev.	Common Market Law Review
EC	European Community
ECHR	European Convention on Human Rights
ECtHR	European Court of Human Rights
ECJ	European Court of Justice
ECR	European Court Reports
EEA	European Economic Area
EFA Rev.	European Foreign Affairs Review
EJIL	European Journal of International Law
EL Rev.	European Law Review
EPC	European Political Cooperation
EU	European Union
DLR	Dominion Law Reports
GATT	General Agreement on Tariffs and Trade
GYIL	German Yearbook of International Law
ICC	International Criminal Court
ICJ	International Court of Justice
ICTR	International Criminal Court for Rwanda
ICTY	International Criminal Tribunal for the former Yugoslavia
IDF	Israeli Defense Force
OJ	Official Journal of the European Communities/Union

NATO	North Atlantic Treaty Organisation
NGO	Non-governmental Organisation
NPP	Nuclear Power Plant
NYIL	Netherlands Yearbook of International Law
PCIJ	Permanent Court of International Justice
SCR	Supreme Court Reports
TEU	Treaty of the European Union
UN	United Nations
UNTS	United Nations Treaty Series
VCLT	Vienna Convention on the Law of Treaties
WLR	Weekly Law Reports
WTO	World Trade Organization
ZaöRV	Zeitschrift für ausländisches öffentliches Recht und Völkerrecht

HIGHEST COURTS AND THE INTERNATIONALISATION OF LAW: CHALLENGES AND CHANGES

A.S. Muller and M.A. Loth*

1. Introduction

Globalisation has a firm grip on our world as well as on our minds. We have become familiar with a world in which boundaries are less relevant and sometimes even not present. In many areas we are adjusting our concepts and ways of thinking and acting accordingly. In other fields, the process of thinking through what is really changing is only just under way. This publication contains the exchanges of views that took place at a colloquium which sought to identify the right questions related to the functioning of the highest national courts. On 30 June and 1 July 2006 a group of current and former judges of highest courts, together with leading academics, met for two days in the impressive *Gotische Zaal* of the Dutch *Raad van State* (Council of State) to debate the changing role of highest courts in an internationalising world.

National legal orders constantly interact with each other and with international and supranational law, with the effect of mutual influence and adjustment, but also conflict and compromise. National law has changed beyond recognition and cannot be studied in isolation from other legal systems, from whatever origin or content. As a consequence, a gradual process of adjusting

* M.A. Loth is Professor of Jurisprudence and Legal Theory, Erasmus University, Rotterdam, and was chairman of the conference. Dr A.S. Muller is the Director of the Hague Institute for the Internationalisation of Law (HiiL). The authors would like to thank Elaine Mak, Ph.D. candidate at the Erasmus University, Rotterdam, and Ramona Apostol, intern at HiiL, for their assistance in writing this introduction.

A.S. Muller and M.A. Loth (eds.), Highest Courts and the Internationalisation of Law

practices and theories is under way. Much of the focus, however, is on the consequences of the internationalisation of law (substantial or procedural) for national law. With a few notable exceptions, insufficient attention is being paid to consequences of this for our legal institutions and, most prominently, our highest judiciaries.

Traditionally highest courts have the task of safeguarding the unity of law within the territory of their jurisdiction, thus serving basic principles of law, such as equality before the law and legal certainty. 'Law' in this paradigm, is understood to mean national law (including international law as declared applicable through national constitutions). It is for this reason that most judiciaries are organised hierarchically, with a high or supreme court at the top, controlling the rulings of lower courts. This rather simple picture is thoroughly disturbed by the internationalisation of law, in several different ways.

First, the whole idea of unity of law has changed, since law includes also a considerable amount of law from international or supranational origin that is an integral part of the national legal systems involved through a variety of national constitutional provisions. This creates a plurality of legal sources of different origins and contents, partly complementary, partly overlapping, and sometimes even conflicting. Highest courts need to deal with this and navigate a more or less coherent route in concrete cases involving conflicting interests. The reality of the ever-increasing 'moveability' of the actors in the legal system (individuals, companies, etc.), adds a further dimension to this 'unity problem': not only must those highest national courts be coherent in interpreting the plurality of legal sources within their own legal system, they must also assure a degree of coherency in relation to other systems. It would be odd for an enterprise to be confronted with completely different interpretation of the same treaty provision in three different states in which it operates.

Next, there are complications of an institutional nature. The internationalisation of law and the challenges it creates for highest national courts raises serious questions which relate to their legitimacy. A number of aspects come to the fore. On the broadest level, questions arise regarding the relationship between the national judiciary and the legislature. While the legislature and the executive are involved in the lawmaking process on the international and supranational level (the details depending on national constitutional provisions), the judiciary has the last word in interpreting regulations, of whatever origin or content, into a coherent body of law. International legislation is often broadly formulated, leaving much room for interpretation in concrete cases and bestowing upon courts a degree of norm setting, as opposed to strict interpreting. Secondly, national courts are more easily put into the position where they need to look at 'foreign' precedents (either because there are no national precedents or because there are well-known strong foreign precedents which are hard to neglect). This raises questions as to the legitimacy of using precedents and referring to law that is not 'of the national system'. Another aspect of the questions which arise in the legitimacy context concerns the relationship between highest national courts and the international courts that hover above them. Highest courts are not alone any more, but are confronted with international or supranational courts, such as the European Court of Justice (ECJ) or the European Court of Human Rights (ECtHR). These courts play their own distinctive roles, of course, which is the result of the treaties by which they are constituted, as well as their own understanding of their role and function. As a result, highest courts not only have to reinvent their constitutional relationship with the national legislature, they also have to adjust their rulings as well as their self-image to even 'higher' courts (so to speak).

The context in which highest courts must function today has stimulated an impressive body of transnational judicial dialogue. Of course, comparative law has always been part and parcel of the daily work of judges. Highest courts do take each others' rulings into account, if not always explicitly, then at least implicitly. The internationalisation of law, however, has stimulated the emergence of a judicial transnational discourse, in which highest courts play a considerable role. 'Courts are talking to one another all over the world,' writes Anne-Marie Slaughter.[1] This raises interesting questions, of a theoretical as well as a practical nature. What forms does the judicial dialogue take? Who participates in this discourse? What role is played by new networks and what role by new technologies (notably the internet and other aspects of ICT)? What are its consequences for the relations between different courts and for the coherency of law itself?

2. The Colloquium

The colloquium was opened by the then Dutch Minister of Justice, H.E. Minister Piet Hein Donner. In his opening address, he highlighted the traditional

[1] A.-M. Slaughter, 'A typology of transjudicial communication', 29 *University of Richmond Law Review* (1994) p. 99.

relation between society, law and government and its evolution within an internationalised society. Traditionally, the effective functioning of law is considered to be strictly dependent on the existence of working social mechanisms and institutions and the purpose of law is to facilitate social interaction and channel it towards social morality. In this context, the role of supreme courts is that of guardians of the proper functioning of this complex process of interaction. In the present age, though, the pressure of globalisation challenges this paradigm of the nation state. Within this new reality, alternative versions of the principles of *trias politica* and democracy emerge. Despite major challenges, the emerging forms of multilevel governance perform the same functions as the traditional mechanisms; dispersion of power, separation of functions and systems of checks and balances. In this context, law can also continue performing its traditional function of influencing behaviour and implementing sets of moral values into the common consciousness. An important role in this respect is played by judicial networks, which, Donner underlines, must be viewed in connection to the other social ordering mechanisms of the national, as well as of the global community. And within these emerging judicial networks, the role of supreme courts shifts towards guarding the proper functioning of the interaction process between national and transnational and international levels.

Different aspects of the colloquium theme – as also set out above – were discussed in three sessions; one on coherency, one on legitimacy, and one on the transnational judicial dialogue.

2.1 Coherency

The first session concerned the question of 'Coherency; the Role of Highest Courts and Constitutional Provisions'. This question was dealt with from different perspectives by H.E. Judge Willibrord Davids, President of the Supreme Court of the Netherlands; Dr Antoine Garapon, Secretary General of the *Institut des Hautes Etudes sur la Justice*, Paris, speaking on behalf of H.E. Judge Olivier Dutheillet de Lamothe, Judge of the *Conseil d'Etat* of France; H.E. Judge Wilhelmina Thomassen, Judge of the Supreme Court of the Netherlands and former Judge of the European Court of Human Rights; H.E. Judge Ernst Hirsch Ballin, then Judge of the Dutch Council of State, President of the Administrative Law Division of the Council of State, and Professor of International Law (Tilburg University, the Netherlands); and Dr Robert Schütze, Lecturer on European Law (Durham University, UK).

Two main questions arose from the discussion on the theme of coherency. The first looked at what the notion of 'coherency' does or should mean. The second dealt with the manner in which, whatever definition one agrees on, it can be achieved. Concerning the first point, it was concluded that 'coherency' should not be equated with an almost perfect unity. It was argued that inconsistency in itself is not a bad thing and that therefore harmonisation measures should be directed at achieving compatibility rather than a perfect unity of legal provisions originating in different legal orders. In case of conflict of norms, the various existing national and international systems offer different solutions concerning the question of which norm should prevail. To reach 'coherency' in the defined sense, the 'willingness to cooperate in transnational dialogue' is a prerequisite, especially in the light of the proliferation of courts on the national and the international level. In this regard, it was also noted that supreme courts should acquire a greater responsibility regarding the implementation of international law. At the same time, the questions already referred to above, relating to the diversity of interpretations, the change of debate when a case is transferred from the national to the international level, the diversity of (legal) cultures, different sources of legitimacy and shifts in the separation of powers also surfaced.

2.2 **Legitimacy**

During the afternoon session, the question of 'The Paradigm of Separation and the Position of Highest Courts' was dealt with by H.E. Judge Mirjam Skrk, Vice-President of the Constitutional Court of the Republic of Slovenia; H.E. Judge Dorit Beinisch, Judge of the Supreme Court of Israeli; Dr Anton Hol, Professor of Legal Theory (Utrecht University, The Netherlands); and H.E. Judge Pauliine Koskelo, President of the Supreme Court of Finland.

The legitimacy of the judiciary was considered in the light of its role in a changing society. It was concluded that, given the diversification of powers within states, Montesquieu's characterisation of the judiciary as the '*bouche de la loi*' can no longer be maintained. The judiciary is the lynchpin between the general law and its application in a concrete case. In a society where the judiciary can – willingly or unwillingly – come closer to policy making, its legitimacy can no longer be mainly an 'input legitimacy,' concentrating on institutional measures justifying the resolution of conflicts by judicial authorities.[2] The 'output legitimacy', i.e., the justification of judicial decisions (among other things) through their motivation, is becoming more and more important, demanding more transparency, for example, through concurring and dissenting opinions. However, although the shift in the balance of power has resulted in a greater role for the judiciary, it still remains a balance, albeit one with changed nuances.

2.3 Transnational dialogue

The third and last session of the seminar dealt with the question of 'Transnational Interaction'. In this session, presentations were made by Professor Dieter Grimm, Professor of Public Law (Humboldt University of Berlin, Germany) and former Judge of the German Constitutional Court; H.E. Judge Anita Usăcka, Judge of the International Criminal Court and former Judge of the Constitutional Court of Latvia; Dr Andrea Lollini of the University of Bologna, Italy; Dr Carlos Ruiz Miguel, Professor of Constitutional Law (Santiago de Compostela University, Spain); and H.E. Judge Guy Canivet, President of the French *Cour de Cassation*.

The discussion focused on the tension between ways of interaction and limits to interaction. Concerning the ways of interaction, it was pointed out that, in a universalist interpretation, 'law' can be defined as a 'cross-boundary collection of general principles.' Such a perspective may provide the groundwork for the development of universalist jurisdictions. An interesting example that was brought forward in which the transnational judicial dialogue is officially sanctioned and widely used, is South Africa. There, the Statute of the Constitutional Court allows the use of certain aspects of foreign law as precedent, a power which has been creatively applied. Attention was also focused on the limits to transnational judicial interaction. They can be caused by legal authority and language, but also by the fact that national courts operate in a 'thick' cultural and legal context while international courts operate in a 'thinner' context. A further issue that came up concerned the framework in which the dialogue takes place: how does one avoid arbitrariness in borrowing arguments from foreign case law?

The question of the role of supreme courts in an internationalised world appears to feed two separate discussions at the same time. In the first place,

[2] M. de S.O.L'E. Lasser, *Judicial Deliberations, A Comparative Analysis of Judicial Transparency and Legitimacy* (Oxford University Press 2004).

a dialogue is taking place concerning the question of interpretation of provisions originating in different legal systems. In the second place, the formal relations between participants in this dialogue form a topic of discussion.

The inspiring exchanges of views during the colloquium have strengthened the conviction that the subject area forms a valuable field for further research and initiatives. It is hoped that this volume can act as an inspiration.

3. The Contributions

The contributions are discussed below, taking as a basis the three clusters of issues that formed the framework of the colloquium; coherency, legitimacy, and judicial dialogue. The first heading takes the perspective of the quest for coherency between different legal systems. The second heading looks at the changing role of supreme courts not so much from the perspective of the relations between legal systems, but rather of relations between different courts. In other words, the perspective shifts from substantial law to institutions. The third heading includes contributions which focus on the relationship between the interaction amongst courts and the coherency of law. In the final section, two contributions which deal with courts in exceptional circumstances are discussed.

3.1 The quest for coherency

In his contribution, H.E. Minister Ernst Hirsch Ballin analyses the evolution of the concept of supremacy, a key tool in ensuring the coherency of law. Supremacy in its most genuine form finds expression in dualistic national legal systems, such as in the USA. Here, the existence of a supreme court, with exclusive and full competence to decide on the interpretation of laws and on the extent of its own competence, is not only uncontested, but is even considered necessary. Within other national legal systems, though, the pressure of international and supranational legal orders gives rise to more relative forms of supremacy. Some national legal systems proclaim their national courts to be the final gatekeepers in relation to supra- or international courts, while others open their constitutions for the supremacy of supra- and international law. Yet other national legal systems do not perceive the relationship between courts in terms of absolute hierarchy, but rather in terms of complementary competences. The European legal order offers a relevant example of such a relation of judicial cooperation, within which supremacy is distributed depending on the extent of the material competence. This does not presuppose a shift of supremacy towards supranational levels, but rather a shift towards 'qualified precedence' or 'primacy'. In the context of interconnected legal orders, Minister Hirsch Ballin concludes, an absolute form of hierarchy is not a viable option anymore, and this relativisation of the concept of supremacy is a welcome development.

H.E. Judge Willibrord Davids addresses the provisions of the Dutch constitution on the relation between supranational and national law (particularly Article 94 of the Constitution). These provisions attribute preference to international law over Dutch law if, and only if, it concerns self-executing provisions. Whether this is the case is decided by the judiciary. For this, the wording of the provision at hand is of crucial importance, but not only its wording. By introducing some examples, Judge Davids argues that in case a general constitutional issue is the subject of an international treaty, it is considered to be the aim and purpose of that treaty to give it the effect of a self-executing provision, notwithstanding the fact that this may not be self-evident from a strict textual reading of the provision in question.

In a comparable fashion, H.E. Judge Olivier Dutheillet de Lamothe addresses the relation between European law and French law, particularly against the background of Article 88 of the French Constitution. Based on this provision, the Constitutional Council has ruled that 'the transposition of a Community directive into domestic law results from a constitutional requirement' and that 'the transposition of a directive cannot run counter to a rule or a principle inherent to the constitutional identity of France.' Since this position is also adopted by Spanish, Italian and German Constitutional Courts, De Lamothe concludes, the European Union has built up an 'ordered pluralism' (in the phrasing of Delmas-Marty).

Dr Robert Schütze addresses the relationship between European Community law and public international law. By declaring that the Community constitutes a new legal order, the European Court of Justice has chosen 'middle ground' between the international and national legal orders, which raises new questions. The first part of this contribution addresses the status and effect of international norms that are directly binding on the Community (for example, international agreements concluded by the Community, and customary international law). As a result of the Community's monist stance, international norms binding on the Community are also binding on the Member States as part of Community law. The second part considers the question of whether the Community considers itself bound by international agreements concluded by the Member States. It is argued that the Community legal order has acknowledged a doctrine of functional succession for international agreements concluded by all its Member States. Finally, the 'middle ground' position of the Community legal order is evaluated. In the light of the self-declared autonomy and identity of the Community legal order, the author is critical regarding the subordination of the Community to the UN Security Council (by the Court of First Instance, in the *Yusuf* case). This may re-open the debate on the ultimate arbiter of constitutionality in Europe. This debate had been settled in favour of the absolute supremacy of Community law due to 'constitutional guarantees' offered in exchange. Since no equivalent human rights protection is guaranteed on the international level, the chosen 'middle ground' requires that the Community legal order should be entitled to review United Nations law against European standards.

3.2 Legitimacy and the *trias politica*: the shift to courts

In the second series of contributions the focus is shifted to the courts as institutions. Minister Donner, in his opening speech, sets the framework for discussion, by portraying the general picture of the evolving role of law and of highest courts within increasingly internationalised societies.

In the same line, Professor Hol raises the increasing pressure on national courts to take into consideration foreign decisions and the role legitimacy plays as an underlying motivation. Professor Hol identifies the general reasons for national courts to refer to foreign decisions as the source of argumentation and the need of coherency of different legal orders, both pre-requisites of the overarching quest for legitimacy. Next, he focuses on types of legitimacy, on the legitimizing function of courts and the methodology to fulfil it. In a national context, the function of national courts to legitimise their decisions implies a mediation effort in solving/reducing tensions between the objective of law and the perceptions of citizens towards law and justice. The best methodology to fulfil this role is to use reasoning and persuasiveness, as within modern, democratic societies the authority of judicial decisions is not self-evident, but is increasingly under scrutiny. Therefore, explaining the rationale behind a judicial solution increases the legitimacy and the acceptance of the decision and avoids accusations of arbitrariness. In the context of globalisation, which stimulates internationalisation of law and trans-nationality, and increases consciousness of interdependence, foreign decisions are becoming more than just a source of inspiration. They are becoming a source of legitimacy. This is not only obvious in the application of international law, where national judges make efforts of consistency in order to avoid negative (economic) consequences, but also in the case of transnational law and even purely national decisions with an international impact. Ignoring new judicial developments cannot be an option for national judges without jeopardizing the legitimacy of the courts themselves. In this context, it is important to mention the difficulties of choosing the right foreign decisions in the quest for coherency and legitimacy, as there is no universal yard-stick for measuring rightness and judges do not possess a full insight into law and its moral implications within different legal systems. At the national level, supreme courts might perform this function of selection, but at the transnational level, the yardstick might be reasoning and persuasion through judicial dialogue and exchange of arguments.

Against the background of the general observations of the previous article, H.E. Judge Miriam Skrk highlights the role of the Constitutional Court of Slovenia as intermediary between national and international law, more particularly in the review and interpretation of international treaties. She demonstrates that it has a rather broad jurisdiction in this respect. The Constitutional Court is empowered to examine the constitutionality and legality of all abstract legal acts passed by the legislature, including laws and ratified treaties, governmental regulations, and abstract acts passed by local communities. It is also competent to examine the constitutionality of treaties before their ratification (*a priori* review) and to decide on complaints against judgments of regular courts under the proviso that all legal remedies have been exhausted. Case law with respect to *a priori* review of the constitutionality of treaties demonstrates that the Constitutional Court has substantively reviewed the challenged provisions of treaties in accordance with international law and its own case law. Concerning *a posteriori* review of treaties (indirect review), the case law of the Constitutional Court has been restrained despite the fact that the Court confirmed its jurisdiction to undertake such review. The case law of the Constitutional Court in this field, Judge Skrk concludes, points to the problems regarding international law which Slovenia as a relatively new state has faced.

In her contribution, H.E. Judge Wilhelmina Thomassen starts from the observation that the unifying role of national supreme courts has changed – as we noticed before – and asks what it takes to create order in the chaos of rules and regulations to ensure legal security. First and foremost, she advocates more knowledge of international law, including knowledge of its interpretation by other courts, as well as an activist approach in implementing international law in the national legal system, which in their turn require mutual consultation. Apart from the unifying role of supreme courts, there is also the role of providing for an effective remedy for individuals. Moreover, an activist attitude of a supreme court towards human rights constitutes a contribution to the debate on fundamental values at the national level and to the further interpretation of the European Convention on Human Rights, thus contributing to the freedom of individuals and society as a whole.

In his contribution, Professor Dieter Grimm, a former judge, is more critical about the role of the European Court of Human Rights. Against the background of the cases of *Princess Caroline of Monaco* and of *Görgülü*, Grimm discusses the question of whether differences exist between domestic courts and international courts that should lead to different judicial behaviour and role-perception. Grimm argues that the task of the Court is to be the guardian of the limits which the European Convention on Human Rights draws to state action in favour of individual freedom, but not to harmonise the law in the 46 States in its jurisdiction. That is why the margin of appreciation that States enjoy is such an important notion. In his view, the Court trespassed on that margin of appreciation in the *Caroline* case, since it did not strike the balance between competing interests, but imposed one extreme of the spectrum on Europe as a whole. He argues that, in comparison with domestic courts, the European Court of Human Rights has three disadvantages. First, the chambers system does not always guarantee consistency in its jurisprudence. Second, the judges of the Court do not have the full range of information about the case they have to decide, since the files of the national proceedings are not submitted to the Court. And thirdly, and connected with the latter point, the Court does not necessarily always have a full overview of the interests concerned and the arguments raised in the litigation; the losing party is represented, the winning party not. Contrary to the European Court of Human Rights, national courts do not only operate on the basis of a more developed national legal order and a shared method of interpretation, they also act within the context of a common legal culture, which is largely missing on the international level. As a result, specific interests and freedoms involved may be distorted, Professor Grimm concludes, as happened in the *Caroline* case.

In her contribution, H.E. Judge Pauliine Koskelo also addresses the role of Supreme Courts in the judicial system of modern societies. Against the background of the challenge of a growing complexity of the tasks of the Supreme Court, she focuses on the implications for the role of Supreme Courts in the context of international law, where Supreme Courts play a role as an 'intermediary' between complex non-domestic sources of law and the domestic administration of justice. As a result of the internationalisation of national law, a new role is to be identified for national judges, since they are called upon to ensure that supranational and international law is respected in the administration of justice. The guiding role for Supreme Courts can be summarised as 'ring the bell' and 'spread the message,' and asks for a more outward looking professional horizon. From this perspective, Judge Koskelo argues, it follows that transnational interaction between professionals of the judicial system is not only useful, but even necessary (both horizontally and vertically; both constructive as well as critical):

> Horizontal and vertical interaction across borders is needed in order for judges to understand their role and to help them adopt a professional identity and a mental approach that is in line with the demands and responsibilities that follow from the current, increasingly internationalised and multilayered system of legal sources.

3.3 **Judicial dialogue**

This brings us to the third series of contributions, on the relation between the coherence of law and judicial interaction. In her contribution, H.E. Judge Anita Usăcka links several concepts mentioned before, such as the concepts of globalisation, interaction and coherency. Starting with the observation that the globalisation of the judiciary has stimulated different kinds of interaction between judges – both horizontally and vertically – she rightly stresses that this presupposes as well as contributes to a universalist conception of law, implying that law is best understood as a body of principles which transcend national boundaries. She then deals with several anti-universalist arguments, rejecting them as inadequate and not convincing. Taking the International Criminal Court (ICC) as example, Judge Usăcka shows how the law it applies is constituted by general principles derived from the national law of the legal systems of the world. Also, procedurally, the ICC leans heavily on the experience of other international criminal courts, such as the International Criminal Court for the former Yugoslavia (ICTY), the International Criminal Court for Rwanda (ICTR), or the Special Court for Sierra Leone. She concludes by emphasizing the advantages of both horizontal and vertical dialogue between national and international courts. It allows judges to share expertise and to improve the quality of their jurisprudence, but the importance of judicial dialogue goes beyond that: 'Moreover, they allow for the creation and implementation of common values, which are shared among the societies worldwide and are not limited to a particular legal system,' Judge Usăcka writes. She further asserts that 'by globally enforcing general principles of law, both international courts and domestic courts foster the coherency of the law, both on the domestic level as well as on the international level.'

The notion of judicial dialogue is placed at the centre of the contribution of H.E. Judge Guy Canivet: 'Courthouses become the place of an organised dialogue where everyone can represent his or her arguments, get to know his or her rights and make the law evolve'. Judge Canivet continues by specifying the challenges highest courts face in making the law coherent, which implies the reconciliation of the internal and international order, the competition of legal systems, solving social phenomena, and European harmonisation. For this purpose new methods and instruments are developed by (*inter alia*) the *Cour de Cassation.* Examples are; systems to ensure up-to-date knowledge of European jurisprudence, capacity for research into comparative law, the development of international databases for access to foreign jurisprudence (such as the Francophone base JURICAF, the portal to European case law), and participation in the network of Supreme Court Presidents (to create a discussion forum, reinforce mutual relations, work on shared subjects of the courts involved, and contribute to the judicial architecture of Europe and to build relations with the EU institutions). Judge Canivet concludes by including in the judicial dialogue also the very symposium of which this book is the result:

> The vocation of the Hague Institute for the Internationalisation of Law and the subject of the symposium naturally suggest that the European and International networks of professors, of researchers and the networks of judges create a veritable cooperation'.

3.4 **Case studies**

H.E. Judge Dorit Beinisch sketches an impressive picture of the role of the Israeli Supreme Court in the fight against terrorism. 'A democracy that ignores basic principles of human rights', Judge Beinisch writes, 'is liable to give terrorism the victory it seeks.' Starting from this basic assumption, the Israeli Supreme Court tries to uphold principles of law, international (humanitarian) law included, in the face of war and terror. Four aspects of judicial review make the Court particularly responsive to the needs of our time, namely (1) broad access to justice, (2) judicial review exercised in real time, rather than retrospectively, (3) the status as the highest court of the land, and (4) the use of international law as both substantive law and interpretive guide. Several examples show the Court's critical potential of review, even against the Israeli executive and military. In the many cases concerning the legal consequences of the construction of the separation fence (the so-called 'Wall'), the Court has showed itself willing to apply international standards, as interpreted by the International Court of Justice (ICJ), though it developed a more nuanced approach for the great variety of cases. 'In exercising judicial review,' Judge Beinisch concludes, 'the Court's basic premise is that the law is not silent before the guns of war.'

Dr Lollini, in his contribution, examines in detail how judges communicate with foreign jurisdictions, taking the Canadian Supreme Court and the South African Constitutional Court as examples. The Canadian court is of importance since it very often uses foreign law or extra-systematic parameters in its judgments. The South African Constitutional Court is of special importance because of a constitutional provision (Article 39 of the 1996 Constitution), stating that the Constitutional Court, when interpreting the Bill of Rights, *must* promote the 'values that underlie an open and democratic society', *must* consider international public law and *may* take foreign law into consideration. Clearly, the South African Constitutional Court is supposed to be in need of legitimacy and examples, as part of a phase of legal and cultural learning. Dr Lollini continues by showing that these courts use a special technique for comparison, referred to as the 'setting of two extremes' technique. The courts introduce in their reasoning two extremes consisting of foreign constitutional interpretations of similar cases and principles. The two extremes limit the range of interpretation, and facilitate the choice of one of the two alternatives or, on the contrary, an in-between position. The subsequent analysis of two examples where the aforementioned courts use this technique illustrates that it facilitates both the limitation of the playing field, and the introduction of specific legal or extra-legal characteristics of the situation in the given legal system. At the same time, of course, it implies the participation in a discourse between different courts, and the combined effort to elaborate on a universal corpus of legal principles and precedents.

4. Conclusion

The contributions to this volume differ in subject, perspective and conclusion. In fact, they display the diversity of the international community that their writers represented at the conference. However different their focus is, though, they linger on a coherent set of topics and issues. And what is more important, they all referred (explicitly or implicitly) to what might be called a shared picture of what internationalised law is and will be, what the responsibility of highest courts is in that regard (however different their responsibilities may be), and what this means for the legal community involved, and even the international community at large. This shared picture is well drawn in the article of Anne-Marie Slaughter. According to Slaughter, the transnational discourse presupposes certain common elements. First, there is a shared self-image of the courts as autonomous and independent. Next, there is a greater reliance on persuasive than on coercive authority, that is, authority which attracts adherence as opposed to obliging it. Third, there is a conception of a common judicial enterprise, a shared conviction of rule of law values, enhanced by common methods of legal reasoning. This discourse creates a true transnational community, next to the existing ideological, cultural and social ones. Slaughter leaves us with the following picture:

> Imagine a world of regular and interactive transjudicial communication – among national courts, between national courts and supranational tribunals, and among supranational tribunals. It would be a world in which courts perceived themselves independent of, although linked to, their fellow political institutions, open to persuasive authority, and engaged in a common enterprise of interpreting and applying national and international law, protecting individual rights, and ensuring that power is corralled by law. National differences would be recognised and often given priority, but would not obscure common problems nor block the adoption of foreign solutions. Courts would relate to one another in ways that would circumvent and constrain other branches of national governments and that could forge an independent link between national and international institutions. In this conception, the phenomenon of transjudicial communication is a pillar of a compelling vision of global legal relations. It is a vision that is particularly potent in the human rights field, but potentially extends to all fields.[3]

To a certain extent this picture was shared by the participants in the conference, discussing the judicial dialogue and at the same time conducting it.

---

[3] Slaughter, loc. cit. n. 1, at p. 132.

Perhaps it was this that contributed to the constructive spirit essential for fertile debate. In any case, it was a fertile debate, and the volume before you is the fruit of it.

SUPREME COURTS IN AN INTERNATIONALISED WORLD

Opening speech by J.P.H. Donner*

EXCELLENCIES, LADIES AND GENTLEMEN,

Less than nine months ago, I had the privilege to speak in this magnificent hall, the Gothic Hall of the Council of State, on the occasion of the official start of the Hague Institute for the Internationalisation of Law – an institute that is to play a leading role as a pioneer research institute for questions on the internationalisation of law. The present colloquium, with an exciting, topical and challenging subject, an impressive list of prominent speakers, and an honourable audience, is proof of its ambitions. I am sorry that I will not be able to attend the entire colloquium. If I speak rapidly, I may still finish this address before the Prime Minister visits the Queen and puts my function at the disposal of the Queen, so it will be my last address in office.

This seminar will examine the role that supreme courts are to play in the ongoing process of internationalisation of law, and the concomitant questions regarding their legitimacy, autonomy and the separation of powers. Organised society as we know it is unthinkable without law and legislation. The intimate relation between society, law and government is expressed in the earliest histories of nations. Thus, Herodotus tells us of the creation of the Median nation by a wise and skilful judge, Deiocus. To realise his ambition to become king of the Medians he started by travelling throughout the country in order to settle disputes as a judge. In this way he became famous throughout the territory of the Medians. People travelled from afar in order to submit cases to his judgment. In the end he was virtually the only accepted

* H.E. Minister Donner was the Minister of Justice of the Netherlands at the time of the Colloquium.

A.S. Muller and M.A. Loth (eds.), Highest Courts and the Internationalisation of Law

judge in the country. Then he went on strike, arguing that he did not even have time to deal with his own affairs. As the country rapidly reverted to chaos and mayhem, people came to offer Deioces the crown. He did not accept immediately. But as the pressure increased he indicated that he would accept if the people would first build him a palace and a capital. Thus the capital of Media, Ecbatana, was built and Deioces became king.

As often, the history of Herodotus looks more like legend than true facts, though in the end they always appear to contain more truth than seems to be the case at first sight. But whether it is true or not, the story of Deioces illustrates the relation between society, law and government. Organised society needs all kinds of mechanisms and institutions in order to function and allow individuals to live together in peace and cooperate for mutual benefit. They constitute what could be considered the social capital; norms, markets, associates and innumerable other forms of organisation and coordination. Rights and statutory law create the opportunity for these social mechanisms to function, but at the same time they cannot exist without these social mechanisms.

The effectiveness of law, and indeed, the viability of the democratic and constitutional state, depend on the extent to which citizens are prepared and willing to cooperate. If the state does not want to revert to large-scale coercion, of which it is probably not capable anyway, it is required that the great majority of the population more or less voluntarily complies with the most important rules, which again presupposes civic engagement, horizontal and vertical trust, a set of shared values and a sense of a common fate, briefly: moral attitudes.

The question of where these moral attitudes come from, has been raised in Western philosophy since Socrates. He argued that in the end each individual is the final arbiter between good and evil. Morality cannot be enforced, it can only be guided or supported. Moral insights can only be found through reflection and consent of the person involved. Moral attitudes cannot be organised; a sense of public responsibility cannot be imposed; trust cannot be enforced. Thus, the prerequisites for the vitality of a society cannot be produced on purpose. A complicated situation, captured by the former judge of the German *Bundesverfassungsgericht*, Ernst-Wolfgang Bockenforde, in one phrase:

> The liberal, secular state lives from presuppositions which it cannot itself guarantee.

Social morality and moral attitudes come about as a by-product of social interaction. Law, indeed government as a whole, is meant to serve and facilitate this interaction and the growth of these moral attitudes – on which they depend for their own functioning. But law can as easily frustrate this growth and turn it into a downward spiral. In the end laws and governments should be judged by this effect, whether they promote or frustrate this process of social interaction and moral attitudes.

At the national level, we have developed procedures, institutions and systems of such complexity that we sometimes forget that they depend on these social mechanisms and moral attitudes, and that their ultimate reason is to facilitate peaceful society and social interaction that is more than a zero sum. Democracy, the rule of law, constitutionalism and the division of powers all are meant to support this process and to prevent it from stagnation. The judiciary, and the supreme courts at the pinnacle of the judicial system, are often in many respects the guardians of the proper functioning of this process, and of the coherence and stability of the national systems.

In the present age we are faced by this complex phenomenon of globalisation, worldwide social interaction and concomitant problems, and by the internationalisation of law. All of a sudden, this precious precision clockwork seems to have become obsolete. Or can the same clockwork be reproduced at the international or even global level – a world state, with a global government, an international court with worldwide jurisdiction and a unified legal order? This seems a quite remote possibility, and to me altogether undesirable as well.

Ours are interesting times. Surely, we will have to look for other solutions than the precision clockwork type. In this quest we will encounter devilish dilemmas; between unity and diversity, predictability and chaos, coherence and fragmentation, structure and process, frozen and fluid. Multilevel thinking seems to become one imperative, as well as thinking in terms of governance – and governability – instead of government. At the national level, the role of governments can be seen as a hierarchical regulator, as well – and more and more – as a coordinating provider of frameworks. At the international level we will we have to develop and rely on new forms of governance without government, while for the time being the question will be: how governable is the global society?

Similarly, there is a need to organise the interaction of different national legal systems and international law-making organisations, both horizontally and vertically.

What about the *trias politica* and the democratic legitimacy of law in this context? Maybe we find a clue to answering the previous questions while responding to this latter one. A democratic state and the *trias politica*, as I stated before, should be understood as mechanisms to disperse power. Again, let us try not to focus on the forms but on their purpose – dispersion of power over multiple actors, separation of functions, systems of checks and balances, and all this, in order to enable fruitful social interaction between individuals and communities.

Surely, at the international level we should not look for possibilities to reproduce the old forms, but we have to be alert and be able to identify emerging new ways to perform those functions; dispersion of power and systems of checks and balances. On the international scene, a multitude of actors, old and new, have made their appearance, interacting and networking; information spreads in no time and worldwide.

Civil society, non-governmental organisations, lobby and pressure groups, good governance, naming and shaming, corporate social responsibility for people and planet, democracy understood as contestatory power, sovereignty understood as responsibility – those are just a few catchwords that describe this new reality, harbouring exciting opportunities for installing new, probably loosely structured, forms of dispersion of power and systems of checks and balances. Present day transnational judicial reality is an exciting one.

To conclude. On the one hand, globalisation is to be understood as an intensification of social interaction that poses new challenges for governance, coordination and problem resolution. On the other hand, law is meant to serve and facilitate social interaction and thereby the coming about and reproduction of moral attitudes. It influences behaviour and interaction, to perform in more beneficial ways, and reflects and installs shared sets of values in the common consciousness.

Within this broad context, I would like to maintain that law still can perform its traditional functions – as a guarantor of predictability, an objective measuring standard, and a clear guide for behaviour – provided that it is narrowly linked to, and interacting with, the other social ordering mechanisms. This implies that the multiple relations of law with the societal dynamics are clearly perceived, understood, and processed accordingly.

Clearly, we should focus our attention not only on the various legal systems of different societies, and the ways that they are – and are to be – linked, but also on the various and dynamic social ordering mechanisms linked to them, as well as on the social ordering mechanism of the global community.

In the emerging complex and multilevel judicial network, the supreme courts have an important role to play, being the hub between the national and the trans- and international levels, provided with extensive connections on either side. I wish you all the success you need in your exciting and significant quest.

Part I
The Quest for Coherency

SUPREME COURTS IN AN INTERNATIONALISED WORLD: CHALLENGES FOR THE *TRIAS POLITICA* AND THE COHERENCY OF LAW?

E.M.H. Hirsch Ballin*

Supremacy is a bothersome concept. It sounds absolute but, in terms of human activity, it always relates to a specific domain. Those who consider themselves *supreme* usually look more kindly on it than those who are *subordinate*. Nevertheless, within a national legal order, having a supreme court that ensures the uniformity of the law is often seen as a theoretical and practical necessity.

This view is related to the idea that legal systems are closed and self-sufficient, delimited by specific rules of recognition. Standards that apply within another legal system, that of international law, for example, have no legal force in a national legal order unless one of the rules of recognition says that they do – subject to certain conditions. In this context, it is appropriate to have a supreme court that is exclusively and fully competent to decide on the validity and interpretation of legal standards. Should there be more than one such body, with complementary jurisdiction, then, according to this view, a rule of recognition should indicate which body is competent to decide on the demarcation of powers between them.

The United States Supreme Court provides a practical and significant example of this type of arrangement. Although it has to accept internal restrictions on its jurisdiction in relation to the federal states, it is itself the ultimate arbiter in any disputes in this area. Furthermore, as the highest federal court

* H.E. Minister Hirsch Ballin is the current Minister of Justice of the Netherlands and is a former Judge of the Dutch Council of State and Professor of International Law at Tilburg University, The Netherlands.

A.S. Muller and M.A. Loth (eds.), Highest Courts and the Internationalisation of Law

of the Union, it rules on all areas of law, including the interpretation of the Constitution, and of treaties, which according to that same Constitution form part of the 'supreme Law of the Land'. Article VI, Section 2 of the US Constitution formulates this *supremacy clause* (the 'linchpin of the Constitution') as follows:

> This Constitution, and the Laws of the United States which shall be made in Pursuance thereof; and all Treaties made, or which shall be made, under the Authority of the United States, shall be the supreme Law of the Land; and the Judges in every State shall be bound thereby, any Thing in the Constitution or Laws of any State to the Contrary notwithstanding.

The first sentence of Article III, Section 1, states, accordingly, that there will be a single highest court for the interpretation of the 'Law of the Land':

> The judicial Power of the United States shall be vested in one supreme Court, and in such inferior Courts as the Congress may from time to time ordain and establish.

It is clear that this view of supremacy fits perfectly with the traditional concept of the fully sovereign state. Indeed, the words *supremacy* and *sovereignty* come from the same root. In the modern world, however, the supremacy of a single judicial body is increasingly difficult to maintain. Both the international legal order and supranational legal orders are exerting growing pressure on national systems to conform to the rulings of external bodies such as the International Court of Justice and the European Court of Justice, on national law and its application as well as on international questions. From the national vantage point, people sometimes try to argue that the national courts, as gatekeepers, have the last word (see, for example, the *Solange* case law of the German Federal Constitutional Court). It is also possible for national constitutions to open the door, as it were, for international and supranational law (see Articles 92 to 94 of the Dutch Constitution), but they can no longer claim genuine supremacy. It is now accepted in Dutch case law, for example, that provisions of European law fall outside the scope of Article 93 and 94 of the Constitution and by themselves have direct effect.

For other reasons too, the concept of the supremacy of judicial bodies requires qualification. Our French colleagues present here today represent the *Cour de Cassation* and the Council of State. Both are the highest courts in their respective fields, but have no hierarchical relationship to each other. The same kind of arrangement exists in the Netherlands and other countries where jurisdiction is divided according to legal domain. While each of these courts is supreme in its own field, their judges know that in other fields their counterparts in the country's other highest court (or even the European Court of Justice or the European Court of Human Rights) have the last word in interpreting legal norms. Although this system is unwieldy, it has the advantage of limiting the subject-matter competence required of any individual. Even the best judges are human, and have their limitations.

Does this perhaps imply a shift of supremacy towards supranational levels, so that the European Court of Justice, for example, is now the supreme court of the European Union? I believe that conclusion would be mistaken. According to EU law, it takes qualified precedence over national law, rather than being by definition superior. European and national law act in concert. Depending on the field of application, European law may take precedence over national law, or national law may give effect to European law. For this reason Article I-6 of the Treaty establishing a Constitution for Europe – signed but destined, probably, never to come into force – avoided the word *supremacy* in describing the relationship between the law of the European Union and that of the Member States:

> The Constitution and law adopted by the institutions of the Union in exercising competences conferred on it shall have primacy over the law of the Member States.

Accordingly, the ECJ sees itself more as a partner in judicial cooperation than as the supreme court of the EU. Nor is it really possible any more to impose a hierarchical structure on public international law, either for the national courts or for the European courts (see for instance the judgment of the Court of First Instance, given on 21 September 2005, case T-306/01).

These examples are but a few of many. In fact, the term *primacy* is a useful one since it leaves room for different assessments of precedence in specific situations, while *supremacy* suggests a hierarchical structure. But to the extent that *supremacy* is still a meaningful term, it has become a very relative concept in twenty-first-century law – a fact that we need not be at all unhappy about.

THE DUTCH CONSTITUTION AND THE SUBORDINATION OF NATIONAL LEGISLATION IN CONFLICT WITH PROVISIONS OF INTERNATIONAL TREATIES

W.J.M. Davids*

For national judges it is of great importance to know when and how to regard regulations of public international law. It is relatively simple for judges to recognise whether private international law is applicable in a certain case, when in relations subject to private law international aspects such as different nationalities or places of residence of parties are at stake in one way or another. Provisions of public international law can also be applicable in cases of just a national character. The Dutch Constitution contains an article that deals with this topic:

> Statutory regulations in force within the Kingdom shall not be applicable if such application is in conflict with provisions of treaties that are binding on all persons or of resolutions by international institutions.[1]

As far as I know this provision is rather unique; a similar one cannot be found in most other constitutions. The provision is also remarkable for another reason. In the Netherlands judges are not allowed to give preference to the Constitution above a law adopted by parliament.[2] In the Dutch view it is up to the legislative authorities – the Council of Ministers, the Council of State and both houses of the Parliament – and not up to the judge to ensure that a law is in conformity with the Constitution.

* H.E. Judge Davids is President of the Supreme Court of the Netherlands.

[1] Article 94 Dutch Constitution.

[2] Article 120 Dutch Constitution: 'The constitutionality of Acts of Parliament and of treaties shall not be reviewed by the courts.'

A.S. Muller and M.A. Loth (eds.), Highest Courts and the Internationalisation of Law

However, as has been noted already, it is up to the judge to ensure that a law is not in conflict with provisions of treaties that are binding on all persons or resolutions by international institutions. This provision has a long history. It is beyond the bounds of the time allotted to me to go into further detail about this history. The first fundamental debate in Parliament was around 1950, at the time a new constitution was prepared. In these same years, shortly after World War II, one may observe that treaties of more general, almost constitutional, interest came into force; a development that has not stopped since.

In the first place I mention the European Convention on Human Rights, yet a number of other treaties belong to this category as well. These were treaties to prevent all manner of atrocities which were experienced during the war, such as forced labour, torture, discrimination, abuse of more vulnerable people like women and children, etc. It is obvious that treaties of this kind contend with topics which (similar to human rights) often find a place in constitutions of a classical enlightened nature. They are of a different character than the more specific treaties which aim to regulate more specific issues, for instance, taxation in international relations, environmental standards, rates of air traffic, or alimony in favour of children.

Treaties of a general, constitutional nature are formulated in general terms. This circumstance makes them less fit to be seen as self-executing or 'binding on all persons' as laid down in the Dutch Constitution. On the other hand, as a consequence of the topic itself, these 'constitutional' treaties deserve to have preference above a national law. Without such preference the very nature of these treaties would be neglected. A certain vagueness in the wording of a treaty cannot be decisive for the question whether the treaty is self-executing or not. In my view, national constitutional law and public international law, as far as human rights and democratic values are concerned, are of the same nature and must be handled in an equal manner in the national field.

To illustrate this I will give some examples derived from Dutch national practice. In the Netherlands there is a political party with an orthodox Christian protestant reformed basis. According to the bylaws of this party, on religious grounds only men, not women, are allowed to obtain membership. Due to the fact that this party is represented in Parliament it obtains financial support from the government on the basis of a national law. Several institutions, most of which are directed towards the protection of women's rights, submitted a request to the County Court of The Hague[3] seeking a decision that the financial support from the Dutch government is in conflict with Article 7(a) and (c) of the international Convention on the Elimination of All Forms of Discrimination against Women which reads:

> States Parties shall take all appropriate measures to eliminate discrimination against women in the political and public life of the country and, in particular, shall ensure to women, on equal terms with men, the right:
> (a) To vote in all elections and public referenda and to be eligible for election to all publicly elected bodies;
> [...]
> (c) To participate in non-governmental organisations and associations concerned with the public and political life of the country.

We can see that even the wording of this provision, 'States Parties shall take all appropriate measures...', indicates that it is directed to the Parties. Nevertheless, the County Court applied Article 94 of the Constitution and gave preference to the rather vague wording of Article 7 of the Convention that is addressed to the States Parties to the Convention.

There are numerous other examples of a similar character. In a case of the extradition of a person suspected of drug-related offences to the United States, the Dutch Supreme Court gave preference to the applicable extradition Treaty over the national law on extradition.[4] The national law states that a Dutch national will not be extradited unless that person is allowed to return to the Netherlands for the execution of his sentence in his own country. The applicable extradition Treaty, however, did not contain such limitation.

On the basis of Article 26 of the International Covenant on Civil and Political Rights, the Special Court on Social Security Matters decided that – contrary to the regulations of national law – not only widows but also widowers were entitled to receive a pension. This decision was taken notwithstanding the very complicated technical consequences of actuarial science and considerable financial consequences for public funds.

In a refugee case, the Dutch Supreme Court concluded that Article 33 of the Convention relating to the Status of Refugees, which concerns the prohi-

---

[3] Rechtbank 's-Gravenhage, 7 September 2005, LJN: AU 2088, HA ZA 03/3395.
[4] Centrale Raad van Beroep, 7 December 1988, LJN: AK 8481.

bition of expulsion or return, is self-executing based on its aim and purpose.[5]

I would like to conclude that in Dutch case law the following growing tendency can be observed. Where a general, constitutional issue is subject to an international treaty, it is the aim and purpose of such a treaty that make it self-executing, notwithstanding the more general terms in which the treaty was written. Where a specific issue is at stake within a treaty, the wording of such a treaty is of major importance in determining whether the treaty may be considered as self-executing.

[5] Hoge Raad, 13 May 1988, LJN: AD 0305.

THE PRIMACY OF COMMUNITY LAW OVER NATIONAL CONSTITUTIONS: THE CASE OF FRANCE

O. Dutheillet de Lamothe*

The French Constitution has been amended to allow the ratification of the Treaty of Maastricht. It now provides for a specific constitutional basis for the European Community. According to Article 88-1 of the Constitution:

> The Republic shall participate in the European Communities and in the European Union constituted by States which have freely chosen, under the treaties that established them, to exercise some of their powers in common.

In an important decision of 10 June 2004, the Constitutional Council ruled that it follows from Article 88-1 of the Constitution that 'the transposition of a Community directive into domestic law results from a constitutional requirement.'[1] This has two consequences: one negative, the other positive.

On the one hand, the Council has ruled that it has no jurisdiction to review the conformity to the Constitution of legislative provisions 'which merely draw the necessary conclusions from the unqualified and precise provisions of the directive'. The reason for this is that only the European Court of Justice has jurisdiction to review the conformity of a Community regulation to both the treaties, in terms of the powers established, and Article 6 of the Treaty on European Union[2] in terms of the fundamental rights guaranteed.

On the other hand, the Constitutional Council, to which referral has been made for review of a statute designed to transpose a Community directive into domestic law, is under a duty to comply with this constitutional require-

* H.E. Judge Dutheillet de Lamothe is Judge of the *Conseil d'Etat* of France.

[1] Decision No. 2004-496 DC, 10 June 2004, *Journal Officiel* 22 June 2004, p. 11182.

[2] Article 6 amended by the Treaty of Nice in 2001

A.S. Muller and M.A. Loth (eds.), Highest Courts and the Internationalisation of Law

ment. Since it is required by the Constitution to give a ruling within one month, the Constitutional Council may only find a statutory provision unconstitutional under Article 88-1 of the Constitution if this provision is 'obviously incompatible with the directive which it is intended to transpose.'[3]

The Constitutional Council has expressly ruled that 'the transposition of a directive cannot run counter to a rule or principle inherent to the constitutional identity of France', for example, the principle of secularism in the French meaning of the word.

This position of the French Constitutional Council is similar to the position adopted by the Spanish, Italian, and German constitutional courts. The Spanish Constitutional Tribunal has ruled in its decision of 13 December 2004 on the conformity to the Constitution of the Treaty establishing a Constitution for Europe that Article I-5 of the Treaty consecrates the guarantee of the existence of the Member States and of their fundamental structures as well as their values, principles and fundamental rights which could in no way be infringed by the transfer of powers to the European Community.[4] The Italian Constitutional Court, which thoroughly recognises the primacy of Community Law, has reserved the right to safeguard 'the supreme principles of the Italian legal order.'[5] The German Constitutional Court had paved the way. According to its case law, which has developed gradually, the German Constitutional Court has ruled that as long as the European Court of Justice exercises review of the respect for fundamental rights at the Community level, it does not have to control whether a Community law violates the fundamental rights guaranteed by the German Constitution. However, this renunciation to review remains conditional.[6]

Consequently, the process of Community integration has built up, to quote the beautiful words of Mrs Delmas-Marty, an 'ordered pluralism': a pluralism of national legal orders integrated into one single Community legal order. The national values proper to each Member State mark the limits of this integration. It is this basic reality that Article I-5 of the Treaty establishing a Constitution for Europe recognises:

> The Union shall respect the national identities of its Member States, inherent in their fundamental structures, political and constitutional [...]

---

[3] Decision No. 2006-540 DC, 27 July 2006, *Journal Officiel* 3 August 2006, p. 11541.

[4] Declaration 13 December 2004, DTC 1/2004, *Boletín Oficial del Estado*, No. 3, 4 January 2005.

[5] Corte Constituzionale, Sentenza No. 232, 13 April 1989.

[6] *Solange I*, BVerfGE 37, Judgment of 29 May 1974.

ON MIDDLE GROUND – EUROPEAN COMMUNITY LAW AND PUBLIC INTERNATIONAL LAW*

R. Schütze**

1. Introduction: Foreign Affairs and European Constitutional Law

Foreign affairs are 'border' affairs – in a geographical and a constitutional sense. Traditionally, they are subject to distinct legal principles, for the political questions posed might not be susceptible to judicial answers.[1] In a similar vein, international law may not automatically be domestic law, for a national legal order might require prior domestic 'validation' before it could pass the national legal border.[2] In our globalised world of intense international economic interdependence, the traditional distinctions between 'internal' and 'external' affairs has lost much of its nineteenth-century clarity. Today, international treaties play a decisive role in international coordination, and the establishment of international organisations has solidified the transition from an international law of co-existence to a cooperative international law.[3] The constitutional response of many national legal orders – in particular, of their supreme courts – has, therefore, been to 'open up' to international law.

The European Community embodies that cooperative spirit on a regional international scale. The Treaty of Rome (1957) formed part of international

* In honour of Sir F.G. Jacobs. I would like to thank C. Warbrick, J. Murkens, A. Dashwood, B. de Witte, M. Cremona, A. Antoniadis and the organisers of the Hague Colloquium.

** Dr Robert Schütze is Lecturer on European Law, Durham University, United Kingdom.

[1] T.M. Franck, *Political Questions/Judicial Answers* (Princeton University Press 1992).

[2] H. Triepel, *Völkerrecht und Landesrecht* (Leipzig, C.L. Hirschfeldt 1899).

[3] W.G. Friedmann, *The Changing Structure of International Law* (London, Stevens 1964).

A.S. Muller and M.A. Loth (eds.), Highest Courts and the Internationalisation of Law

law, although the European Court of Justice was eager to emphasise that the 'Community constitutes a new legal order of international law.'[4] 'By contrast with ordinary international treaties, the EC Treaty has created its own legal system which, on the entry into force became an integral part of the legal systems of the Member States and which their Courts are bound to apply.'[5] However, what was the relationship between the new legal order and the *old* legal order of international law? '[T]he Community's founding fathers ha[d] kept silent about the effects of international law in the Community legal order.'[6] Would the Community legal order constitute a (closed) 'self-contained regime' or would it be an 'open system'?[7]

If Community law were merely regional international law, the question of the status and effect of international law within the Community legal order would have to be answered by international rules on the conflict of treaties and by principles governing the internal law of international organisations. 'In contrast, the conception of Community law as a distinct body of law compels an altogether different approach.'[8] Has the Community legal order thus assumed an 'autonomous' position *vis-à-vis* international law?

This chapter will analyse the European Community's relationship with public international law. Importantly, the Community's constitutional choice will have a federal dimension: 'Interposing itself, in many areas, between

---

[4] *NV Algemene Transport- en Expeditie Onderneming van Gend & Loos v. Netherlands Inland Revenue Administration*, Case 26-62 [1963] ECR 1, 12.

[5] *Flaminio Costa* v. *E.N.E.L.*, Case 6/64 [1964] ECR 585, 593.

[6] J. Klabbers, 'International law in Community law: the law and politics of direct effect', 21 *Yearbook of European Law* (2001) p. 263 at p. 271.

[7] On the theory of self-contained regimes in international law, see: B. Simma, 'Self-Contained Regimes', 16 *NYIL* (1985) p. 111, defining the concept as 'a category of agreements, namely those embracing, in principle, a full (exhaustive and definite) set of secondary rules' (at p. 117).

[8] A. Peters, 'The position of international law within the European Community legal order', 40 *GYIL* (1997) p. 9 at p. 11 (emphasis added). For the view that considers Community law as part of traditional international law, see: D. Wyatt, 'New Legal Order, or old?', 7 *EL Rev.* (1982) p. 147 arguing that the Community legal order is 'quite explicable in terms of traditional international legal theory and practice' (at p. 148). For a strong response, see: F.G. Jacobs, *European Community Law and Public International Law – Two Different Legal Orders?* (Vortrag am Institut für Internationales Recht an der Universität Kiel, 20 April 1983) p. 6 (emphasis added): '[I]t seems to me that those writers who have stressed the resemblance of the EC Treaty to ordinary international treaties have really missed the point. It is not the provisions of the Treaty, taken in themselves, but the Community legal *system*, as developed by the Court, that is novel…'

municipal law and traditional international law, Community law [could] become a conduit for the incorporation and application of international law in the municipal sphere.'[9] Placed on a systemic 'middle ground' between the international and the national legal orders, the EC legal system may profoundly transform the status of international norms before they enter into the domestic legal orders of the Member States. The first part of this chapter will analyse the status and effect of international norms that are formally binding on the Community. The two legal sources discussed are international treaties concluded by the Community and customary international law. The second part changes perspective and investigates when the Community has considered itself materially bound by international agreements concluded by its Member States. The Community legal order had originally developed a doctrine of functional succession for international agreements concluded by all its Member States. The doctrine had been developed for GATT (1947) and has recently been extended to United Nations Security Council Resolutions. A third part will finally try to assess the 'middle ground' position of the Community legal order.

2. International Norms formally binding on the Community: Monism and the Politics of Direct Effect

2.1 International Agreements as Direct Sources of Community Law

The capacity of international organisations to engage in treaty-making was recognised as long ago as 1949 for the United Nations and today seems universally accepted.[10] The 1957 Treaty of Rome did acknowledge the legal personality of the European Community, yet the Community's capacity to establish contractual links with third countries was not taken to imply its treaty-making competence for all matters falling within the scope of the EC Treaty. Prior to the Single European Act (1986), the Community's treaty-

[9] D. Bethlehem, 'International Law, European Community Law, National Law: Three Systems in Search of a Framework – Systemic Relativity in the Interaction of Law in the European Union', in M. Koskenniemi (ed.), *International Law Aspects of the European Union* (The Hague, Kluwer Law International 1998) p. 169 at p. 172.

[10] Cf., Reparation for Injuries suffered in the Service of the UN, Advisory Opinion [1949] ICJ, 174.

making powers were confined to international agreements under the Common Commercial Policy and Association Agreements with third countries or international organisations.[11] The restrictive attribution of treaty-making powers to the Community level protected a *status quo* in which the Member States were the protagonists on the international relations scene.

This picture has dramatically changed. In the past three decades, the European Courts have led – and won – a remarkable campaign to expand the Community's treaty-making powers through the doctrine of 'parallel external powers.'[12] The classic version of the doctrine recognises an implied competence of the EC to enter into international agreements wherever the EC enjoys an internal legislative competence, *in foro interno in foro externo.*[13] External powers run 'parallel' to internal powers. This widening of the Community's treaty-making powers has a significant 'internationalist' dimension. The Community's international treaties will not only be binding on the Community; they will – within Community law – bind the Member States of the Community.[14] International obligations of the Community will operate on the Member States *qua* Community law and will, consequently, enjoy supremacy over all national law, including national constitutional law.[15] International treaties will not, however, be absolutely supreme over Community law. While the Community legal order has accepted the priority of international treaties over secondary Community law, it continues to place international treaty norms below its 'constitutional charter', the EC Treaty.[16]

---

[11] Cf., Articles 113 and 238 of the original EEC Treaty.

[12] R. Schütze, 'Parallel external powers in the European Community: From "Cubist" perspectives towards "naturalist" constitutional principles?', 23 *Yearbook of European Law* (2004) p. 225.

[13] D. McGoldrick, *International Relations Law of the European Union* (London, Longman 1997) p. 48.

[14] Article 300(7) EC provides: 'Agreements concluded under the conditions set out in this Article shall be binding on the institutions of the Community and on Member States.'

[15] *Internationale Handelsgesellschaft mbH* v. *Einfuhr- und Vorratsstelle für Getreide und Futtermittel*, Case 11/70 [1970] ECR 1125.

[16] *Opinion 1/91 (EEA Agreement),* [1991] ECR 6079, para. 21. Consider also Article 300(6) EC: 'The European Parliament, the Council, the Commission or a Member State may obtain the opinion of the Court of Justice as to whether an agreement envisaged is compatible with the provisions of this Treaty. Where the opinion of the Court of Justice is adverse, the agreement may enter into force only in accordance with Article 48 of the Treaty on European Union.'

2.2 The Direct Effect of International Agreements – A Political Question?

Today, international agreements have become important legislative instruments. Many legal orders have 'opened-up' to a monist position. Under monism, international treaties are *constitutionally* recognised as an autonomous legal source of domestic law. The European Court of Justice has, from early on, chosen a monist road: international agreements concluded by the Community enter the Community legal order without the need for an additional transposition or validation. International treaties 'form an integral part of the Community legal system' from the date of their entry into force.[17] Community agreements are, therefore, directly applicable in the Community legal order. The capacity of international treaties directly and generally to affect the lives of European citizens permitted an external form of Community legislation.[18]

Yet, even in a monist legal order, not all international treaties will be directly effective. Particular treaties may lack direct effect for 'when the terms of the stipulation import a contract, when either of the parties engages to perform a particular act, the treaty addresses itself to the political, not to the judicial department; and the legislature must execute the contract before it can become a rule for the Court.'[19] Where a treaty is addressed to the legislative branch, it will not be self-executing as its norms will not be operational for the executive or the judiciary. The doctrine of self-execution or direct effect is a 'monist' doctrine. Dualist systems deny the legal validity of an international treaty within the domestic legal order *a priori*. Dualism insists on a validating domestic act and international agreements are, therefore, not direct instruments of domestic legislation. Monist legal systems, on the other hand, recognise the legal validity of (properly concluded) international treaties in the national legal order. However, the *effectiveness* of a particular international treaty in the national legal order will depend on the extent to which it has been given direct effect.[20] The doctrine of direct effect

---

[17] *Haegemann* v. *Belgium*, Case 181/73 [1974] ECR 449, para. 5.

[18] For an analysis of the legislative quality of international agreements in the Community legal order, see: R. Schütze, 'The morphology of legislative power in the European Community: Legal instruments and the federal Division of Powers', 25 *Yearbook of European Law* (2007) p. 91 at pp. 131-144.

[19] *Foster* v. *Neilson* (1829) 27 U.S. (2 Pet.) 253 at 314.

[20] The direct effect of an international treaty within the domestic legal order is, ultimately, a domestic decision. See: Y. Iwasawa, 'The Doctrine of Self-Executing Treaties in the United

represents, therefore, a yardstick for the actual openness of a legal system: it is a *chiffre* for the intensity of its monist creed.

The question whether a Community agreement has direct effect has been monopolised by the European Court of Justice. The Court has justified the 'centralisation' of the direct effect question by reference to the uniformity of the Community legal order. The effects of the Community's international agreements 'may not be allowed to vary [...] according to the effects in the internal legal order of each Member State which the law of that State assigns to international agreements concluded by it. Therefore it is for the Court, within the framework of its jurisdiction in interpreting the provisions of agreements, to ensure the uniform application throughout the Community.'[21] Once an agreement has been considered to unfold direct effect, it will thus also be directly effective in the national legal orders of the Member States. Individuals will be able to challenge Community as well as national legislation on the ground that it violates an international treaty.

What are the conditions for direct effect in the Community legal order? The signatory parties to the agreement may have positively settled this issue themselves and the Community Courts have recognised the binding effect of that political decision.[22] If the political authorities have not expressly decided the issue, the Court has devised a two-stage test.[23] In the first stage, the Court examines whether the agreement *as a whole* is capable of containing directly effective provisions. Here, the Court employs a policy test that looks at the nature, aim, purpose, spirit or general scheme of the treaty.[24] This

States: A Critical Analysis', 26 *Virginia Journal of International Law* (1985) p. 627 at p. 651: 'States determine how to implement their international legal obligations on the municipal level. It is well recognised that domestic law determines the "validity" and "rank" of treaties in domestic law.' If this is so, domestic law should also determine the 'direct applicability' of treaties in domestic law. This corresponds to the position of the European Court of Justice: 'Although each contracting party is responsible for executing fully the commitments which it has undertaken it is nevertheless free to determine the legal means appropriate for attaining that end in its legal system, unless the agreement, interpreted in the light of its subject-matter and purpose, itself specifies those means' (*Portugal* v. *Council*, Case 149/96 [1999] ECR 8395, para. 35).

[21] *Hauptzollamt Mainz* v. *Kupferberg & Cie*, Case 104/81 [1982] ECR 3641, para. 14.

[22] Ibid., para. 17.

[23] For an excellent analysis, see: Peters, loc. cit. n. 8, at pp. 53–54 and pp. 58–66.

[24] Cf., *International Fruit Company and others* v. *Produktschap voor Groenten en Fruit*, Case 21–24/72 [1972] ECR 1219, para. 20 as well as *Germany* v. *Council*, Case 280/93 [1993] ECR 3667, para. 105.

evaluation is as much political as judicial in nature as it will have political effects. Direct effect is a 'political question.' Once the political question hurdle has been crossed, the Court turns to examining the possible direct effect of a specific provision of the agreement.[25] Individual provisions must represent a 'clear and precise obligation which is not subject, in its implementation or effects, to the adoption of any subsequent measures.'[26]

The Community Courts have overall been 'favourably disposed towards direct effect' and created an atmosphere of 'general receptiveness to international agreements.'[27] The illustrious exception to this constitutional rule is the WTO agreement, where the Community Courts persist in denying that multilateral agreement a safe passage through the Community policy test. The most famous judicial ruling in this respect is, without doubt, *Germany* v. *Council* (*Bananas*);[28] yet, it was only in a later decision of the European Court of Justice that a clear constitutional rationale for the refusal of direct effect emerged. In *Portugal* v. *Council*, the Court found it crucial to note that:

> [...] some of the contracting parties, which are among the most important commercial partners of the Community, have concluded from the subject-matter and purpose of the WTO agreements that they are not among the rules applicable by their judicial organs when reviewing the legality of their rules of domestic law. Admittedly, the fact that the courts of one of the parties consider that some of the provisions of the agreement concluded by the Community are of direct application whereas the courts of the other party do not recognise such direct application is not in itself such as to constitute a lack of reciprocity in the implementation of the agreement[.]
> However, the lack of reciprocity in that regard on the part of the Community's trading partners, in relation to the WTO agreements which are based on reciprocal and mutually advantageous arrangements' and which must ipso facto be distinguished from agreements concluded by the Community [...] may lead to disuniform application of the WTO rules.

---

[25] The two prongs of the test can be well seen in *Hauptzollamt Mainz* v. *Kupferberg & Cie*. In paras. 18–22, the Court undertook the global policy test, while in paras. 23–27 it looked at the conditions for direct effect of a specific provision.

[26] *Demirel* v. *Stadt Schwäbisch Gmünd*, Case 12/86 [1987] ECR 3719, para. 14.

[27] P. Eeckhout, *External Relations of the European Union. Legal and constitutional foundations* (Oxford University Press 2004) p. 301.

[28] *Germany* v. *Council*, Case 280/93 [1994] ECR 4973.

> To accept that the role of ensuring that Community law complies with those rules devolves directly on the Community judicature would deprive the legislative or executive organs of the Community of the scope for manoeuvre enjoyed by their counterparts in the Community's trading partners.[29]

While confirming the monist philosophy of the EC legal order, the Court – rightly or wrongly – tempered the full effect of this monist creed.[30] In light of the economic consequences of granting direct effect to the WTO agreement, this was too 'fundamental' a political question for the Court to decide. The judicial self-restraint acknowledged a constitutional prerogative of the legislative and executive branch of the Community to answer this question. The judgment equally demonstrated that the very concept of direct effect 'is itself inherently political, in the sense that its meaning, in any given case, is contested, and is indeed bound to be contested.'[31]

2.3 Indirect Effects of International Agreements in the Community Legal Order

Norms may have direct or indirect legal effects. An international treaty lacking direct effect may still enjoy an indirect effect in a legal order.[32] From this perspective, a Community treaty lacking direct effect can still be seen as an integral part of Community law. The lack of direct effect simply means exactly that: the treaty has no *direct* effect. It cannot be directly relied upon as a source of rights or a standard of review in the Community legal order. A treaty without direct effect requires a medium – an internal Community measure – to unfold its effect in the Community legal order.

---

[29] *Portuguese Republic* v. *Council of the European Union*, Case C-149/96 ECR [1999] 8395, paras. 43-46 (emphasis added).

[30] The academic response to the Court's position *vis-à-vis* the WTO has been mixed. Compare the negative assessment by S. Griller, 'Judicial Enforceability of WTO Law in the European Union: Annotation to Case C-149/96, *Portugal* v. *Council*', 3 *Journal of International Economic Law* (2000) p. 441, with the response and positive evaluation by P. Eeckhout, 'Judicial Enforcement of WTO Law in the European Union: Some further Reflections', 5 *Journal of International Economic Law* (2002) p. 91.

[31] J. Klabbers, 'International Law in Community law: The law and politics of direct effect', 21 *Yearbook of European Law* (2001) p. 263 at p. 264.

[32] These indirect effects pose serious difficulties for the view that identifies direct effect with 'incorporation.'

What are the indirect effects a Community agreement can unfold? Two constitutional principles spring to mind in this context. First, there is the principle of 'consistent interpretation.'[33] In *Commission* v. *Germany* (IDA),[34] the Court defined the principle in the following terms: '*When the wording of secondary Community legislation is open to more than one interpretation ...* the primacy of international agreements concluded by the Community over provisions of secondary legislation means that such provisions must, *so far as possible, be interpreted in manner that is consistent with those agreements.*'[35] Secondly, there is the 'principle of implementation.'[36] In two exceptional circumstances an international agreement that lacks direct effect – typically an agreement related to the WTO – will provide an *indirect* standard of review for the legality of a Community measure. This indirect review occurs 'where the Community *intended to implement a particular obligation* assumed in the context of the WTO, or where the *Community measure refers expressly to the precise provisions* of the WTO agreements.'[37] The legality of the internal Community measure is reviewed 'in the light of' the international treaty.[38]

According to the first prong of the implementation principle, established in *Nakajima*,[39] a WTO agreement will prevail over inconsistent Community legislation, where the latter intends to implement the former. In that case, the Anti-Dumping Code of the WTO was in issue. The Court pointed out that the applicant was 'not relying on the direct effect of those provisions', but on Article 230 EC, i.e., on an '*infringement of the Treaty or any rule of law relating to its application.*'[40] The Community measure had been adopted in order to comply with the international obligations of the Community, and therefore it was judged 'necessary to examine whether the Council went beyond the legal framework thus laid down.'[41] We encounter a variation on that theme in *FEDIOL*.[42] A Community regulation had been adopted in the

---

[33] For a discussion of the principle, see: Eeckhout, op. cit. n. 27 at pp. 314-316.

[34] *Commission* v. *Germany (IDA),* Case 61/94 [1996] ECR 3989.

[35] Ibid., para. 52 (emphasis added).

[36] Eeckhout, op. cit. n. 27, at p. 316.

[37] *Portugal* v. *Council*, Case C-149/96 [1999] ECR 8395, para. 49 (emphasis added).

[38] Ibid. In *Germany* v. *Council*, Case 280/93 [1994] ECR 4973, para. 111, the Court uses the phrase 'from the point of view of'.

[39] *Nakajima All Precision* v. *Council*, Case 69/89 [1991] ECR 2069.

[40] Ibid., para. 28.

[41] Ibid., para. 32.

[42] *FEDIOL* v. *Commission*, Case 70/87 [1989] ECR 1781.

aftermath of 'the conclusions of the European Council of June 1982, which considered that it was of the highest importance to defend vigorously the legitimate interests of the Community in the appropriate bodies, in particular GATT.'[43] Article 2(1) of the regulation prohibited all 'illicit commercial practices' defined as 'any international trade practices attributable to third countries which are incompatible with international law or with the generally accepted rules.' The specific reference to international law in the Community measure, so the Court claimed, did entitle it to review the actions of the Commission in the light of the GATT rules. As the Community legislator had instructed the Commission to let its action be guided by the international norms, judicial review of these actions would also involve the interpretation and indirect application of GATT.[44]

What is the constitutional rationale behind these cases? What is clear is that it was not the international agreements *themselves* that provided the direct basis for review. The treaties were only an *indirect* standard, since the Community measures were reviewed 'in the light of' these treaties. The international norms were mediated through a Community measure. Could one, therefore, not argue that *through the act of implementation* the EC institutions have 'used and forfeited the international scope of manoeuvre?'[45] According to this view, it is the self-binding of the Community institutions – manifested in a specific domestic act by the Community – that provides the intellectual basis for the judicial review of the Community acts.[46] The review of the Community rules will be determined by the intention of the Community legislator to implement the international norms. Only '*because of that intention*, the international rule can be directly invoked to control the validity of the implementing legislation.' This approach is '*midway* between a monist and a dualist system of integrating international law.'[47] However, it seems closer to the monist than the dualist end of the spectrum

[43] Preamble of Council Regulation No. 2641/84 on the strengthening of the common commercial policy with regard in particular to protection against illicit commercial practices (*OJ* L 252, 1).

[44] *FEDIOL* v. *Commission*, Case 70/87 [1989] ECR 1781, para. 20.

[45] Eeckhout, op. cit. n. 27, at p. 319.

[46] The constitutional concept of 'self-binding', albeit in the context of the executive branch, is well-known in German public law.

[47] C. Timmermans, 'The EU and Public International Law', 4 *EFA Rev.* (1999) p. 181 at p. 190 (emphasis added). Eeckhout neatly refers to the 'dualist streak' of the Court's approach: 'Whether one calls that type of effect direct or indirect, it is clear that, in theory at

2.4 Customary International Law in the Community Legal Order

International treaties are not the only source of public international law. They are complemented by custom and general principles of law.[48] In contrast to the express provision under Article 300(7) EC for Community treaties, no similar constitutional commitment existed for customary international rules. Yet it seemed uncontested that the European Community, endowed with international legal personality and as such subject to international law 'must respect international law in the exercise of its powers' including internationally recognised custom.[49] What, however, is the *internal* legal status of customary rules in the Community legal order? Has the monist stance adopted in relation to international treaties been extended to this second source of international law?

After a period of sibylline ambiguity on the issue,[50] the European Courts had to deal with the issue more squarely. In *Opel Austria*, the Court of First

---

least, it involves more than mere consistent interpretation' (P. Eeckhout, 'The domestic legal status of the WTO Agreement: Interconnecting legal system', 37 *CML Rev.* (1997) p. 11 at pp. 44 and 42).

[48] For the concepts of international custom and general principles of law, see: I. Brownlie, *Principles of Public International Law* (Oxford University Press 2003) pp. 6-12 resp. 5-18.

[49] *Poulsen and Diva Navigation Corp.*, Case C-286/90 [1992] ECR I-6019, para. 9. Some consider that there exists '[a]n unwritten Community rule which corresponds to [Article 300 (7)] [that] foresees the incorporation of customary international law into the Community legal order' (Peters, loc. cit. n. 8, at p. 21).

[50] In one of the first cases dealing with the status of customary international in the Community legal order, the Court found that 'it is a principle of [customary] international law, which the [EC] Treaty cannot be assumed to disregard in the relations between Member States, that a State is precluded from refusing its own nationals the right of entry or residence' (*Van Duyn* v. *Home Office*, Case 41-74 [1974] ECR 1337, para. 22). In *Ahlstrom Osakeyhtio and others* v. *Commission of the European Communities (Wood-pulp)*, Joined cases 89, 104, 114, 116, 117 and 125–129/85 [1988] ECR 5193, non-Community undertakings had challenged the validity of a Commission decision on the ground that it breached the international legal principles limiting the jurisdiction of the Community. It was argued that 'the application of the competition rules in this case was founded exclusively on the economic repercussions within the common market of conduct restricting competition which was adopted outside the Community'. The ECJ did not analyse the substance of the international customary rules on territorial jurisdiction. It was content in finding that 'the Community's jurisdiction to apply its competition rules to such conduct is covered by the territoriality principle as universally recognised in public international law' (at paras. 15, 18). In *Poulsen and Diva Navigation Corp*, the Court was asked to determine the effect of 'general rules recognised by international custom' on Community legislation. The Court held, as a preliminary point, that 'the

Instance (CFI) was asked to annul a Community measure on the ground that it violated the customary international law principle of good faith. The CFI referred to Article 18 of the first Vienna Convention and held that it codified 'the principle of good faith [as] a rule of customary international law whose existence is recognised by the International Court of Justice' and 'is therefore binding on the Community.'[51] This principle, however, seemed not sufficient a ground for invalidation for the Court considered it necessary to add: 'The principle of good faith is the corollary in public international law of the principle of protection of legitimate expectations which, according to the case-law, forms part of the Community legal order.'[52] Indeed, in the subsequent analysis, the Court would exclusively refer to the *Community* general principle of legitimate expectations.[53]

Customary public international law did not operate directly, but was applied indirectly *via the medium* of Community law. This mediated application of international custom betrayed a judicial preference to regard the latter as a mere 'source of inspiration.' Customary international norms were 'channelled' into a Community principle.[54] However, this 'transformation ap-

---

European Community must respect international law in the exercise of its powers' and that, consequently, the relevant Community legislation 'must be interpreted, and its scope limited, in the light of the relevant rules of the international law of the sea.' The Community measure had to be interpreted 'so as to give it the greatest practical effect, within the limits of international law' (at paras. 9 and 11). For a panoramic view over the European Court's references to general principles of international law during this period, see: J.-P. Puissochet, 'La Place du Droit international dans la Jurisprudence de la Cour de Justice des Communautés Européennes', in: Claus Gulman (ed.), *Scritti in onore di Giuseppe Federico Mancini* (Bologna, Dr. A. Giuffré 1998), p. 781.

[51] *Opel Austria GmbH* v. *Council of the European Union*, Case T-115/94 [1997] ECR II-39, para. 90. The Court of First Instance referred to a PCIJ judgment of 25 May 1926, *German interests in Polish Upper Silesia*, CPJI, Series A, No 7, 30 and 39. Article 18 of the Vienna Convention on the Law of Treaties provides: 'A State is obliged to refrain from acts which would defeat the object and purpose of a treaty when: (a) it has signed the treaty or has exchanged instruments constituting the treaty subject to ratification, acceptance or approval, until it shall have made its intention clear not to become a party to the treaty; or; (b) it has expressed its consent to be bound by the treaty, pending the entry into force of the treaty and provided that such entry into force is not unduly delayed.'

[52] *Opel Austria GmbH*, Case T-115/94 [1997] ECR II-39, paras.123-124.

[53] In the case of *Opel Austria GmbH*, the Court would additionally mention the principle of legal certainty.

[54] Eeckhout, op. cit. n. 27, at p. 327.

proach'[55] did not answer the question whether international custom could have direct effects within the Community legal order.

The status and effect of customary international norms was again at issue in *Racke*.[56] The Community had concluded a Cooperation Agreement with the Federal Republic of Yugoslavia for an unlimited period of time, which nonetheless allowed either party to terminate the agreement six months after having notified the other party of its unilateral decision to terminate. Claiming that the war in the Federal Republic of Yugoslavia constituted a radical change in the conditions under which the agreement had been concluded, the Community had adopted a series of measures to suspend the agreement without having complied with the six-months rule. The questions posed in this preliminary reference from the German Federal Finance Court related, thus, to the validity of the Community legislation suspending the agreement. Was the Community entitled to terminate unilaterally the agreement by reference to the customary international rule of *rebus sic stantibus*?

The European Court of Justice affirmed its jurisdiction to examine the Community measure against international custom binding on the Community: 'Rules of customary international law concerning the termination and the suspension of treaty relations by reason of a fundamental change of circumstances are binding upon the Community institutions *and form part of the Community legal order*.'[57] The Court thereby confirmed the monist relationship between the Community legal order and customary international rules binding on the Community. But when would these rules have direct effect? Once more, the Court tried to evade this very issue.[58] It acknowl-

[55] J. Wouters & D. van Eeckhoutte, 'Giving effect to Customary International Law through European Community Law', in: J.M. Prinssen and A. Schrauwen (eds.), *Direct Effect – Rethinking a Classic of EC Legal Doctrine* (Groningen, Europa Law 2002) p. 183 at p. 210.

[56] *Racke GmbH & Co.* v. *Hauptzollamt Mainz*, Case C-162/96 [1998] ECR 3655 (henceforth, *Racke*).

[57] *Racke*, para. 46.

[58] How difficult the question of direct effect of customary international law would have been can be seen in the Opinion of Advocate General F. Jacobs. Pointing out that 'most rules of customary international law do not create rights for individuals and therefore do not have direct effect', the Advocate General turned to the law of treaties: 'In the light of those principles, there must also be limits to the effect of rules of customary international law relating to treaties. The overall nature and purpose of the law of treaties is to lay down rules applying in the relations between States (and international organisations). The law of treaties is clearly not intended to create rights for individuals. It is true that its application may have the effect of creating such rights, namely in those cases where a domestic legal system accepts that

edged that Article 62(1) of the Vienna Convention codified international custom,[59] but referred to the 'complexity' of the customary rules that would allow the Community a margin of discretion in applying these rules. Hence, only where the Council had made 'manifest errors of assessment concerning the conditions for applying those rules' would the Court invalidate the (suspending) Community measure.[60] The Court, thereby, reconciled – at least rhetorically – two contradictory wishes. While on the one hand accepting that an individual can 'invoke…, in order to challenge the validity of the suspending regulation, obligations deriving from rules of customary international law which govern the termination and suspension of treaty relations,'[61] it nonetheless wished to recognise a discretionary power of the Community to (mis-)interpret the meaning and scope of international custom. This desire to allow for a margin of discretion, while wishing to exercise *some* judicial

international agreements concluded in conformity with the law of treaties are capable of conferring rights on individuals. However, that is but an indirect effect, by no means intended at the level of international law. It is the provision of the agreement (lawfully concluded) which has direct effect. The overall nature and purpose of the law of treaties would therefore seem not to be conducive to direct effect. (It may be noted in passing that there may be other types of rules of customary international law which do intend to confer rights on individuals, for example rules of international humanitarian law.) In addition, the particular rules in issue must contain clear and precise obligations. In the circumstances of the present case, it is not obvious that that condition is satisfied. The notion of *rebus sic stantibus* is notoriously difficult and contested; indeed it has often been described as the *enfant terrible* of international law. Its scope has perhaps been formulated more clearly in Article 62 of the Vienna Convention, but even that provision contains concepts which easily lend themselves to widely diverging interpretations. What is a fundamental change of circumstances? What are circumstances which constituted an essential basis of the consent of the parties? And when does the change in circumstances radically (...) transform the extent of obligations still to be performed? It may therefore be doubted whether the conditions for the application of the doctrine of *rebus sic stantibus* are sufficiently clear and precise to confer rights on individuals' (ibid., paras. 80, 84-85).

[59] This Article provides: 'A fundamental change of circumstances which has occurred with regard to those existing at the time of the conclusion of a treaty, and which was not foreseen by the parties, may not be invoked as a ground for terminating or withdrawing from the treaty unless: (a) the existence of those circumstances constituted an essential basis of the consent of the parties to be bound by the treaty; and (b) the effect of the change is radically to transform the extent of obligations still to be performed under the treaty.'

[60] *Racke*, para. 52. As regards the procedural rules laid down in Article 65 of the Vienna Convention, the Court simply held that 'the specific procedural requirements there laid down do not form part of customary international law' (ibid., para. 59).

[61] *Racke*, para. 51.

review, may explain why the Court was so eager to separate its analysis from the question of the direct effect of the customary international rules.

From this, we may conclude the following: while recent jurisprudence has confirmed that rules of customary international law 'form part of the Community legal order', the European Courts have yet to provide a clear dogmatic response to the question of direct effect. Some even see a 'clear determination of the Courts to avoid the issue of direct effect.'[62] However, this evasive strategy did ultimately fail in *Racke*, where the European Court of Justice allowed an individual to invoke customary international law. This is, in spite of all judicial protestations to the contrary, the doctrine of direct effect.[63] However, a host of questions remains unresolved. Will international custom only bind the Community, or will it – as part of the Community legal order – equally bind the Member States?[64] What is the hierarchical rank that customary international law enjoys in the Community legal order? It could

---

[62] P. Koutrakos, *EU International Relations Law* (Oxford, Hart 2006) p. 248. K. Lenaerts & E. de Smijter, 'The European Union as an Actor under International law', 19 *Yearbook of European Law* (1999) p. 95 at p. 126 argue that in *Racke* 'the Court appears to have qualified its earlier case law to the extent that it no longer made reliance on a provision codifying a rule of customary international law conditional on the relevant provision's being directly effective. Rather, it considered that circumstance to be irrelevant where the purpose of reliance on the particular provision is to obtain the enforcement by the Court of rights claimed under a directly effective rule of Community law, which in *Racke* was the relevant provision of the EEC-Yugoslav Agreement. A rule of customary international law can thus always be invoked by an individual in the framework of a claim based in another rule of Community law.' Interestingly, some of the Court's pronouncements have been interpreted along the lines of the *Nakajima* case law: '[I]t seems as if the invocability of a rule of customary international law to review the legality of a Community act is furthermore restricted to the situation in which this Community act is, in fact, an implementation of the invoked rule of customary international law. After all, the contested regulation explicitly stated to have been taken account on the basis of *rebus sic stantibus*. Therefore, one may wonder whether the *Racke* case does not in any way boil down to an application of the *Nakajima* case law vis-à-vis customary international law' (Wouters & van Eeckhoutte, loc. cit. n. 55, at p. 203).

[63] P. Pescatore, 'The doctrine of "direct effect": an infant disease of Community law', 8 *EL Rev.* (1983) p. 155.

[64] A. Epiney has argued in favour of the restrictive first alternative: 'Denn die Grundsätze des allgemeinen Völkerrechts sind zwar Bestandteil der Gemeinschaftsrechtsordnung im oben genannten Sinn; für die Mitgliedstaaten unmittelbar als solche verbindlich sind sie jedoch insofern nicht, als sie (nur) die Gemeinschaft als Völkerrechtssubjekt binden; eine "Durchgriffswirkung" auf die Mitgliedstaaten dürfte zu verneinen sein.' (A. Epiney, 'Zur Stellung des Völkerrechts in der EU', 10 *Europäische Zeitschrift für Wirtschaftsrecht* (1999) p. 5 at p. 8).

be argued that the Community Courts should extend the constitutional principles governing the status of international treaties to international custom,[65] yet this is not a matter of constitutional necessity.[66]

3. 'External' International Treaties and Community Succession: From the GATT to the United Nations?

What is the relationship between the Community legal order and international treaties to which the European Community is not a party? While not formally binding on the Community, these treaties may overlap with the competences of the Community and thus come into the 'orbit' of the Community legal order.[67] The European Court of Justice has, however, held that '[b]efore the incompatibility of a Community measure with a provision of international law can affect the validity of that measure, the Community must first of all be bound by that provision.'[68] However, this raises an important question: has the Community considered itself to be bound by international treaties to which it has not formally given consent? The question will only arise for international treaties to which all the Member States are parties. In the past, the ECJ had accepted a 'succession doctrine' in relation to GATT (1947). The famous passage in the decision in *International Fruit* reads:

> The Community has assumed the functions inherent in the tariff and trade policy, progressively during the transitional period and in their entirety on the expiry of that period, by virtue of [Articles 131 and 133] of the Treaty. By conferring those powers on the Community, the Member States showed their wish to bind it by the obligations entered into under the general agreement. Since the entry into force of the E[]C Treaty and more particularly, since the setting up of the common

---

[65] Ibid.

[66] The status of international law in the German legal order, for example, differs depending on its legal source. While general principles of international law assume a hierarchical position between the German Constitution and federal legislation, the transformed or implemented international treaty has traditionally been placed at the hierarchical rank of normal legislation.

[67] I borrow this expression from N. Lavranos, who – in turn – borrowed it from B. de Witte.

[68] *International Fruit Company NV* v. *Produktschap voor Groenten en Fruit*, Joined Cases 21–24/72 [1972] ECR 1219, para. 7.

> external tariff, the transfer of powers which has occurred in the relations between Member States and the Community has been put into concrete form in different ways within the framework of the General Agreement and has been recognised by the other contracting parties. ... It therefore appears that, in so far as under the E[]C Treaty the Community has assumed the powers previously exercised by Member States in the area covered by the General Agreement, the provisions of that agreement have taken effect of binding the Community.[69]

Functional succession emanated from the exclusive nature of the Community's powers under the Common Commercial Policy (CCP).[70] With the Community today being formally bound by GATT under the WTO Agreement, the succession doctrine seemed a dead letter. For three long decades it had not been extended to either of the two other two major legal 'satellites' of the Community legal order: the European Convention on Human Rights (ECHR) and the United Nations (UN). Recent developments, however, indicate a change of direction in relation to the latter. The second part of this chapter will, therefore, concentrate on the status and effect of United Nations Security Council Resolutions in the Community legal order.

3.1 Constitutional Design: The United Nations and the Community Legal Order

The European Community is not a member of the United Nations.[71] All Member States of the European Community are, however, members of the

[69] Ibid., paras. 14-16 and 18 (emphasis added). In *Amministrazione delle Finanze dello Stato* v. *Societa Petrolifera Italiana SpA (SPI) and SpA Michelin Italiana (SAMI),* Joined Cases 267/81, 268/81 and 269/81 [1983] ECR 801, para. 17, the ECJ clarified that, following the introduction of the common customs tariff on 1 July 1968, the Community had 'assumed its full powers in relation to the sphere covered by GATT.'

[70] The Court of Justice had not yet 'officially' declared the CCP as an exclusive competence of the Community. The doctrine of succession was rather a precursor to that development, see: R. Schütze, 'Dual Federalism constitutionalised: The emergence of exclusive competences in the EC legal order', 32 *EL Rev.* (2007) p. 3 at pp. 6-10. On the application of the idea of 'succession' in the Community legal order generally, see: R. Schütze, 'EC Law and International Agreements of the Member States – An Ambivalent Relationship?', 9 *Cambridge Yearbook of European Legal Studies* (2006) p. 387 at pp. 397-406.

[71] According to Article 4 of the UN Charter, only States can become full members. Before formal amendment of the UN Charter, the Community must 'settle for a more modest participation in the work of the world organization' (P. Brückner, 'The European Community and the United Nations', 1 *European Journal of International Law* (1990) p. 174 at p. 176).

United Nations. According to Article 48(2) of the UN Charter, decisions of the Security Council 'shall be carried out by the Members of the United Nations directly and through action in the appropriate international agencies of which they are members.'[72] The fulfilment of United Nations obligations is, thereby, mandatory. Article 103 of the UN Charter specifies that '[i]n the event of a conflict between the obligations of the Members of the United Nations under the present Charter and their obligations under any other international agreement, their obligations under the present Charter shall prevail.'

What is the legal relationship between the United Nations and the Community legal order? Sandwiched between the United Nations and the national legal orders, how will the Community layer affect the obligations under the United Nations Charter? Have the Community Courts considered United Nations law binding on the Community, even if 'the singular and independent nature of the Community legal order, which has been made clear from the beginning by the case law of the Court of Justice, points in the opposite direction?'[73]

The potential competence overlap between the United Nations and the Community legal orders has principally materialised in the form of economic sanctions adopted by the United Nations Security Council. These measures have a commercial nature and may thus fall within the Community's common commercial policy competence. However, because of their foreign policy objective, economic sanctions were originally regarded to have remained within the exclusive foreign affairs competence of the Member States.[74] Under the 'Rhodesia doctrine,'[75] economic sanctions were considered to be beyond the scope of the CCP. They were adopted under Article 297 EC allowing a Member State to adopt national measures 'to carry out obligations it

[72] Article 48(2) UN Charter.

[73] J.P. Puissochet, 'The Court of Justice and international action by the European Community: The example of the embargo against the Former Yugoslavia', 20 *Fordham International Law Journal* (1996) p. 1557 at p. 1568.

[74] An excellent historical overview of the European Community's approach towards economic sanctions can be found in P. Koutrakos, *Trade, Foreign Policy and Defence in EU Constitutional Law: The legal regulation of sanctions, exports of dual-use goods and armaments* (Oxford, Hart 2001) pp. 58-91.

[75] P.J. Kuyper, 'Sanctions against Rhodesia: the EEC and the implementation of general international legal rules', *CML Rev.* (1975) p. 231.

has accepted for the purpose of maintaining peace and international security.'[76]

The pitfalls of a missing harmonised approach for economic sanctions soon led to a second constitutional formula. The Member States would attempt to coordinate their national foreign policies within the framework of the European Political Cooperation (EPC). If a unanimous diplomatic decision to impose sanctions emerged, it would then be 'translated' into a Community measure based on Article 133 EC.[77] The *Community* character of these measures remained, however, ambivalent. Indeed, the standard formula in the preambles of the EC sanctions regulations adopted during this phase would refer to 'the Community and its Member States hav[ing] agreed *to have recourse to a Community instrument* in order to ensure uniform implementation throughout the Community.'[78] Did this mean that the Member States had only 'borrowed' the Community organs to adopt a '*sui generis*' legal instrument?[79] With the constitutional relationship between the EPC and Article 133 EC not clarified, it was 'not surprising that the question of

---

[76] The Article provides: 'Member States shall consult each other with a view to taking together the steps needed to prevent the functioning of the common market being affected by measures which a Member State may be called upon to take in the event of serious internal disturbances affecting the maintenance of law and order, in the event of war, serious international tension constituting a threat of war, or in order to carry out obligations it has accepted for the purpose of maintaining peace and international security.'

[77] Under this original two-step process, 'the EPC mechanism under international law principles precede[d] the proper legislative process within Community law.' It has been taken to 'reflect the compromise between the Member States' interests to preserve their sovereignty as to matters of security policy on the one hand, and the interests of the EC to guarantee the uniform application of law within the whole of the Community on the other' (S. Bohr, 'Sanctions by the United Nations Security Council and the European Community', 4 *EJIL* (1993) p. 256 at p. 266).

[78] E.g., Council Regulation (EEC) No. 2340/90 of 8 August 1990 preventing trade by the Community as regards Iraq and Kuwait (*OJ* L 213, 09/08/1990 at 1) Recital 4.

[79] On this point, see: P. Koutrakos (op. cit. n. 74, at p. 74) arguing that 'trade sanctions against third countries were treated as a *sui generis* category of measures'. According to the author this gave rise to the paradox that economic sanctions, while actually being imposed on the basis of Article 133 EC were 'in effect being dissociated from the Common Commercial Policy.' 'In effect, the arrangement under consideration negated the Community's exclusive competence over the Common Commercial Policy as far as the imposition of sanctions was concerned' (ibid., 66). Interestingly, the Member States even adopted a declaration to the effect that recourse to Article 133 'did not constitute a precedent' which 'finally enabled the Council to adopt the regulation[s] on sanctions' (Kuyper, loc. cit. n. 75, at p. 398).

the legal foundation or basis for Community action in relation to economic sanctions has been much debated'.[80]

More solid constitutional foundations were given during a third phase. Setting up a 'Common Foreign and Security Policy' (CFSP) for the newly erected European Union, the Maastricht Treaty cemented the constitutional practice for economic sanctions in Article 301 EC. The article stipulates the following:

> Where it is provided, in a common position or in a joint action adopted according to the provisions of the Treaty on European Union relating to the common foreign and security policy, for an action by the Community to interrupt or to reduce, in part or completely, economic relations with one or more third countries, the Council shall take the necessary urgent measures. The Council shall act by a qualified majority on a proposal from the Commission.

Today, virtually all UN Security Council Resolutions imposing economic sanctions will be implemented on the basis of this provision.[81] Yet, the nature of the competence – as well as the character of the measures adopted under it[82] – has remained mysterious. Commentators are divided on whether the article provides for an exclusive competence of the Community.[83] Its

---

[80] Puissochet, loc. cit. n. 73, at p. 1561.

[81] K. Lenaerts and E. De Smijter, 'The United Nations and the European Union: Living Apart Together', in K. Wellens (ed.), *International Law: Theory and Practice. Essays in Honour of Eric Suy* (The Hague, Nijhoff 1998) p. 439 at p. 448, even assert that 'the Member States introduced a Community law obligation for the Community institutions to implement UN economic sanctions into [Article 301] EC.'

[82] In line with the pre-Maastricht *status quo*, Koutrakos considers measures adopted under Article 301 EC as 'a *sui generis* genre of measures.' The 'political genesis' of these measures within the Second Pillar 'attributes a quality to the measure adopted under Article 301 EC that distinguishes it from all other Community measures' (Koutrakos, op. cit. n. 74, at p. 77).

[83] In favour of an exclusive competence are K. Lenaerts and E. De Smijter (loc. cit. n. 81, at p. 454): 'Within the European legal order the Community enjoys exclusive competence in this area [economic sanctions]', as well as N. Lavranos, *Legal interaction between decisions of international organizations and European law* (Groningen, Europa Law 2004) p. 100. Against exclusivity is P. Eeckhout, pointing out that '[t]here are no indications in Article 301 that this will be the case; on the contrary, the reference to the prior decision under the CFSP suggests that Community competence is conditional. That is clearly a strong argument against exclusivity: if there is no CFSP sanctions decision, for example because there is no unanimity, the Community cannot adopt sanctions. Surely, this signifies that the Member States, which as the Court recognised remain competent in the area of foreign and security policy, have the

relationship with Article 133 is not clarified.[84] The same holds true for its relationship with Article 297 EC.[85] The constitutional design for economic sanctions, therefore, still raised many questions that the Community Courts would eventually have to answer.

3.2 The Community Judiciary and UN Security Council Resolutions

3.2.1 *The Traditional Approach: Community autonomy with an 'internationalist' streak*

The normative positioning of the European judiciary began with the European Court of Justice's decision in *Bosphorus*.[86] This was the first case dealing with a Community sanctions regulation and concerned the UN embargo against the Federal Republic of Yugoslavia. Adopted before the European Union Treaty entered into force, the regulation was still based on Article 133 EC.[87] Executing the Community measure, Ireland impounded an aircraft

---

power to adopt sanctions' (Eeckhout, op. cit. n. 27, at p. 448). In the light of the constitutional relationship between the CFSP and the First Pillar, the case against exclusivity is much stronger.

[84] The question at issue is whether Article 133 EC continues to provide an alternative legal basis for economic sanctions where Article 301 EC is inapplicable because Member States reached no agreement within the CFSP provisions of the TEU. For an affirmative answer, see: K. Lenaerts & E. de Smijter (loc. cit. n. 81, at p. 449): 'It is therefore safe to state that when the Council does not come to a unanimous CFSP decision on the implementation of UN economic sanctions, this does not prevent the EC from taking the necessary action against a third State. The absence of such CFSP decision merely excludes the applicability of [Article 301] EC. It does not paralyse the Community, since the latter remains free to use its *normal* competence on the common commercial policy laid down in [Article 133], *juncto* [Article 300] EC.'

[85] The case has been made that 'Article 301 EC has not precluded a Member State from relying upon Article 297 EC in order to justify national measures imposing unilateral sanctions on a third country' (Koutrakos, op. cit. n. 74, at p. 86). For a discussion of Article 297 EC generally, see: P. Koutrakos, 'Is Article 297 EC a "Reserve of Sovereignty"?', 37 *CML Rev.* (2000) p. 1339 at p. 1339.

[86] *Bosphorus Hava Yollari Turizm ve Ticaret AS* v. *Minister for Transport, Energy and Communications and others*, Case C-84/95 [1996] ECR 3953.

[87] Council Regulation (EEC) No. 990/93 of 26 April 1993 concerning trade between the European Economic Community and the Federal Republic of Yugoslavia (Serbia and Montenegro) (*OJ* 1993 L 102, 14) was based on UN Security Council Resolution 820 (1993).

belonging to Bosphorus, a Turkish company, on the ground that it had been leased from a 'person or undertaking in or operating from the Federal Republic of Yugoslavia (Serbia and Montenegro).'[88] Claiming, *inter alia*, that its fundamental right to property was violated, Bosphorus argued that the Community regulation that implemented the UN obligations of the Member States was void. The ECJ, referring to its case law on fundamental rights in the Community legal order, approached its legality review in the following way:

> Any measure imposing sanctions has, by definition, consequences which affect the right to property and the freedom to pursue a trade or business, thereby causing harm to persons who are in no way responsible for the situation which led to the adoption of the sanctions.
> Moreover, the importance of the aims pursued by the regulation at issue is such as to justify negative consequences, even of a substantial nature, for some operators.
> The provisions of Regulation No. 990/93 contribute in particular to the implementation at Community level of the sanctions against the Federal Republic of Yugoslavia adopted, and later strengthened, by several resolutions of the Security Council of the United Nations. ...
> As compared with an objective of general interest so fundamental for the international community, which consists in putting an end to the state of war in the region and to the massive violations of human rights and humanitarian international law in the Republic of Bosnia-Herzegovina, the impounding of the aircraft in question, which is owned by an undertaking based in or operating from the Federal Republic of Yugoslavia, cannot be regarded as inappropriate or disproportionate. [89]

The Court showed respect for the autonomy of the Community legal order. It did not address the legal status of UN Security Council Resolutions in the Community legal order, but focused on the legality of the Community measure's. Importantly, the ECJ seemed to treat the sanctions regulation as a 'real' Community measure. First, the Court had no difficulty in establishing its jurisdiction. Second, the Court reviewed the measure in the light of the Community standard of fundamental rights. Finding that fundamental rights are 'not absolute and their exercise may be subject to restrictions justified by

[88] Article 8 of Council Regulation No. 990/93.

[89] *Bosphorus*, Case C-84/95 [1996] ECR 3953 paras. 21-26.

objectives of general interest pursued by the Community',[90] the ECJ nonetheless considered the balance struck between the foreign policy objective and the adverse interference with individual rights reasonable. Even if a lower degree of judicial scrutiny was applied,[91] the Court had thus no qualms to review indirectly the substance of the UN Security Council Resolution.

The message seemed clear: where the Member States decided to have recourse to a Community instrument to fulfil their obligations arising under the United Nations *qua* Community law, they would have to comply with the constitutional principles of the Community legal order. The solution would safeguard the autonomy of the Community legal order in an approach that paralleled the Community legal order's relationship to the European Convention on Human Rights.[92]

This judicial approach was confirmed in *Centro-Com*.[93] In a preliminary reference from the English Court of Appeal, the European Court was requested to interpret the relationship between UN Security Council Resolution 757 (1992) and the implementing Community measure in the form of Council Regulation 1432/92 prohibiting trade between the European Economic Community and the Republics of Serbia and Montenegro. The Sanctions Regulation had exempted products intended for medical purposes from the prohibition, but required prior authorisation 'issued by the competent authorities of the Member States.'[94] The United Kingdom, in accordance with its United Nations Act 1946, had adopted the Serbia and Montenegro (United Nations Sanctions) Order 1992. The Order prohibited any person

---

[90] Ibid., para. 21.

[91] For a critique of the standard of review, see I. Canor, '"Can two walk together, except be agreed?" The relationship between international law and European law: The incorporation of United Nations sanctions against Yugoslavia into European Community law through the perspective of the European Court of Justice', 35 *CML Rev.* (1998) p. 137 at p. 162: 'However, it can be sensed from the decision of the Court that it was so "impressed" by the importance of the aims of the Regulation, that it was prepared to justify any negative consequences … This attitude implies that no serious balancing test was carried out by the Court, and that it expressed an almost total indifference to the way the Community organs exercised their discretion in the political – foreign affairs – sphere when implementing the Resolution. It should not be the case that by invoking foreign affairs needs, the Council and the Commission is given carte blanche to infringe individual rights.'

[92] Puissochet, loc. cit. n. 73, at p. 1571.

[93] *The Queen, ex parte Centro-Com Srl* v. *HM Treasury and Bank of England*, Case C-124/95 [1997] ECR 81.

[94] Article 3 Council Regulation 1432/92 (*OJ* 1992 L 151, 4).

from supplying or delivering any goods to a person connected with Serbia or Montenegro, except under the authority of a licence granted by the Secretary of State.

Centro-Com, an Italian undertaking, had exported fifteen consignments of pharmaceutical goods and blood-testing equipment to Montenegro. The payments for those exports were to be debited to a bank account held by the National Bank of Yugoslavia with Barclays Bank. While eleven consignments had been duly paid, reports of abuse of the authorisation procedure led to a change of United Kingdom policy. Henceforth, the British authorities would only authorise payment for those medical products that were exported from the United Kingdom. This was claimed to allow better control over goods exported to Serbia and Montenegro. The question submitted to the European Court of Justice was whether the CCP, as implemented by the Community Sanctions Regulation, precluded the United Kingdom from adopting such a scheme – even if it was designed to ensure the national implementation of Security Council Resolution 757 (1992).

The ECJ analysed the three-layer problem in two steps. In a first part of the judgment it focused on the relationship between national foreign security measures and the CCP. The British government had argued that the national measures had been taken by virtue of its competence in the field of foreign and security policy and that the validity of these measures 'cannot be affected by the exclusive competence of the Community in relation to the common commercial policy.'[95] While accepting the competence of the Member States in the field of foreign policy, the Court significantly added that 'the powers retained by the Member States must be exercised in a matter consistent with Community law.'[96] Moreover, this time, the Court showed its true colours and provided the constitutional rationale behind its reasoning:

> [W]hile it is for the Member States to adopt measures of foreign and security policy in the exercise of their national competence, those measures must nevertheless respect the provisions adopted by the Community in the field of the common commercial policy provided for by [Article 133] of the Treaty.
> It was indeed in the exercise of their national competence in matters of foreign and security policy that the Member States expressly decided to have recourse to

---

[95] *Centro-Com*, Case C-124/95 [1997] ECR 81 para. 23.
[96] Ibid., para. 25.

> a Community measure, which became the Sanctions Regulation, based on [Article 133] of the Treaty.
> As the preamble to the Sanctions Regulation shows, that regulation ensued from a decision of the Community and its Member States which was taken within the framework of political cooperation and which marked their willingness to have recourse to a Community instrument in order to implement in the Community certain aspects of the sanctions imposed on the Republics of Serbia and Montenegro by the United Nations Security Council.
> It follows from the foregoing that, even where measures such as those in issue in the main proceedings have been adopted in the exercise of national competence in matters of foreign and security policy, they must respect the Community rules adopted under the common commercial policy.[97]

In essence, the Court recognised that the Member States had 'retained' powers as regards foreign and security policy. Thus, even if these measures fell within Article 133 EC, the Member States would not be excluded *a priori* in spite of the exclusive nature of the CCP. The Court thereby gave an implicit judicial blessing to the constitutional symbiosis between the intergovernmental EPC and the supranational CCP.[98] Significantly, however, it found that where the Member States wilfully use the Community's legal instruments to fulfil *their* obligations within the United Nations legal order, they must equally wilfully submit to the constitutional logics of the Community legal order. From there, the Court moved on to the second step in its analysis. The Court found that the Community legislation on the matter was exhaustive. The Sanction Regulation had been 'designed to implement, uniformly throughout the Community' the relevant aspects of the sanctions imposed by the UN Security Council.[99] The United Kingdom was, therefore, precluded from adopting stricter national measures.[100]

---

[97] Ibid., paras. 27-30.

[98] 'The Court could afford to dispense with lengthy discussions, as the constitutional development of the Community ha[d] rendered this point moot. With the coming into force of the Maastricht Treaty in the European Union, [Article 301] EC ha[d] introduced a legal basis for a *Community* embargo' (C. Vedder & H.-P. Folz, 'Case Note on *Centro-Com* and *Ebony Maritime*', 35 *CML Rev.* (1998) p. 209 at p. 215).

[99] *Centro-Com*, Case C-124/95 [1997] ECR 81 para. 47.

[100] The Court, however, did not fully close the door in relation to Article 307 EC. While pointing out that 'when an international agreement allows, but does not require, a Member State to adopt a measure which appears to be contrary to Community law, the Member State must refrain from adopting such a measure' (ibid., para. 60), it nonetheless admitted that – at

In sum, under the traditional approach, the following constitutional picture emerged: the Community did not consider itself materially bound by the UN Charter and Security Council Resolutions were not part of the Community legal order. When Member States 'had recourse' to Community instruments to implement UN Resolutions, they could use Article 133 EC, but this 'communitarisation' also implied the obligation to adhere to the Community's constitutional rules. The constitutional message was thus if 'transposing international law into Community law strengthens international rules by allowing them to partake in the special effects of Community law,'[101] these rules must equally partake in the special obligations of Community law – including those fundamental human rights recognised in the Community legal order.

3.3 A new approach? *Yusuf* and the subordination of the Community Legal Order

The judicial commentary on the pre-Maastricht constitutional design protected the autonomy of the Community legal order, while paying attention to the international obligations of the Member States. This metaphorical 'middle ground' stance has recently been abandoned by the Court of First Instance. In *Yusuf*,[102] the Court established a significantly different position when interpreting the constitutional provisions inserted by the European Union Treaty.

The case was brought by alleged Taliban terrorists, whose assets had been frozen. The contested Community regulations – as well as the CFSP common position – had reproduced the relevant UN Security Council Resolu-

least under the preliminary proceedings procedure – it was for the national courts 'to determine which obligations are imposed by an earlier agreement on the Member State concerned and to ascertain their ambit so as to be able to determine the extent to which they thwart application of the provisions of Community law in question' (ibid., para. 58). In the final analysis, it was for the national court to decide on 'whether, in the circumstances of the case before it, in which exports were approved by the United Nations Sanctions Committee and authorised by the competent authorities in the country of export, both the change of policy and the four decisions refusing to allow funds to be released are necessary in order to ensure that the Member State concerned performs its obligations under the Charter of the United Nations and United Nations Security Council Resolution 757 (1992)' (ibid., para. 59).

[101] Peters, op. cit. n. 8, at p. 34.

[102] *Ahmed Ali Yusuf and Al Barakaat International Foundation* v. *Council and Commission*, Case T-306/01 [2005] ECR II-3533 (henceforth, Yusuf).

tions.[103] The Community measures had been based on Articles 301, 60 and 308 EC.[104] The applicants had challenged the legality of these measures, *inter alia*, on the ground that their fundamental rights had been violated. The Community organs, having intervened in the proceedings, argued that 'the Charter of the United Nations prevail[s] over every other obligation of international, Community or domestic law' to the effect that Community human rights standards should be inoperative.[105]

How did the CFI re-position the Community legal order? While admitting that under public international law the EC was not bound by UN Security Council Resolutions, the Court still found that 'the Community *must be considered to be bound* by the obligations under the Charter of the United Nations in the same way as its Member States, *by virtue of the Treaty establishing it*.'[106] How did the Court come to this novel interpretation? The Court repeated that all the Member States of the Community were bound under Chapter VII of the Charter and, referring to Articles 297 and 307 EC, it considered

[103] Cf., UN Security Council Resolution 1390/2002 laying down the measures to be directed against Osama bin Laden, members of the Al-Qaeda network and the Taliban and other associated individuals, groups, undertakings and entities.

[104] Common Position 2002/402/CFSP led to the adoption of Council Regulation (EC) No. 881/2002, imposing certain specific restrictive measures directed against certain persons and entities associated with Osama bin Laden, the Al-Qaeda network and the Taliban, and repealing Regulation No. 467/2001 (*OJ* 2002 L 139, 9). Article 2 of the Regulation provides: 'All funds and economic resources belonging to, or owned or held by, a natural or legal person, group or entity designated by the Sanctions Committee and listed in Annex I shall be frozen. No funds shall be made available, directly or indirectly, to, or for the benefit of, a natural or legal person, group or entity designated by the Sanctions Committee and listed in Annex I. No economic resources shall be made available, directly or indirectly, to, or for the benefit of, a natural or legal person, group or entity designated by the Sanctions Committee and listed in Annex I, so as to enable that person, group or entity to obtain funds, goods or services.'. Annex 1 wrongly mentioned a certain 'Ali, Yusaf Ahmed' and in May 2003, the Commission adopted (Commission) Regulation 866/2003 amending Council Regulation 881/2002 (*OJ* L 124, 19), whose Annex I now mentioned the correct name of 'Ali Ahmed Yusaf (alias Ali Galoul), Kralingegrand 33, S-16362 Spanga, Sweden; date of birth 20 November 1974; place of birth: Garbaharey, Somalia; nationality: Swedish; passport no: Swedish passport 1041635; national identification No. 741120-1093.' The Council Regulation had been adopted under a triple legal base. Recourse to Article 308 EC was deemed necessary as the Community legislator believed that Articles 301 and 60 would not allow for smart sanctions. For an analysis of the competence aspect of the cases, see: A. Garde, 'Casenote on *Yusuf* and *Kadi*', 65 *Cambridge Law Journal* (2006) p. 281.

[105] *Yusuf*, para. 227.

[106] *Yusuf*, para. 243 (emphasis added).

that the Community 'must, therefore, in that capacity, take all measures necessary to ensure that those resolutions are put into effect'.[107] The Court reasoning goes as follows:

> By concluding a treaty between them [the Member States] could not transfer to the Community more powers than they possessed or withdraw from their obligations to third countries under that Charter. On the contrary, their desire to fulfil their obligations under that Charter follows from the very provisions of the Treaty establishing the European Economic Community and is made clear in particular by [Article 297] and the first paragraph of [Article 307] …
> By conferring those powers on the Community, the Member States demonstrated their will to bind it by the obligations entered into by them under the Charter of the United Nations. Since the entry into force of the Treaty establishing the European Economic Community, the transfer of powers which has occurred in the relations between Member States and the Community has been put into concrete form in different ways within the framework of the performance of their obligations under the Charter of the United Nations …
> It therefore appears that, in so far as under the EC Treaty the Community has assumed powers previously exercised by Member States in the area governed by the Charter of the United Nations, the provisions of that Charter have the effect of binding the Community[.][108]

This is, if confirmed by the European Court of Justice, a radical change in the three-level relationship between the United Nations, the Community and the national legal orders. The Court imposed a positive obligation on the Community legislator to implement UN Security Council Resolutions by invoking the functional succession doctrine. The doctrine, established in *International Fruit* for GATT, had long been thought dead. *Yusuf* revives and extends it 'by analogy' to the UN Charter. This extension is highly debatable.[109] While it is true that all the Member States of the European Commu-

---

[107] *Yusuf*, para. 239.

[108] *Yusuf*, paras. 245–253 (references omitted). Significantly, the Court did not refer to the exclusive nature of the Community competence to adopt economic sanctions (under Article 133 EC).

[109] Analysing the European Court's relationship to GATT in *International Fruit* before the CFI had decided *Yusuf*, P. Eeckhout (op. cit. n. 27, at p. 439) claimed that '[m]uch of that reasoning can be transposed to the relationship between the UN Charter and the EC, in so far as Security Council resolutions are concerned.' Therefore, 'the Court might well, if the question were ever to come before it, be inclined to recognise the binding character of the UN Charter and of Security Council resolutions, and find support for such recognition in its own

nity are also members of the United Nations, the Community has not replaced the Member States in foreign affairs by assuming an exclusive competence within this area.

The references to Articles 297 and 307 EC are spurious.[110] The former provision is addressed to the Member States not the Community,[111] while the latter allows Member States to suspend temporarily the supremacy of Community law to fulfil their prior international legal obligations. In fact, even an analogous application of Article 307 EC could hardly explain why the annulment of a *Community* measure would prevent the *Member States* from fulfilling *their* obligations under the UN Charter.[112] The traditional

---

case law.' However, there are weighty arguments against such a position: First, as Eeckhout himself admits, the Community has not replaced the Member States in the UN or in the Security Council. Second, the idea that the Member States 'could not transfer to the Community more powers than they possessed' (*nemo dat quod non habet*) had been rejected by the majority of Community commentators considering 'that the establishment of the Community had led to the emergence of a new governmental power centre which could not be conceptualised as being made up of fragments or splinters of national sovereign authority' (C. Tomuschat, 'Case Note on *Yusuf* and *Kadi*', 43 *CML Rev.* (2006) p. 537 at p. 543). See also: E. Stein, 'European Political Cooperation (EPC) as a Component of the European Foreign Affairs System', 43 *ZaöRV* (1983) p. 49 at p. 66: '[I]t is widely agreed that, in contrast with its position in GATT, the Community has not "replaced" the Member States in the United Nations and thus is not bound as such by a Security Council Resolution.'

[110] For the opposite view, see: C. Tomuschat arguing that, in relation to Articles 307 and 297, 'the exposition of the Court does not show any weakness' (loc. cit. n. 109, at p. 542).

[111] Article 297 EC allows a Member State, *inter alia*, 'to carry out obligations it has accepted for the purpose of maintaining peace and international security' and, therefore, represents a specification of Article 307 EC: 'Whereas [Article 307] of the Treaty of Rome regulates the solution of possible conflicts between two legal orders, [Article 297] confers in a special situation, wide derogative powers to the Member States concerned which can affect all Treaty provisions within the limits set by [Article 298]. ... Under the strict terms of [Article 297] Member States therefore were empowered to adopt measures in order to implement Security Council resolutions on economic sanctions against, for example, Southern Rhodesia. Measures were taken by Member States in this regard which were designated by the Council and Commission as legal. The derogation clause of [Article 297] of the treaty of Rome itself provides, however, for consultation among all Member States[.] ... When these discussions occur they may lead to the adoption of a Community act.' (Bohr, loc. cit. n. 77, at pp. 265-266).

[112] 'But if the Court were to strike down those regulations, why would that impede the performance by the Member States of their UN obligations? Those obligations would remain intact, and surely every Member State could itself decide to take the action (freezing of assets) which is required by the relevant resolutions. (...) Surely there might be some Member States where it would be possible to have review of the domestic measures on human-rights grounds

constitutional rationale behind Article 307 EC has always been to permit Member States to satisfy their international commitments *against* Community law.[113] The 'internationalist' reading suggested by the CFI would seem to force Member States into fulfilment of their international obligations *qua* Community law!

The Community legal order's self-binding *vis-à-vis* United Nations law remains, therefore, highly contestable. Yet, the most astonishing and dangerous part of the judgment relates to the consequences the Court drew from its normative positioning. After a rhetorical concession that the European Community was 'based on the rule of law, inasmuch as neither its Member States nor its institutions can avoid review of the question whether their acts are in conformity with the basic constitutional charter, the Treaty', the CFI then, swiftly, raised the question of 'whether there exist any structural limits, imposed by general international law or by the EC Treaty itself, on the judicial review.' Surprisingly, the Court indeed found the Community 'acted under circumscribed powers,' with the result that the Community legislator had 'no autonomous discretion' and could 'neither directly alter the content of the resolutions at issue nor set up any mechanism capable of giving rise to such alteration.'[114] What were these structural limits? The Court answers this question in the following way:

> Any review of the internal lawfulness of the contested regulation, especially having regard to the provisions or general principles of Community law relating to the protection of fundamental rights, would imply that the Court is to consider, indirectly, the lawfulness of those resolutions. In that hypothetical situation, in fact, the origin of the illegality alleged by the applicant would have to be sought, not in the adoption of the contested regulation but in the resolutions of the Security Council which imposed the sanctions [.]
> In particular, if the Court were to annul the contested regulation, as the applicants claim it should, although that regulation seems to be imposed by international law, on the ground that that act infringes their fundamental rights which are pro-

in domestic constitutional law. But that cannot be of concern to the CFI' (P. Eeckhout, *Does Europe's Constitution Stop at the Water's Edge: Law and Policy in the EU's External Relations*, Fifth Walter van Gerven Lecture, 22).

[113] On Article 307 EC generally, see: Eeckhout, op. cit. n. 27, at pp. 333-342; Koutrakos, op. cit. n. 62, at pp. 301-328; and loc. cit. n. 70. R. Schütze, 'EC Law and International Agreements of the Member States – An Ambivalent Relationship?'

[114] *Yusuf*, paras. 260-265.

> tected by the Community legal order, such annulment would indirectly mean that the resolutions of the Security Council concerned themselves infringe those fundamental rights. In other words, the applicants ask the Court to declare by implication that the provision of international law at issue infringes the fundamental rights of individuals, as protected by the Community legal order.[115]

The Court, thus, declined all jurisdiction to review the Community regulation *because it would entail an indirect review of the Security Council Resolutions*. The justification for this generous self-abdication was that UN law would be binding for all Community institutions, including the Community Courts.

There are at least two objections to this argument. First, when the Court claims that the UN Charter prevails over every other international and domestic obligation of the Member States,[116] this is definitely wrong as regards the 'domestic law' part.[117] International law – not even United Nations law – has never claimed automatic supremacy within the national legal orders. Will the international legal order's neutrality towards the dualism-monism debate not, *mutatis mutandis*, extend to the Community legal order? Interestingly, the Court of First Instance spoke of 'the domestic or Community legal order,'[118] and this might indeed be taken as an acknowledgement 'that *vis-à-vis* the UN system the Community constitutes nothing other than a "domestic" regime, to which the rules can be applied which generally regulate the relationship between international and national law.'[119] This dogmatic problem may partly be evaded by invoking 'structural' auto-limitations

---

[115] *Yusuf*, paras. 266-267 (references omitted, emphasis added).

[116] *Yusuf*, para. 231: 'From the standpoint of international law, the obligations of the Member States of the United Nations under the Charter of the United Nations clearly prevail over every other obligation of domestic law or of international treaty law including, for those of them that are members of the Council of Europe, their obligations under the ECHR and, for those that are also members of the Community, their obligations under the EC Treaty.'

[117] The CFI invokes Article 27 of the Vienna Convention on the Law of Treaties, prohibiting a State from invoking its internal law as a *justification* for a failure to perform a treaty. This provision cannot, however, be interpreted to codify the primacy of international law over domestic law. '[N]o rule of international law tells the subjects of international law which hierarchical status they should attribute to international law *within* their internal legal system,' for 'international law respects the decision as pertaining to the *domaine réservé*' (A. Peters, op. cit. n. 8, at p. 35). Compare also the discussion on direct effect above: *supra* n. 20.

[118] *Yusuf*, para. 228.

[119] Tomuschat, loc. cit. n. 109, at p. 541.

of the Community legal order. Yet, the internationalist solution – which would subject Community *primary* law to compliance with international law – would come at a high price: it effectively downgrades the EC Treaty to an 'ordinary international treat[y].'[120] This vision may explain why the CFI – paradoxically – felt more confident to apply *international* human rights law (in the form of *jus cogens*) than *Community* human rights law.[121] While abdicating its function as a Community court, the CFI was happy to assume its function as a decentralised international court![122]

There is a second objection to the primacy of United Nations law as pronounced by the CFI. The traditional approach had been based on a conscious reflection of the Community legal order's 'middle ground' position. The European Court of Justice was neutral towards the use of a Community instrument by the Member States. However, once the Member States had recourse to Community law to implement UN economic sanctions, they would have to exercise this power in conformity with Community law. This approach translated the systemic middle ground position of the Community legal order into a normative *argumentum ad temperantiam*. The CFI judgment changes this balance dramatically on either side of the scales: the Community legal order would now seem to *require* the Member States to implement their UN obligations *qua* Community law, while it refuses to impose the traditional *quid pro quo* in the form of judicial review in the light of Community human rights.

This reasoning has dangerous *federal* repercussions. These result from the Community legal order's claim to absolute supremacy over the national law of its Member States.[123] As national Supreme Courts are prevented from

---

[120] *Flaminio Costa* v. *E.N.E.L.*, Case 6/64 [1964] ECR 585, 593, by way of contrast, had proclaimed that '[b]y contrast with ordinary international treaties, the E[]C Treaty has created its own legal system.'

[121] Having refused to review the UN measure against Community law indirectly, the CFI found that it was nonetheless 'empowered to check, indirectly, the lawfulness of the resolutions of the Security Council in question with regard to *jus cogens*, understood as a body of higher rules of public international law binding on all subjects of international law, including the bodies of the United Nations, and from which no derogation is possible' (*Yusuf,* para. 277).

[122] For a discussion of G. Scelle's theory of *dédoublement fonctionnel*, see: A. Cassese, 'Remarks on Scelle's Theory of "Role Splitting" (*dédoublement fonctionnel*) in International law', 1 *EJIL* (1990) p. 210.

[123] *Internationale Handelsgesellschaft mbH* v. *Einfuhr- und Vorratsstelle für Getreide und Futtermittel*, Case 11/70 [1970] ECR 1125.

challenging a Community measure in the light of their national human rights standards, the judicial abdication of the *Community* judiciary *vis-à-vis* international law will simultaneously tie the hands of the *national* judiciaries of the Member States. The CFI's refusal to review indirectly the UN Security Council Resolutions in the forms of the Community measures thus immunises them from legal challenges in every single national legal order of the European Community. This will be bad news for those Member States that have not accepted the direct effect and supremacy of UN measures in their domestic legal orders.[124] Moreover, in the future, it may also be bad news for the Community legal order, for the lack of judicial stomach on the part of the CFI may erode the Community legal order's legitimacy in the national legal orders. National Supreme Courts may well decide to suspend EC Sanctions Regulations 'as long as' the Community legal order refuses to safeguard an adequate level of fundamental human rights protection.[125] *Yusuf* thus endangers the autonomy of the Community legal order on either side: it subordinates the Community legal order to United Nations law and risks a serious judicial rebellion from the national legal orders.

4. Conclusion: The Community Legal Order on 'Middle Ground'

The Community legal order is an autonomous legal order and, as such, has had to define its relationship towards international law. Early on, the Community Courts chose a monist road: international norms binding on the Com-

[124] For an analysis of the relationship of the German, Dutch and French legal orders to UN Security Council Resolutions, see: N. Lavranos, op. cit. n. 83, at pp. 100-110.

[125] The famous gesture of defiance of the German Supreme Court in BVerGE 37, 271 (*Solange* I) may come to mind: '*Solange* der Integrationsprozeß der Gemeinschaft nicht so weit fortgeschritten ist, daß das Gemeinschaftsrecht auch einen von einem Parlament beschlossenen und in Geltung stehenden formulierten Katalog von Grundrechten enthält, der dem Grundrechtskatalog des Grundgesetzes adäquat ist, ist nach Einholung der in Art. 177 des Vertrags geforderten Entscheidung des Europäischen Gerichtshofs die Vorlage eines Gerichts der Bundesrepublik Deutschland an das Bundesverfassungsgericht im Normenkontrollverfahren zulässig und geboten, wenn das Gericht die für es entscheidungserhebliche Vorschrift des Gemeinschaftsrechts in der vom Europäischen Gerichtshof gegebenen Auslegung für unanwendbar hält, weil und soweit sie mit einem der Grundrechte des Grundgesetzes kollidiert' (ibid., 285 (emphasis added)).

munity will enter the Community legal order without an additional Community act introducing them into the 'domestic' legal order.

The openness of the Community system is, nonetheless, tempered by the doctrine of direct effect: only self-executing rules can be used as a source of rights or obligations and as a standard of review. The direct effect question is a 'political question' and the European Courts refuse to give direct effect to an international treaty, where doing so 'would deprive the legislative or executive organs of the Community of the scope for manoeuvre enjoyed by their counterparts in the Community's trading partners.'[126] We encountered a similar constitutional filter in the context of international custom. While affirming the monist creed and considering international custom to '*form part of the Community legal order*,'[127] the Courts have also granted the Council the power to make 'manifest errors of assessment concerning the conditions for applying those rules.'[128] Customary international law can, consequently, only be used as a ground for invalidating conflicting Community rules in limited circumstances.

However, to soften the consequences of a lack of direct effect, Community constitutionalism recognises a doctrine of indirect effects, the most important element of which is the duty of consistent interpretation *pro* international law. Community legislation 'must be interpreted, and its scope limited, in the light of the relevant rules of the international law ... so as to give it the greatest practical effect, within the limits of international law.'[129]

The Community's choice to 'open up' towards the international legal order has significant federal repercussions. When the European Court of Justice pierced the dualist veil between the Community and the national legal orders in *Van Gend en Loos*, the Community's constitutional position towards international law would automatically determine the status of these norms in the Member States' legal orders. International norms thus 'incorporated' will automatically enter every single national legal order and will partake in the constitutional effects of Community law. From the perspective of national legal orders, these international norms are communitarised. They enjoy absolute supremacy over national law. Community law, thus, not only

---

[126] *Portuguese Republic* v. *Council of the European Union*, Case C-149/96 [1999] ECR 8395, para. 46.

[127] *Racke*, para. 46.

[128] *Racke*, para. 52.

[129] Poulsen and Diva Navigation Corp, paras. 9 and 11.

'interpose[s] itself, in many areas, between municipal law and traditional international law,' but it also 'become[s] a conduit for the incorporation and application of international law in the municipal sphere.'[130]

In the second part of this chapter, we investigated to what extent the Community has considered itself bound by international agreements concluded by all of its Member States. The Community legal order has recognised a doctrine of functional succession. This doctrine was developed in the context of GATT (1947) and has recently been extended to the United Nations Charter. This is, in itself, a highly contested and contestable decision. More problematic, however, were the conclusions that the CFI drew from this judicial choice in *Yusuf*. The succession doctrine in *International Fruit* never meant that GATT law was hierarchically superior to primary Community law. The ECJ simply found the Community legal order materially bound by that multilateral agreement. GATT law would then share the hierarchical rank of all international agreements – that is, *below* Europe's constitutional charter. The superiority of the EC Treaty would safeguard the autonomy of the Community legal order.

How then did the CFI justify the 'primacy' of United Nations law *in the Community legal order*? The Court misinterpreted Article 103 UN Charter as mandating the supremacy of international law over Community law. The subordination of the Community under the UN Security Council may please some international lawyers. The pro-international law stance will, however, have a high price: the Community legal order could lose its autonomy and its identity in a move that would contradict the very spirit of the constitutional reforms agreed at Maastricht. Had the TEU not obliged the European Union 'to assert *its* identity on the international scene, in particular through the implementation of a common foreign and security policy';[131] an identity that should be 'founded on the principles of liberty, democracy, respect for human rights and fundamental freedoms, and the rule of law, principles which are common to the Member States'?[132]

---

[130] Bethlehem, loc. cit. n. 9, at p. 172.

[131] Article 2 TEU (emphasis added). According to Article 11(1) TEU, the EU is required to 'define and implement a common foreign and security policy covering all areas of foreign and security policy, the objectives of which shall be', *inter alia*, 'to develop and consolidate democracy and the rule of law, and respect for human rights and fundamental freedoms.'

[132] Article 6(1) TEU.

The unconditional surrender to the supremacy of the UN Security Council may, ironically, re-open the debate on the ultimate arbiter of constitutionality in Europe.[133] The relationship between the Community Courts and the national Supreme Courts had been gradually settled in favour of the absolute supremacy of Community law due to the adequate constitutional guarantees offered in exchange by the latter. Yet 'this type of primacy cannot as a matter of course be extended to the international level. No such guarantees are present at the UN level. Respect for international law cannot mean that core precepts of constitutionalism are abandoned.'[134]

In conclusion, 'as long as' the international level has not generated an equivalent standard of human rights protection, the Community legal order should be entitled to review United Nations law against its *European* constitutional standard. Apart from safeguarding the autonomy of the Community legal order, this would also follow from the Community's precious 'middle ground' position. Where Member States decide under the CFSP to 'communitarise' these international norms, they cannot only give them the

[133] Cf., M. Kumm, 'Who is the final arbiter of constitutionality in Europe?: Three conceptions of the relationship between the German Federal Constitutional Court and the European Court of Justice', 36 *CML Rev.* (1999) p. 351.

[134] Eeckhout, op. cit. n. 112, at p. 25. For the (moderately) opposite view, see: Tomuschat, loc. cit. n. 109: 'The reader is positively impressed by the willingness of the Court to apply the same standards that govern the relationship between the Community legal order and the domestic legal orders of the Member States also to the relationship between the UN System and the Community system... However, it should not be overlooked that already at that stage, precisely in *Internationale Handelsgesellschaft*, the existence of fundamental rights as an integral element of the Community legal order was affirmed; furthermore, there existed a full-fledged judicial procedure through which individuals who were victims of Community measures could assert rights which had already been infringed. None of that can currently be found in the UN legal system, or in any event very little. Therefore, what is at stage is not the rivalry between two legal systems each of which satisfies the legitimate needs of individuals as they are recognised ... but rather the choice between a fully developed legal system for the protection of individual rights, on the one hand, and, on the other hand, an embryonic system which is ill-equipped to deal with instances of direct individual grievances' (ibid., 544) However, a little later, Tomuschat congratulates the Court for not having shied away from the responsibility by claiming that only the Member States were bound by the UN Charter: 'What obviously the Court of First Instance wished to achieve was full harmony between the requirements of the UN system and the legal position within the Community system. The Court is to be congratulated for having rejected such *finesseries* and for accepting the primacy of the UN system without any general restrictive caveats – with one exception only [i.e. *jus cogens*]' (ibid., 545).

benefits of supremacy and direct effect. They must equally accept the constitutional responsibilities that come along with the EC, in particular, respect for *Community* human rights.

5. Postscript: Kadi and the European Court of Justice – Towards an 'As-Long-As' Jurisprudence?

While *Yusuf* would only knock at the judicial gates of the European Court of Justice,[135] a second appeal case entered into Europe's highest court. In *Kadi* v. *Council and Commission*,[136] the ECJ will have to deal with the very same issues discussed above.[137] Will the Court confirm the CFI or will it return to the European Union's traditional approach towards the United Nations? Will it adopt an altogether different approach?

On 16 January 2008, Advocate General Poiares Maduro delivered his opinion in *Kadi*. Holding that the 'Treaty is not merely an agreement between States, but an agreement between the *peoples* of Europe', the Advocate General considered that 'the Treaty has created a municipal legal order of trans-national dimensions.' This would not mean that Community law and public international law 'pass by each other like ships in the night.' International law may well inspire Community law, but 'in the final analysis, the Community Courts determine the effect of international obligations within the Community legal order by reference to conditions set by Community law.'[138] In the light of these constitutional generalities, the fundamental ques-

---

[135] Thanks to the diplomatic pressure of the Swedish government, Yusuf was removed from the United Nations terrorist list. On the Community obligation to press for de-listing in the form of diplomatic protection within the UN systems, see: *Chafik Ayadi*, Case T-253/02 [2006] ECR II-2139, where the CFI held 'that particular obligations are imposed on the Member States of the Community when a request for removal from the list is addressed to them ... Member States must thus ensure, so far as is possible, that interested persons are put in a position to put their point of view before the competent national authorities when they present a request for their case to be reviewed' (ibid., paras. 144 and 147).

[136] *Yassin Abdullah Kadi* v. *Council and Commission*, Case C-402/05P (not yet decided).

[137] In the light of the constitutional principles at stake and the strong academic reaction to the *Yusuf* and *Kadi* judgments, it would be unwise for the Court to choose an easy exit and annul the European legislation for lack of competence. While the legal basis argument may have some merit, a responsible constitutional court would feel obliged to clarify the legal uncertainty created by the decisions in *Yusuf* and *Kadi*.

[138] Opinion of Advocate General Poiares Maduro, 16 January 2008 (not yet reported), paras. 21-23.

tion in *Kadi* was whether there was 'any basis in the Treaty for holding that the contested regulation is exempt from the constitutional constraints normally imposed by Community law, since it implements a sanctions regime imposed by Security Council resolutions.'[139]

The Advocate General answered this question in the negative. He first discarded the respondents' principal argument based on Article 307 EC. Three objections are voiced.[140] 'The crucial problem with the argument', according to Maduro, was 'that it presents Article 307 EC as the source of a possible derogation from Article 6(1) EU.'[141] 'Furthermore, it would potentially enable national authorities to use the Community to circumvent fundamental rights which are guaranteed in their national legal orders' – a development that would contradict the European Court's case law, 'according to which the Community guaranteed a complete system of judicial protection in which fundamental rights are safeguarded in consonance with the constitutional traditions of the Member States.' Thirdly and most importantly: 'The obligations under Article 307 EC and the related duty of loyal cooperation flow in both directions: they apply to the Community as well as to the Member States.' This meant that Member States as members of the United Nations and particularly those belonging to the Security Council 'must act in such a way as to prevent, as far as possible, the adoption of decisions by organs of the United Nations that are liable to enter into conflict with the core principles of the Community legal order.'[142]

After having discarded the 'political question doctrine' as a potential argument against the European Court's jurisdiction, the Advocate General addressed the functional differences between the European Court of Human Rights and the European Court of Justice. The former acted on the basis of an international treaty that was 'designed to operate primarily as an interstate agreement which creates obligations between the Contracting Parties at the international level.' The duty of the latter, on the other hand, was 'to act as the *constitutional court of the municipal legal order* that is the Community.' The European Court of Human Rights and the European Court of Jus-

[139] Ibid., para. 25.

[140] Each of the three objections is controversial. However, the following section will only provide a descriptive account of the main arguments of the Advocate General.

[141] According to Article 6(1) EU, the European Union 'is founded on the principles of liberty, democracy, respect for human rights and fundamental freedoms, and the rule of law.'

[142] Opinion of Advocate General Poiares Maduro, 16 January 2008, paras. 31-32.

tice were thus incomparable 'as regards the relationship of their legal system with public international law.'[143] Thus regardless of whether or not the European Court of Human Rights would be obliged not to review United Nations measures, it was the duty of the European Court of Justice to review Community acts implementing United Nations measures in the light of *Community* human rights.

Such a review might well have 'certain repercussions on the international state'; yet, 'these repercussions need not necessarily be negative.' '[A]s the system governing the functioning of the United Nations now stands, the only option available to individuals who wish to have access to an independent tribunal in order to obtain adequate protection of their fundamental rights is to challenge domestic implementing measures before a domestic court.'[144] This approach thus translates the 'as-long-as' jurisprudence to the relationship between European and international law: '[h]ad there been a genuine and effective mechanism of judicial control by an independent tribunal at the level of the United Nations, then this might have released the Community from the obligation to provide for judicial control of implementing measures that apply within the Community legal order.' Yet, *as long as* such a mechanism did not exist, 'the Community institutions cannot dispense with proper judicial review proceedings when implementing the Security Council resolutions in question within the Community legal order.'[145]

If followed by the European Court of Justice, this approach promises a nuanced treatment of legal acts adopted by the United Nations within the European legal order. It would go beyond the traditional approach of the Community legal order – legal autonomy with an 'internationalist' streak – in that it expressly links the degree of judicial scrutiny in the European legal order with the existence of functional equivalents in the international legal order. This approach would guarantee the autonomy of the Community legal order, while providing a constitutional incentive for the international legal order to develop in such a way that would allow the European legal order to continue its 'opening-up' towards international law.

---

[143] Ibid., para. 37 (emphasis added).
[144] Ibid., para. 38.
[145] Ibid., para. 54.

Part II
Legitimacy and the *Trias Politica*: The Shift to Courts

INTERNATIONALISATION AND LEGITIMACY OF DECISIONS BY THE HIGHEST COURTS

A.M. Hol*

1. Argumentation, Coherency, Justice

For what reasons is it important for the highest courts to study each other's decisions? I think at least three reasons have to be mentioned.

The first reason I would like to call the reason of argumentation. Studying the decisions of courts of foreign legal systems can be inspiring, as it can help to find relevant arguments for legal reasoning in a specific case. In this case the decisions of foreign courts are seen as a kind of reservoir of relevant arguments for one's own decisions. Of course, it can be the case that one disagrees with the outcome or the reasoning of the other court. Still, its study can be seen as helpful and inspiring, since a foreign decision can work as a kind of take-off point to help to develop one's own arguments.

A second reason for studying foreign court decisions is motivated by an internal legal dynamic: the need for coherency. It is a feature of a legal system to be as coherent as possible (otherwise one could not speak of a 'system'). Law has to be developed and interpreted in such a way that inconsistencies and incoherencies are avoided. This is not only a requisite of rationality, but also serves the principle of legal certainty. Perhaps the need for coherency not only applies to the national legal system. In a strongly internationalising world, there may also be a need to move towards a more or less coherent international and transnational legal order. This might provide

* A.M. Hol is Professor of Jurisprudence, Utrecht University, The Netherlands. He is also Deputy Justice at the Court of Appeal of Amsterdam and Deputy Judge at the District Court of Haarlem, The Netherlands.

A.S. Muller and M.A. Loth (eds.), Highest Courts and the Internationalisation of Law

a reason to study the legal decisions of foreign courts in order to discover whether the legal solution developed for the national context fits in the international or transnational context. Of course, this search for coherency is not a simple matter. The question always remains as to which decisions should be coherent with which decisions. After all, one could argue that decisions of foreign courts are simply erroneous. The search for coherency is not simply a matter of fitting in decisions in an already existing international or transnational legal system. As expressed by Lord Bingham in the *Fairchild* case, 'the development of the law [...] cannot of course depend on a head-count of decisions.'[1] Already because of the differences in legal traditions and rules, this would not be a very advisable approach. A far more meaningful approach would be to look for common legal principles as a test of coherence. Although serious methodological problems have to be solved concerning how to promote a more coherent international or transnational legal order, coherency still seems to be an important reason for the highest courts to compare each other's decisions. Again, as Lord Bingham said in hi judgement of the case, when underlining the need for a comparison of decisions of foreign courts, 'In a shrinking world [...] there must be some virtue in uniformity of outcome whatever the diversity of approach in reaching that outcome.'[2]

A third reason for studying foreign court decisions can be seen as an overarching one. In the end the need to search for arguments and coherency in comparing foreign court decisions will be inspired by the search for legitimacy. Indeed, one could say that it is the core of legal reasoning to legitimise its outcomes. Presenting effective arguments and showing that the decision is coherent with other decisions and fits well in the legal system is an undeniable prerequisite of any rational, and therefore legitimate, decision. Here, it is important to note that legitimacy is a complex thing, and that it might be helpful to distinguish between two kinds of legitimacy; input and output legitimacy.[3] In the field of law a decision can be legitimised by showing that the solution found is grounded in the legal system itself. This is the case when the decision can be deduced from the existing legal rules in a procedure that conforms to the legal standards. One could say that here it is the

[1] *Fairchild* v. *Glenhaven Funeral Services Ltd* [2002] 3 WLR 89, 3 All ER 305 (HL).

[2] Ibid., p. 32.

[3] M.A. Loth and A.S. Muller, 'Highest Courts and the Internationalisation of Law: challenges and changes', in this volume, section 2.2.

legal system itself that provides the input for legitimacy. But for a decision to be legitimate, making reference to the legal system itself might not be enough. To be legitimate, it is also important that the decision will be acceptable to the parties, and more broadly, to the citizens to whom it might be of importance in the future. Merely referring to the fact that the decision fits well in the legal system might not be enough here. To make it acceptable, it is important that the parties and others consider, or should consider, the decision to be just, never mind its formalistic legal appropriateness. Whether the decision is acceptable or not is a matter of output legitimacy, which is a matter of justice, here understood as both substantive and procedural justice. In the modern globalising and internationalising world it is easy to understand that a national court might be confronted with critical questions regarding its decisions if they differ from decisions of foreign courts in similar cases. This is because it might make the parties, or one of them[4] and others attentive to it, believe that maybe the court has taken the wrong, i.e., an unjust decision. To prevent or answer such a possible criticism, it might be prudent to discuss alternative solutions found by foreign courts in an implicit or even explicit way.

So, in the end, the search for legitimacy might be the first and foremost reason to study the decisions of foreign courts. In the remainder of this paper I will elaborate on this thesis and make some remarks to qualify and also to nuance what I have put forward. I will start by explaining what, in a modern context, is the legitimising function of courts in general. Next, I will say a few things about what this means if we look at a broader international context. At the end I will come to the question of what this all means for how courts search for arguments, strive towards coherency, and seek justice.

2. The Administration of Justice as a Middle Ground

Above I have made a distinction between input and output legitimacy. Input legitimacy refers to the outcome according to the legal system as such. Output legitimacy refers to the acceptance of the outcome by the parties and others. Legal decisions are completely legitimate if both sides coincide. The outcome as generated by the internal dynamics of the legal system itself is

---

[4] The losing party.

completely accepted by the citizens. However, in everyday practice, such harmony between the law and the way it is experienced by citizens will seldom be fully realised. There will often be tensions. This is because the law does not always produce outcomes that are experienced as just in particular cases. Amongst other things, this has to do with the fact that general rules, when applied to an individual case, can lead to an unfair outcome because of specific features of the case not foreseen by the law. There can also be tensions because citizens have a different understanding of what the law should be and what is actually just. It may also be the case that there are tensions because citizens are not always reasonable, and for that reason they have difficulty in acknowledging the more general point of view of the law, which conflicts with the more self-orientated or egocentric perspective of some citizens. One of the functions of the judiciary in deciding cases is to solve or reduce the potential tension between the law and individual citizens, and the way they perceive justice. This can work both ways. In judging cases, judges can, by interpretation, try to adapt the legal system to what citizens think is just, or the other way around, they can try to change citizens' understanding of justice by making them accept the point of view of what they think the law actually is. In this way, the function of the judge can be understood as a mediating function. As a kind of middle ground, the judge tries to bring together the law and the citizen so that the perceptions of what is just coincide. This is what legitimacy is all about.

3. Reasoning and Persuasiveness

If it is the case that legitimacy has to do with bridging a possible gap between the law and the way citizens perceive what is just, I have to say a few words about the way judges can succeed in doing this. In modern societies, authority is no longer self-evident. Authority is neatly bound with relationships with a hierarchical structure and such structures are often found to be problematic in a more horizontal, democratically organised society. Although the authority of the judiciary in many modern countries is hardly questioned, even here one can notice a tendency towards a more critical approach in its functioning. An interesting expression of this more critical attitude towards the authority of the judiciary may be found in the plea for the introduction of the practice of publishing judges' opinions in those countries where, up until now, no such practice exists. This plea can be seen as an expression of an interest in knowing about the (real) reasons for the decisions taken by the authorities. Anyhow, it is evident that in modern societies people are less willing to accept decisions because they are made by a certain institution that has a certain authority. The willingness to accept certain decisions nowadays seems to be motivated more and more by the fact that there are good reasons for doing so. This clarifies why reasoning and providing reasons for decisions is so important when we are discussing modern forms of adjudication. The legitimacy of legal decisions is partly a matter of reasoning and giving reasons. If the judge is ascribed with a mediating task, it is by means of reasoning and persuasion that he or she will have to fulfil it.

4. Legitimacy and Legal Certainty

Before I can come back to what I have said about the reasons for studying the decisions of foreign courts, one more remark is important. So far, I have emphasised the importance of reasoning because this is the way judges should legitimise their decisions. In these reasons it must become clear that the decision is based on the existing law and that it does justice to the parties and others. However, providing reasons also has another function. Since it is often the case that judges do have a kind of discretionary power,[5] and so have the power to decide the case in different directions, the principle of legal certainty requires them to explain why they have chosen a specific solution. To be able to act according to the law and be proactive towards it, it is important that citizens are able to understand the rationale behind a decision. Explaining this rationale is necessary to prevent a decision being perceived as coincidental or arbitrary.

5. The Legitimacy of National Court Decisions in an International Context

Above, I have presented the thesis that it is because of the search for legitimacy that judges in the national context have to study decisions of foreign courts. It is now time to explain why this is so. At first sight, the thesis looks

[5] Amongst other things, this is the case because of the open texture of the law, its vagueness, and the possible contradictions or tensions between legal regulations.

odd. From the point of view of legitimacy it is easy to understand that the reasoning of the judge is shaped by the law in the national context and not the international context. Foreign law is not recognised as a legal source in most countries,[6] so there is no need for judges to justify their decisions by making reference to the decisions of their colleagues abroad. Of course, studying foreign law can be a source of inspiration, but there is no need to do so. However, things are changing. I think at least three developments are relevant here.

First of all, there is the growing internationalisation of the law. Today, national legal systems are strongly interwoven with international legal systems that also influence and determine the content of the national law of the country. Secondly, part of the development of the law is influenced by the cross-border activities of enterprises and lawyers. In their transnational activities, they develop legal regulations and institutions that cannot be easily reduced to the national law of a certain country. Therefore one speaks about transnational law. Thirdly, there has been a growing exchange between citizens of all countries of the world and there is a growing consciousness of the interdependence of all people in the world. It is said that we live in a globalising world. These and other developments will increasingly compel national courts to recognise the law and legal decisions of foreign countries in order to account for their own decisions.

This is evident where international law has to be applied by national courts. Here we are confronted with possibly serious questions as to how this international law should be understood within the national context. First of all, there is the more general problem of legal interpretation. How do judges apply international law, how should it be understood? In matters of legal interpretation, when a national judge clearly neglects certain interpretations by his colleagues abroad, this is difficult to justify. The need to study the decisions of foreign judges even increases if one realises that international law is often a complex mass of treaties and rules that do not always form a neatly arranged whole. There can be serious problems of consistency in overlapping areas of separate treaty regimes. Also, international law is often the product of a kind of piecemeal engineering.[7] Neither can one neglect the fact

---

[6] Here, the references to foreign law in the Swiss Private Law Code and in the South African constitution are interesting.

[7] B.Z. Tamanaha, *On the Rule of Law. History, Politics, Theory* (Cambridge University Press 2004) p. 132.

that treaties are often the product of far-reaching compromises. For these and other reasons, applying international law in the national context can be a kind of Herculean *tour de force*. Studying the decisions of foreign courts can be helpful not only in coming to a well-considered interpretation. Given these complexities it is also important to look at the decisions of foreign countries because of the problems that contradicting decisions can cause at the national level. It is easy to imagine that decisions can have negative (economic) effects, if in other countries certain international regulations are applied in a more profitable way for commerce or other branches of the economy. Given the internationalisation of commerce, enterprises are no longer bound to a certain nation. Transnationality also requires national courts to study other legal systems and their case law. For reasons of the legitimacy of the courts themselves, the recognition of new kinds of legal regulations and practices that can no longer be identified with a certain national legal system is a prerequisite. By neglecting or denying the development of new forms of transnational law, national courts would price themselves out of the market. Of course, it is not only in the case of international or transnational law that national courts will be forced to study the decisions of foreign courts, but also when merely applying national law there can still be the need to do so. In many cases decisions in national cases, applying merely national law, can still have an international impact. This is so when, for example, certain decided cases attract a great deal of public attention or can have far-reaching social or economic consequences. Examples might be wrongful life cases and tobacco litigation. In short, because of the growing interdependence of nations, internationalisation and globalisation, there is a growing need for national courts not only to study each other's decisions in certain cases, but also to account for their own decisions. Studying foreign case law is not only a matter of intellectual interest and finding inspiration but, in the first place, it is a matter of legitimacy.

6. Plurality and a Dialogue between Judges

At the beginning of this paper, I summed up a few reasons for studying the decisions of foreign courts. Studying these decisions can be important in finding arguments for one's own decision, it can help to produce a more coherent legal order at the transnational or international level, and it can lead to better legitimised and justified decisions. Before concluding, I think it is important to come back to these reasons, and to nuance them after the points which I have highlighted above. This is necessary because finding arguments, striving towards coherency, and doing justice is maybe not as simple as suggested. When looking for possible arguments, it is always a question of whether the arguments found are effective and good. One must acknowledge that arguments produced by other courts may be wrong. And what about coherency? If a court wishes to render a decision that is not coherent with decisions already delivered by other courts, the question remains of which of the decisions is incorrect from the point of view of coherency? One could advocate that former decisions make the system incoherent and that in the future foreign courts should adapt their decisions to this new one. If it is indeed important that a decision is acceptable to citizens and that it can be perceived as just, the question still remains whether the decision will satisfy everybody. When it comes to individual cases, people will often disagree as to what is a just outcome. However, a simple yardstick to determine who is right is lacking. If judges were like Hercules, and had a complete insight into what the law is on the national, transnational and international level, and also had a complete insight into the moral implications of the law, in that case, maybe we could have reason to believe that what they decide must be right and just.[8] But in real life judges are not like Hercules.

Two observations can be made here. First of all, it seems to be part of the nature of the law to come to clear-cut decisions. There always comes a time in a particular case when it has to be decided what is 'true' from a legal point of view. At the national level the court system has a hierarchical nature with a highest court at the summit. This court has supremacy over the other courts that decide in specific cases. In the end it is this highest court that decides what is 'true' in a certain case. At the transnational level we lack such a court system with a highest court at the top. This means that when there is a difference in legal outcomes concerning certain issues between nations, there is no possibility of determining which is the right outcome. We will have to live with these differences. This means that if courts think it important to come to a more coherent transnational legal system, this should be realised in another way, not by decisions made by a legal institution, but by reasoning and persuasion.[9]

---

[8] The image was developed in R. Dworkin, *Taking Rights Seriously* (London, Duckworth 1977) pp. 105–130.

[9] J. Allard & A. Garapon, *Les Juges dans la Mondialisation. La Nouvelle Revolution du Droit* (Paris, Ed. du Seuil 2005) p. 58; A.-M. Slaughter, *A New World Order* (Princeton Uni-

The second observation concerns the way court decisions are reasoned in different nations and legal cultures. Many of the highest courts provide detailed and elaborate reasoning for their decisions. One could think of the decisions of the *Bundesverfassungsgericht*. Others only provide very brief and rather formalistic reasoning for their decision. The decisions of the *Cour de Cassation* in France are an example here. In many courts, judges can publish their own opinion on a case, whether it is concurring or dissenting. I only mention the decisions of the House of Lords and of the Supreme Court of Finland. Now, if it is indeed the case that a more coherent transnational legal order can only be produced by persuasion based on arguments and reasons presented by the courts, the way courts present their decisions becomes very important. If one agrees that there is no simple yardstick to decide what is a good decision and what is not, this means that to come to preferable decisions it is only by an exchange of arguments that one can come to a conclusion.[10] To make this exchange of arguments possible it is important that all the relevant arguments for a certain outcome are made public. Of course, this can be done in different ways. It can be done by presenting a carefully elaborated reasoning by the court itself. It can be done by publishing the briefs of the advocate general and the report of the reporting judge, as is done by the French *Cour de Cassation*. Of course, the opinions of the judges are also very informative. Anyway, to come to a more coherent transnational legal order, it is important that the courts develop an exchange of arguments and ideas in what is also called a 'commerce of judges.'[11]

To serve justice and to develop the legal system in an internationalising and globalising world it is important that national courts exchange their ideas and the solutions they have found for difficult legal questions. Since it is not easy to discern what is just and right in legal matters, this exchange should be based on reciprocal respect for the specific solutions found by other national courts. Plurality, and the acceptance thereof, is important for what one could call the 'judicial comity.'[12] This also means that as long as judges cannot agree on having certain transnational legal cases decided by a spe-

versity Press 2004) pp. 75-78. See also M. Delmas-Marty, *La Refondation des Pouvoirs. Les Forces Imaginantes du Droit (III)* (Paris, Ed. du Seuil 2007) p. 42 ff.

[10] The practice of finding the 'truth' by means of debate, exchanging arguments and dialogue rests on the long Aristotelian tradition of dialectical thinking. Modern versions of the approach are known as consensus theories, as developed, for example, by Habermas.

[11] Allard & Garapon, op. cit. n. 9.

[12] Slaughter, op. cit. n. 9, p. 86 ff.

cific national court, a means by which to reach a more coherent legal world order should be based on dialogue between judges.

7. Internationalisation and the Legitimacy of the Decisions of the Highest Courts

Why should national courts study the decisions of other national courts? This was the main question to be answered in this paper. As I have tried to explain, it is the need for legitimacy. Assuming that the world is internationalising, and therefore also shrinking, decisions on the national level will increasingly have consequences at a transnational or international level. If one agrees that one of the principles of the law is that it can present itself as a rational, i.e., a coherent, order, this development requires national courts to study the decisions of other national courts. The practice of comparative studies by the highest courts will become an even more important part of their daily judicial practice than it already is.[13] This developing practice is not an activity without engagement. Comparative law is important because at the end of the day it helps to legitimate the decisions of the courts, and by doing so also the legal system as a whole.

[13] G. Canivet, 'The Practice of Comparative Law by the Supreme Courts: Brief reflections on the dialogue between the judges in French and European experience', 80 *Tulane Law Review* (2006). Of course, academic studies can be of great value here. An interesting example of the value of comparative legal studies in the case of decisions by the highest courts is B.S. Markesinis, J.-B. Auby, D. Coester-Waltjes & S. Deakin, *The Tortious Liability of Statutory Bodies. A Comparative and Economic Analysis of Five English Cases* (Oxford, Hart 1999).

THE CONSTITUTIONAL COURT OF SLOVENIA AND ITS ROLE AS AN INTERMEDIARY BETWEEN NATIONAL AND INTERNATIONAL LAW

M. Skrk*

1. Introduction

My primary goal is to present the role played by the Constitutional Court of Slovenia in the field of international law as applied and interpreted within the national legal order. The Constitutional Court is not the only judicial body in the country that is entitled to apply international law. It must be emphasised that all courts in Slovenia and a number of state authorities are bound to apply international law according to Slovene national law. Following Article 125 of the Constitution, judges are independent in the performance of their judicial function and they are bound by the Constitution and laws. The constitutional demand that a judge is bound by the Constitution and laws is repeated in Article 3 paragraph 1 of the Law on Courts.[1] There, it is additionally stated that in conformity with the Constitution a judge is bound to respect general principles of international law and ratified treaties. However, the most prominent role in this respect must be assigned to the Constitutional Court. According to its position and the jurisdiction assigned to it, the Constitutional Court provides for the formal interpretation of the Constitution and has jurisdiction to examine treaties.

* H.E. Judge Skrk is Vice-President of the Constitutional Court of the Republic of Slovenia.
[1] Official Gazette of the Republic of Slovenia, Nos. 100/05 (ZS-UPB2) and 49/06.

A.S. Muller and M.A. Loth (eds.), Highest Courts and the Internationalisation of Law

2. The Position of the Constitutional Court

Article 160 of the Constitution establishes the jurisdiction of the Constitutional Court. The Constitutional Court of Slovenia may be listed among those constitutional courts that possess a rather broad jurisdiction. Accordingly, the Constitutional Court is empowered to examine the constitutionality (and legality) of all abstract legal acts passed by the legislature, including laws and ratified treaties, governmental regulations, and abstract acts passed by local communities (paragraph 1). It is also competent to examine the constitutionality of treaties before their ratification (paragraph 2), and to decide on constitutional complaints against judgments of regular courts and other concrete decisions under the proviso that all legal remedies have been exhausted (paragraph 3).

The Law on the Constitutional Court defines the Slovene Constitutional Court as the highest body with judicial power for the protection of constitutionality, legality, human rights and fundamental freedoms.[2] Despite the fact that the Constitution, in Article 127 paragraph 1, defines the Supreme Court as the highest court in the State, the Constitutional Court is actually superior to the Supreme Court. If any court, including the Supreme Court, deems a law applicable to the case at hand to be unconstitutional, it must suspend the case and initiate proceedings before the Constitutional Court.[3] The proceedings in the court may be continued after the Constitutional Court has issued its decision. In addition, while examining a constitutional complaint, the Constitutional Court is empowered to reverse the decision of the Supreme Court – or any other court or body of the last instance – and return the case to the competent body if it establishes that fundamental rights and freedoms of the petitioner were violated.[4]

3. The Supremacy of International Law – Article 8 of the Constitution

The fundamental – but not exclusive – provision concerning the relation between international law and Slovene national law is laid down in Article 8 of the Constitution. It stipulates that:

---

[2] Ibid., No. 15/94.

[3] Article 156 Constitution of the Republic of Slovenia (hereafter, Constitution).

[4] Law on the Constitutional Court, Article 59 para. 1.

> [L]aws and regulations must comply with generally accepted principles of international law and with treaties that are binding on Slovenia. Ratified and published treaties shall be applied directly.[5]

In the view of the author, this constitutional provision gives room for either the monistic or dualistic approach in respect of the position of international law within Slovene national law. In principle, Article 8 is based on the supremacy of international law. The Constitutional Court has, as *obiter dictum*, recognised the supremacy of international law over all domestic norms of non-constitutional character, but not over the Constitution.[6]

Article 8 of the Constitution covers two normative fields of international law, namely, 'generally accepted principles of international law' and treaties. General principles of international law, general principles of law (recognised by civilized nations) and norms of customary international law fall within the ambit of 'generally accepted principles of international law.' In its case law, the Constitutional Court has applied this field of international law by means of incorporation, i.e., 'as the part of the law of the land.'[7] The Constitutional Court has, *inter alia*, applied as a measure 'general principles of law recognised by civilized nations' in its decision on the review of the Decree on Military Tribunals.[8] In the *Stolen Children* case, the Constitutional Court examined whether the Supreme Court acted arbitrarily by establishing that the Federal Republic of Germany could not be sued before Slovene courts for kidnapping children during the Second World War and forcibly transferring them to Germany. It dismissed the constitutional complaint and upheld the Supreme Court's position that no rule of customary international law has (yet) emerged on the basis of which the judicial immunity of Germany could be waived before the Slovene courts for acts *jure imperii* committed by German soldiers during the war.[9]

---

[5] Compare with Article 10 para. 1 of the Constitution of the Italian Republic, Article 25 of the German Basic Law, and Article 9 of the Constitution of the Republic of Austria.

[6] Decision No. U-I-6/93 of 1 April 1994 (*Review of the Decree on Military Tribunals of 1944*), Off. Gaz. RS, No. 23/94, B-I, para. 5 of the reasoning. See also Opinion No. Rm-1/97 of 5 June 1997 *(Preventive review of the Association Agreement between Slovenia and the EC and their Member States, Acting within the Framework of the EU – EU Association Agreement*), Off. Gaz. RS, No. 40/97, para. 12 of the reasoning.

[7] 'The law of nations is part of the law of the land', R. Jennings & A. Watts (eds.), *Oppenheim's International Law*, Vol. I, 9th edn. (London, Longman 1992), p. 56.

[8] Decision No. U-I-6/93. Similarly, it applied as a measure 'generally recognised principles of international law' in Decision No. U-I-266/04 of 9 November 2006 (*Review of the Law on Victims of War Violence*), Off. Gaz. RS, No. 118/06.

[9] Decision No. Up-13 of 8 March 2001, Off. Gaz. RS, No. 28/01.

Since treaties today present the most important and the most reliable source of international law, national courts of the highest instance are most often faced with legal issues pertaining to contemporary treaty law. The Constitutional Court of Slovenia is not an exception in this respect. Therefore, the remaining part of our discussion has been dedicated to the role of treaties in the Slovene national law, including their constitutional review.

4. The Jurisdiction of the Constitutional Court in respect of Treaties

4.1 The purpose of the constitutional review of Treaties

In order to be able to avoid the consequences of state responsibility[10] in so far as it appears after concluding a treaty that it was concluded contrary to the internal constitutional order, the internal legal systems of numerous states provide for the review of the constitutionality of treaties. This role is left to the highest domestic courts or constitutional courts in states providing for a system of judicial review. The relation between international and internal law in an individual state is determined by the constitution of that state and the case law of domestic courts.

Certainly, the majority of contemporary constitutions of democratic states acknowledge the supremacy of international law. Treaties are above domestic laws or are on an equal level with them. In the first case no contradiction between a law and a treaty can occur as the treaty has primacy over the law. In the Slovene internal legal order, a treaty ratified by the National Assembly is on a level higher than the domestic law.[11] If, according to an internal legal order, treaties are on the same level as (federal) laws, in the event of a conflict, general rules on resolving conflicts between the legal regulations of an equal level apply (*lex specialis derogat legi generali, lex posterior derogat legi priori*). However, it is not possible in the internal legal order of Slovenia for a treaty to be on a level higher than the Constitution.[12]

[10] Here I mean state responsibility according to international law (*responsabilité de l'État*).

[11] Article 8, para. 2 of Article 153, and Article 160 para. 1.2 of the Constitution.

[12] See *supra* n. 6. See also A. Graseli, in Šturm (ed.), *Komentar Ustave Republike Slovenije* [Commentary on the Constitution of the Republic of Slovenia] (Fakulteta za podiplomske državne in evropske študije, Ljubljana 2002) p. 140.

4.2 Preventive (*a priori*) constitutional review of Treaties

4.2.1 *Some general observations*

The Slovene Constitution provides *expressis verbis* for the preventive review of the constitutionality of treaties. Among EU Member States such jurisdiction is regulated in France and Spain.[13] Article 160 paragraph 2 of the Slovene Constitution provides that:

> In the process of ratifying a treaty, the Constitutional Court, on the proposal of the President of the Republic, the Government or a third of the deputies of the National Assembly, issues an opinion on the conformity of such treaty with the Constitution. The National Assembly is bound by the opinion of the Constitutional Court.

The jurisdiction of the Constitutional Court to review treaties preventively is also provided in Article 21 paragraph 2 and Article 70 of the Law on the Constitutional Court.

The purpose of the *a priori* review of the constitutionality of a treaty is preventative, i.e., to prevent in good time an unconstitutional international legal obligation from being adopted in the Slovene internal legal order.[14] By ratification a treaty becomes part of the internal law.[15] Here I mean ratification as an internal legal act. Ratification as an international act, equally as acceptance, approval or accession, is one of the possible forms in which a state approves at the international level that it is bound by a treaty.[16] There are also other means of approval. A state can give its approval that it is bound by a treaty by signature or exchange of instruments that form the treaty, or by any other means if so agreed by the parties.[17] Instruments of ratification (or

---

[13] See Opinion No. Rm-1/97, para. 11 of the reasoning.

[14] Ibid., para. 13 of the reasoning.

[15] For a slightly different temporal approach taken by the Constitutional Court, see ibid. '18. The provisions of a treaty by its entry into force in international law become part of the internal legal system of the Republic of Slovenia provided that they have been ratified in conformity with the internal law of the Republic of Slovenia ...'

[16] See Article 2 para. 1(b) of the Vienna Convention on the Law of Treaties (VCLT), signed in Vienna on 23 May 1969, Off. Gaz. SFRY, Treaties and Agreements, No. 30/72, Off. Gaz. RS, No. 35/92, Treaties, No. 9/92. Compare with Articles 14–17 of VCLT.

[17] Ibid., Article 11.

of accession) are issued by the President of the Republic of Slovenia.[18] Thus, a high degree of autonomy of parties in the area of concluding treaties follows from the means by which a state approves, at the international level, that it is bound by a treaty. In this respect, the authorised representatives of the state must also consider prescribed internal legal procedures. The Slovene internal legal order does not recognise the conclusion of a treaty by virtue of signature alone.[19]

In accordance with Slovene national law, the ratification of treaties is in the first place entrusted to the legislature. Pursuant to the same procedure as for the adoption of other laws, the National Assembly ratifies treaties by law by a majority of votes cast by those deputies present, provided that a majority of deputies are present at the session, except where a different type of majority is provided by the Constitution or by law.[20] Therefore, the legislature is granted in the Constitution the same authority for the adoption of laws and for the ratification of those treaties whose ratification falls within its powers. Until the adoption of Article 3.a – the so-called 'European article' – the Constitution did not differentiate between procedures for the ratification of individual types of treaties which are ratified by the National Assembly. At present, in Article 3.a paragraph 1 of the Constitution it is envisaged that pursuant to a treaty ratified by the National Assembly by a two-thirds majority vote of all deputies, Slovenia may transfer the exercise of part of its sovereign rights to international organisations which are based on respect for human rights and fundamental freedoms, democracy and the principles of the rule of law, and may enter into a defensive alliance with states which are based on respect for these values.

The Constitution does not grant the government an explicit authority to conclude treaties.[21] On the basis of the Law on Foreign Affairs[22] the government ratifies the following by a decree: treaties from its competence; treaties that are concluded for the implementation of acts of international organisations

---

[18] Article 107 para. 1.5 of the Constitution and Article 76 of the Law on Foreign Affairs (ZZZ-1), Off. Gaz. RS, No. 45/01.

[19] See the Law on Foreign Affairs. However, in Article 72 of the Law, the provisional application of a treaty prior to its entry into force has been established, for the conclusion of which the government is empowered.

[20] Article 86 Constitution.

[21] Article 153 para. 2 of the Constitution indirectly refers to the power of the government to conclude treaties.

[22] Article 75 para. 5 Law on Foreign Affairs.

binding on Slovenia; the so-called implementing treaties (those which are concluded for the implementation of already existing treaties); treaties on inter-ministerial cooperation; treaties which regulate issues concerning diplomatic and consular relations; implementing treaties in the area of defence and internal affairs; and, treaties which regulate international cooperation in the area of culture, science, and education. The government may not enter into treaties that require the adoption of new laws or the amendment of existing laws.[23] Prior to the ratification of a treaty that is within the competence of the government, the Ministry of Foreign Affairs must send a copy of its text to the working body of the National Assembly that is competent with regards to foreign affairs.[24]

Up to the time of writing, the Constitutional Court has in four cases carried out preventive review of the constitutionality of treaties which were in the process of ratification by the National Assembly. The Constitutional Court made its first, landmark decision of this type in the case of the preventive review of the EU Association Agreement between Slovenia, the European Community, and the (then fifteen) Member States of the EU.[25] Subsequently, the Constitutional Court has preventively reviewed a further three bilateral treaties. It reviewed the conformity of the 'Agreement between the Republic of Slovenia and the Republic of Croatia on Border Traffic and Cooperation' with Section II of the Basic Constitutional Charter on the Sovereignty and Independence of the Republic of Slovenia and with the Constitution.[26] In addition, it reviewed the conformity with the Constitution of the 'Treaty between the Government of the Republic of Slovenia and the Government of the Republic of Croatia on the Regulation of Status-Related and Other Legal Relations Connected with Investments in the Krško Nuclear Power Plant, its Use and Decommissioning,'[27] In a fourth case, the Constitutional Court reviewed the 'Agreement between the Republic of Slovenia and the Holy See on Legal Issues.'[28]

---

[23] Ibid., para. 7.

[24] Ibid., para. 6.

[25] The Europe Agreement establishing an Association between the Republic of Slovenia, of the one part, and the European Communities and their Member States, Acting within the Framework of the European Union, of the other part, Rm-1/97, *supra* n. 6.

[26] Opinion No. Rm-1/00 of 19 April 2001 (*Review of the Transboundary Cooperation Agreement with Croatia*), Off. Gaz. RS, No. 43/01.

[27] Opinion No. Rm-2/02 of 5 December 2002 (*Review of the Treaty on the Krško NPP*), Off. Gaz. RS, No. 117/02.

[28] Opinion No. Rm-1/02 of 19 November 2003 (*Review of the Vatican Agreement*), Off. Gaz. RS, No. 118/03.

The Constitutional Court established unconstitutionality only in the case of the EU Association Agreement (Rm-1/97). The subject of the review was treaty provisions regarding the acquisition of real estate and land in the Republic of Slovenia by citizens of the Member States of the EU (natural persons and legal entities), in view of the fact that the initial text of Article 68 paragraph 2 of the Constitution did not allow aliens to acquire property rights to land except by inheritance provided that the condition of reciprocity was fulfilled.[29] The Constitutional Court found that Article 45.7c and items I and II of Annex XIII of the EU Association Agreement were inconsistent with the constitutional provision insofar as they allowed the purchase of land by citizens of the Member States of the EU. An opinion establishing the unconstitutionality of a treaty is binding on the National Assembly. The National Assembly may not ratify the treaty if the Constitutional Court pronounces that certain provisions of the treaty are inconsistent with the Constitution. The possibility that remains in such a case for the National Assembly is to amend the Constitution prior to the ratification of the unconstitutional treaty. Such an amendment was made by the legislature in the case of the EU Association Agreement.[30] The other possibility remaining for the legislature is to ratify the treaty by reservation in that part in which the Constitutional Court established unconstitutionality, provided that such reservation is permissible under international law. Otherwise, the competent authorities can start new negotiations on the subject of the treaty.[31]

Would the Constitutional Court also be empowered to review preventively a treaty from the competence of the Government? The Constitutional Court has not yet addressed this issue in its case law. However, it seems that it follows from Article 160 paragraph 2 of the Constitution that the Constitu-

[29] Article 68 para. 1 of the 1991 Constitution provides: 'Aliens may acquire ownership rights to real estate under conditions provided by law.'

[30] Article 68 of the 1997 Constitution (Off. Gaz. RS, No. 42/97), which applied until the entry into force of the Constitutional Act Amending Chapter I and Arts. 47 and 68 of the Constitution (Constitutional Act on Arts. 3.a, 47, 68, Off. Gaz. RS, No. 24/03), provided: '(1) Aliens may acquire ownership rights to real estate under conditions provided by law or if so provided by a treaty ratified by the National Assembly, under the condition of reciprocity. (2) Such law and treaty from the preceding paragraph shall be adopted by the National Assembly by a two-thirds majority vote of all deputies.' The existing Article 68 of the Constitution determines that aliens may acquire ownership rights to real estate under conditions provided by law or a treaty ratified by the National Assembly.

[31] Regarding the legislature's possibilities of conduct in the event of an established unconstitutionality of a treaty, see more precisely in Rm-1/97, para. 38 of the reasoning.

tional Court does not have such jurisdiction. A position that the preventive review of the constitutionality of treaties is only envisaged for treaties from the competence of the National Assembly seems to follow from the grammatical interpretation and is based on the second sentence of the above provision, which determines that the National Assembly is bound by the opinion of the National Assembly. In this respect it certainly cannot be excluded that by virtue of other methods of interpretation the Constitutional Court would take a different position. Therefore it is also necessary to consider the rule that the Constitutional Court itself decides on its jurisdiction (*compétence de la compétence*).

The subject of review concerning the preventive review of treaties is the treaty itself and not the draft law on its ratification. Due to its lack of jurisdiction the Constitutional Court rejected the petition to review the constitutionality of the Draft Law on Ratification of the EU Association Agreement.[32]

The Constitutional Court is *ratione temporis* empowered to review a treaty that is in the process of ratification, '[...] i.e., at the time when the treaty has already been signed and when a draft law for its ratification was submitted but not yet adopted by the National Assembly.'[33] As the Constitution provides that the National Assembly is bound by an opinion of the Constitutional Court, the National Assembly may not decide on ratification until it has received the opinion of the Constitutional Court.[34] Generally, the subjects of review are only those treaty provisions which are contested. The entity proposing the review must also state the constitutional provisions to which the alleged violations refer.[35]

The Constitutional Court establishes the conformity of treaty provisions with the Constitution at the time of its decision, regardless of the time when (and if) the treaty enters into force.[36] The entering into force of a treaty depends on the will of the parties and is determined or envisaged in the treaty.[37]

---

[32] Order No. U-I-203/97 of 16 September 1997. Collection of Decisions (OdlUS), VI/2, 115.

[33] Rm-1/97, para. 16 of the reasoning. Compare with Article 75 para. 1 of the Law on Foreign Affairs.

[34] Ibid.

[35] See the Rules of Procedure of the Constitutional Court (Off. Gaz. RS, No. 93/03 and 98/03 corr.).

[36] Rm-1/97, para. 17 of the reasoning.

[37] Article 24 para. 1 VCLT.

In the review of the EU Accession Agreement, the Constitutional Court stated that the opinion it issued according to Article 160 paragraph 2 of the Constitution is not a consultative opinion, but a Constitutional Court decision, of which the character in terms of effects is substantively the same as its other decisions.[38] It is different, however, from other decisions in that the Constitutional Court may not interfere with the treaty itself in the same way that it may interfere with internal legal acts.[39] The opinion pursuant to Article 160 paragraph 2 of the Constitution '[...]does not only oblige the National Assembly, but to the same extent concerning the scope and reasons of review also obliges the Constitutional Court – it has *res judicata* effects.'[40]

The jurisdiction of the Constitutional Court is limited to the review of the conformity of a treaty with the Constitution, not with international law.[41] The review of the conformity of a treaty with international law remains in the domain of the International Court of Justice in The Hague or other international courts, tribunals, and arbitrations.

4.2.2 *Some constitutional legal issues arising from the case law of the Constitutional Court*

In the area of the (preventive) review of treaties it is practically impossible to draw a sharp line between the issues having the character of constitutional law and those having the character of international law. It concerns an area of law in which the two fields of law co-exist. At this point I would like to emphasise two issues of a constitutional law nature which the Constitutional Court has faced concerning the preventive review of the constitutionality of treaties. I assume that other national courts which have jurisdiction to review the constitutional aspects of treaties face similar problems.

In the review of the EU Association Agreement, the government raised the question of whether ratification of the Agreement, which also contained

---

[38] Rm-1/97, para. 15 of the reasoning.

[39] Ibid.

[40] Ibid. An opinion which by its nature is a Constitutional Court decision has *erga omnes* effects.

[41] 'Also in the event of reviewing the conformity of a treaty with the Constitution the Constitutional Court acts as a state authority governed by internal law. This is exactly why the Constitutional Court will carry out a review of a treaty from the viewpoint of its conformity with the Constitution, but not also from the viewpoint of international law.' ibid., para. 15 of the reasoning.

the commitment of the Republic of Slovenia to amend the Constitution, was constitutionally admissible. Namely, it was thought that the National Assembly would ratify the EU Association Agreement prior to amending Article 68 of the Constitution,[42] and with the ratification also adopt an interpretative declaration in which it would make a commitment to amend the Constitution before the entry into force of the Agreement in terms of international law. The response of the Constitutional Court was negative. The Court took the position that the National Assembly may not approve a treaty by which the state would make a commitment to fulfil an international obligation upon the authorisation of the National Assembly, if it is aware of the fact that at the time of deciding on approval that it is inconsistent with the Constitution. Otherwise the National Assembly would prejudice a decision of the drafters of the Constitution, which is not permissible.[43]

The second issue refers to a technique of decision-making by the Constitutional Court. This is whether, in the (preventive) review of a treaty, the Constitutional Court may reach an interpretative decision. The particularity of the opinion in the review of the EU Association Agreement lay also in the fact that the Constitutional Court, within the part of the opinion in which it did not find unconstitutionality, used interpretative operative provisions.[44]

The interpretative decision was introduced into the constitutional review of treaties by the French *Conseil Constitutionnel.*[45] Instead of establishing the unconstitutionality of a treaty provision, the Constitutional Court provides for an interpretation of the contested provision that is consistent with the Constitution.[46]

The actual *sous réserve* interpretation was used by the Constitutional Court in its review of the Vatican Agreement. In item I of the operative part of the opinion, the Court decided that Article 1 of that Agreement, according to which the Republic of Slovenia and the Holy See confirm the principle that the state and the Catholic Church are each within its own system independent and autonomous, and according to which the Catholic Church acts in

[42] In the initial text it prohibited aliens from acquiring real estate except by inheritance provided that the condition of reciprocity was fulfilled; see *supra* n. 26.

[43] Rm-1/97, paras. 35 and 36 of the reasoning.

[44] It concerns Items II and VI of the operative part.

[45] *La décision de non-contrariété sous réserve*, see Rm-1/02, para. 35 of the reasoning.

[46] Ibid. and note 45, cited according to Gaïa, Le Conseil constitutionnel et l'insertion des engagements internationaux dans l'ordre juridique interne (Paris Economica, 1991) pp. 123-127.

the Republic of Slovenia freely under canon law and in conformity with the legal order of the Republic of Slovenia, *is not inconsistent with the principle of sovereignty under Article 3 of the Constitution or with the principle of the separation of the state and religious communities under paragraph 1 of Article 7 of the Constitution insofar as it is interpreted* (emphasis added) that the Catholic Church shall in its activities in the Republic of Slovenia respect the legal order of the Republic of Slovenia, as it follows from the reasoning of the opinion.[47] In item II of the operative part, the Court decided that the interpretation of Article 1 of the Agreement, which is in conformity with the Constitution, is the starting-point for the review of the conformity of other provisions of the Agreement which are the subject of review. Finally, in item VII the Court decided that in the implementation of the Agreement the state authorities of the Republic of Slovenia would have to respect the contents of the Agreement provisions, as interpreted by the Constitutional Court. From paragraph 35 of the reasoning it follows that the Constitutional Court decided to use the so-called interpretative opinion on the basis of its findings made in the decision-making process, according to which Article 1 of the Vatican Agreement may be interpreted in two different manners, one which is consistent and the other which is inconsistent with the Constitution. By excluding the latter the Court was able to conclude as a final result that the challenged provisions of the Vatican Agreement were in fact in conformity with the Constitution.

4.3 Posterior (*a posteriori*) constitutional review of Treaties

4.3.1 *Some general observations*

The Constitution does not envisage the posterior review of the constitutionality of treaties. This type of review has been developed, however, by the Constitutional Court in its case law. It involves an indirect review through the jurisdiction to review laws and regulations, i.e., on the basis of a challenged law or decree on ratification. The jurisdiction of the Constitutional Court is based on paragraphs 1.1 and 1.3 of Article 160 of the Constitution.[48]

---

[47] The operative part refers to paras. 32 and 33 of the reasoning. Article 7 para. 1 of the Constitution contains the so-called 'separation clause' by determining that the state and religious communities are separate.

[48] F. Testen, in Šturm (ed.), op. cit. n. 12, pp. 1112–1113.

As regards the posterior review of constitutionality, the Constitutional Court reviews a treaty through the act on the ratification of a treaty. In the Slovene legal system this can be a law on ratification adopted by the National Assembly or a decree of the government. From the aspect of international law such review raises the question of the hierarchy of treaties, which is an exception in international law,[49] on which parties may reach an agreement.

An act on ratification, either a law or a decree, transposes international obligations contained in a treaty into the national law. Such an act only presents a framework (*chapeau*) and usually contains three to four articles. Their contents are, in addition to introductory provisions, usually limited to include *vacatio legis* – which usually differs from the date on which a treaty enters into force – and the possible determination of an internal authority which is authorised to implement a treaty. The operative part of the act on ratification contains the text of the treaty in Slovene and in a foreign language.[50]

Thus the posterior review of the constitutionality (and legality) of treaties through an act on ratification raises certain fundamental theoretical questions on the relation between international law and the constitutional system of the state. Specifically, this relates to the fact that the supremacy of international law is laid down in the Constitution, and in view of the fact that the state is bound to fulfil its international legal obligations in good faith. Also in the posterior review of the constitutionality of a treaty, the Constitutional Court does not review its consistency with international law, but with the Constitution.

4.3.2 *Case law of the Constitutional Court*

The review of the constitutionality (and legality) of the Decree on Ratification of the Agreement between the Republic of Slovenia and the Republic of Croatia on Military Pensions,[51] on the basis of Article 160 paragraph 1.3 of the Constitution,[52] represents the first case of the posterior review of a treaty

[49] See Article 103 of the UN Charter: 'In the event of a conflict between the obligations of the Members of the United Nations under the present Charter and their obligations under any other international agreement, their obligations under the present Charter shall prevail.'

[50] Article 77 para. 1 of the Law on Foreign Affairs.

[51] Off. Gaz. RS, Treaties, No. 13/92.

[52] 'The Constitutional Court decides:... on the conformity of regulations with the Constitution and with laws.'

in the case law of the Constitutional Court.[53] The Constitutional Court stated in the reasoning that such an agreement has a higher position in the hierarchy of legal acts than regulations but below that of the Constitution and a law.[54] Therefore, it allowed the possibility that the Court could review the constitutionality and legality of such a treaty and not only its conformity with the Constitution. Furthermore, the Constitutional Court asserted that through the review of the constitutionality and legality of the decree on ratification, it reviewed also the constitutionality of the treaty. Moreover, the Court stated that such an indirect review of the constitutionality of a treaty had already been practised in the case law of the Italian Constitutional Court and the German Federal Constitutional Court. In this case the Constitutional Court only reviewed the conformity of the Agreement with the Constitution (and not its legality) and decided that the challenged decree on the ratification of the agreement was not inconsistent with the Constitution.

In the review of the Decree on the Ratification of the Agreement on Military Pensions (No. U-I-147/94), the Constitutional Court did not take a position on whether it is empowered to review the constitutionality of treaties ratified by laws. In the case of the preventive review of the EU Association Agreement discussed above, the Constitutional Court took the position that, on the basis of Article 160 paragraph 1.1 of the Constitution,[55] it is empowered to review the conformity of a law on the ratification of a treaty with the Constitution. Concerning this it allowed the possibility that if in the process of such review the Constitutional Court should find that a treaty provision is in conflict with the Constitution, it may abrogate the law on ratification of the mentioned treaty, but such decision of the Constitutional Court has effect only in the internal legal system.[56] In that case the Constitutional Court has not yet taken a position concerning the question of whether the review of the constitutionality of a law on ratification is possible prior to the entry into force of the treaty on the international level.[57] In this event, the jurisdiction

[53] Decision No. U-I-147/94 of 30.11.1995, Off. Gaz. RS, No. 3/96.

[54] Article 153 para. 2 of the Constitution (The Conformity of Legal Acts) provides that: 'Laws must be in conformity with generally accepted principles of international law and with valid treaties ratified by the National Assembly, whereas regulations and other general legal acts must also be in conformity with other ratified treaties.'

[55] Ibid. n. 52.

[56] Rm-1/97, para. 13 of the reasoning.

[57] Ibid. It follows from the reasoning that this practice was introduced by the German Federal Constitutional Court.

to review a law on ratification would also have a preventive significance, to promptly prevent the undertaking of an unconstitutional obligation arising from international law by the state before the treaty enters into force according to international law.[58] The Constitutional Court addressed this issue in the case of the review of the constitutionality of the law on ratification of the EU Association Agreement, as it was allegedly adopted following an unlawful and unconstitutional procedure. The Court decided that it was indeed competent to review the constitutionality of the procedure of the adoption of the law on ratification prior to the entry into force of the agreement whose ratification was approved by it.[59] However, the Constitutional Court discontinued the proceedings on the grounds of lack of legal interest by the petitioner.

The Constitutional Court repeated that it is empowered to carry out the posterior review of the constitutionality (and legality) of a treaty in accordance with paragraphs 1.1 and 3 of Article 160 of the Constitution when it reviewed the Agreement between the Government of the Republic of Slovenia (Slovene Ministry of Defence) and the Government of the State of Israel (Israeli Ministry of Defence).[60] The Constitutional Court was also called upon to review the constitutionality of a law on ratification in two other cases.[61] However, in both cases it rejected the petitions due to the lack of a legal interest.

4.3.3 *The review of the Decree on the Ratification of the Code of Fishermen – change in the case law?*

I have already mentioned that in the review of the Decree on the Ratification of the Agreement on Military Pensions, the Constitutional Court allowed the possibility that it would also review its legality in a manner such as follows from the Court's jurisdiction to review regulations. Then the Constitutional Court decided to review only the constitutionality of the Agreement.

---

[58] Ibid.

[59] Order No. U-I-197/97 of 21 May 1998, Collection of Decisions (OdlUS), VII/1, 93.

[60] *Review of the Israeli Agreement,* Order No. 128/98 of 23 September 1998. Collection of Decisions (OdlUS) VII/2, 173. See more on this Agreement below in Section 6.

[61] Order No. U-I-190/97 of 30 September 1997, petition to review the EU Association Agreement). Ibid., VI/2, 119; Order No. U-I-44/01 of 18 November 2004 (unpublished), petition to review the Act on Ratification of the Social Insurance Agreement between the Republic of Slovenia and the Republic of Croatia (Off. Gaz. RS, No. 71/97, MP, No. 21/97).

The Constitutional Court again faced the issue of a possible review of the constitutionality and legality of an international agreement, or a decree of the government by which that agreement was ratified, in relation to the petition for review of the constitutionality and legality of the Decree on the Ratification of the Code of Conduct of Fishermen engaged in Fshing Oerations.[62] In that case the Constitutional Court decided that it did not have the jurisdiction to examine the legality of a treaty ratified by a decree of the government, as no grounds for such jurisdiction exist in the Constitution. Furthermore, the Constitutional Court asserted that its jurisdiction to review the legality of a treaty cannot be derived from the review of the government decree by which that treaty is ratified.[63] This entails that a law and a treaty ratified by a government decree would be inconsistent. However, the Constitutional Court is not empowered to review such inconsistency.[64] The Constitutional Court reserved for itself the jurisdiction to review inconsistency between the law and the treaty ratified by the government decree only if such inconsistency entails a violation of Article 2 of the Constitution.[65]

The abovementioned decision results in a departure from the position that the Constitutional Court took in the case of the review of the Decree on the Ratification of the Agreement on Military Pensions. In the latter decision it hypothetically allowed the possibility also to review the legality of treaties that are ratified by the government decree. The decision in the case of the review of the Code of Fishermen thus signifies an important contribution to the supremacy of international law, which stems from Article 8 of the Constitution.

Given the position of the Constitutional Court, that it has no jurisdiction to review the legality of a treaty ratified by a government decree (which in terms of the hierarchy of the internal legal acts ranks lower than a law), the question is raised whether, as regards the Slovene national law, this position might lead to an 'equalisation' of a treaty ratified by a government decree

---

[62] The Code had been adopted on the basis of an agreement between the Presidents of the Republic of Slovenia and the Republic of Croatia of 10 September 2002 on the provisional regime of implementation of the provisions of Arts. 47 to 52 of the Transboundary Agreement, and was extended by the parties until the beginning of 2004 (Off. Gaz. RS, No. 119/02, Treaties, No. 28/02 et seq.). The Code ceased to apply prior to the entering of Slovenia into the EU.

[63] Order No. U-I-376/02 of 24 March 2005, Off. Gaz. RS, No. 46/05.

[64] Ibid.

[65] Ibid.

with a law? A comparison with other legal systems also points to similar questions and does not give a clear answer to this question.[66] This should be decided by a domestic court in every single case. Nevertheless the domestic court's decision of any type does not change the obligation of the state concerning the fulfilment of international obligations from a treaty.

5. Some International Legal Issues arising from the Case Law of the Constitutional Court and its Contribution to the Coherent Application of International Law in the National Legal System

5.1 Self-executing and non-self-executing Treaties

With regard to treaties, the theory of international law makes a distinction between self-executing and non-self-executing treaties concerning whether their provisions are directly applicable in internal law or whether for their implementation it is necessary to adopt implementing legislation. Whether treaties can have direct effect in a national legal system depends on the constitutional provisions of an individual state and on which branch of government is empowered with approving such a treaty. A majority of states in which the ratification (approval) of a treaty is entrusted to the legislature are, in the theory of international law, classified as monist states, since the legislature's approval of a treaty does not require the adoption of a special internal regulation for the entry into force of the treaty. As regards dualist states, the most typical representative being the United Kingdom, ratification (approval) is entrusted to the executive branch of government and a treaty cannot have any legal effect in the internal law without the adoption of internal legislation which confers on it the effect of validity.[67] However, even in states whose constitutions allow the direct effect of treaties provided that they have been duly ratified, not all treaties have the same effect.[68] It

[66] Ibid. For the case law of the USA, Croatia and Germany, see note 14 of the separate opinion of Judge Škrk.

[67] A. Aust, *Modern Treaty Law and Practice* (reprint, Cambridge University Press 2002), pp. 150-151. In the UK the authority to conclude treaties is exercised by the Foreign Minister.

[68] T. Buergenthal, 'Self-executing and non-self-executing treaties in national and international law', 235 *Recueil des Cours, Académie de droit international* (1992) IV, p. 317.

cannot be determined in advance on a purely abstract level whether or not a treaty is directly applicable. This is decided by national courts in every single case.[69]

The Constitutional Court addressed the issue of the direct effect of treaties in its review of the EU Association Agreement, in connection with the obligation of the state to fulfil a treaty obligation according to international law as otherwise it would commit an international wrongful act. From the reasoning of the Court's opinion it follows that the fulfilment of a treaty can be achieved in such a manner that upon its entry into force, treaty provisions become part of the internal legal order, i.e., if these provisions are by the nature of things self-executing, as they regulate the rights and obligations of natural and legal persons.[70] If treaty provisions are non-self-executing, for the fulfilment of treaty obligations, the adoption of internal legal measures is required. The Constitutional Court assessed that, from the view of the fulfilment of an international obligation according to international law, it is essential that the state fulfils the obligation, whereby it is not decisive whether such fulfilment is achieved by the direct effect of treaty provisions in the national law or by the adoption of required internal legal acts.[71]

5.2 *Interpretation of Treaties*

The Constitutional Court took a position concerning the interpretation of a treaty which is subject to constitutional review during the process of ratification in the case of reviewing the Transboundary Cooperation Agreement with Croatia. For the interpretation it applied the interpretative provisions of the Vienna Convention on the Law of Treaties (VCLT), as the Agreement which was the subject of the (preventive) review had not yet become part of the internal legal system of the Republic of Slovenia.[72] The Constitutional Court resorted to the same approach in the review of the Treaty on the Krško Nuclear Power Plant (NPP)[73] and the Vatican Agreement.[74] In particular it based its

---

[69] Aust, op. cit. n. 67, at p. 159.

[70] Rm-1/97, para. 22 of the reasoning.

[71] Ibid. The Constitutional Court took a position concerning self-executing and non-self-executing treaties when it reviewed the Law on Marriage and Family Relations. See Decision No. 312/00, Off. Gaz. RS, No. 42/03.

[72] Rm-1/00, para. 25 of the reasoning.

[73] Rm-2/02, para. 33 of the reasoning.

[74] Rm-1/02, para. 12 of the reasoning.

approach on Article 31 of the VCLT. In the review of the Treaty on the Krško NPP, on the basis of the interpretative provisions of Article 31 VCLT, the Constitutional Court took the position that it reviews the conformity of a treaty with the Constitution according to the contents of the treaty as it follows from its text.[75] A treaty preamble forms the context for the purpose of the interpretation of a treaty, in addition to the text, annexes, agreements, and instruments which have been made in connection with its conclusion (Article 31 (2) VCLT).

The Constitutional Court has reviewed the significance of the preamble of a treaty three times' in the cases of the Transboundary Cooperation Agreement with Croatia, the Krško NPP, and the Vatican Agreement. In the (preventive) review of the Transboundary Cooperation Agreement with Croatia, the Constitutional Court had to take a position concerning Article 1 of the Agreement, which determines the transboundary area on the land and the sea,[76] from the point of view of whether it prejudiced a future state border between Slovenia and Croatia due to the fact that the States were concluding a transboundary cooperation agreement prior to concluding a treaty on the state border. The Constitutional Court decided that the contested provision of Article 1 of the Agreement was to be interpreted in the context of the preamble, from which the intention to enter into the Agreement is evident, and considering its contents as a whole.[77] The purpose of entering into the Agreement was in the first place to improve the living conditions of the people of both states living near the border, and not to determine the state border between them. As already mentioned, the Constitutional Court decided that the Transboundary Cooperation Agreement was not inconsistent with the Constitution.[78]

In the review of the Vatican Agreement, the Constitutional Court addressed the preamble from two aspects: first, from the aspect of its conformity with the Constitution and, second, from the aspect of the interpretation of the context of the Agreement. The government proposed the review of the constitutionality of the preamble as it did not contain a declaration that, by the

[75] Rm-2/02, para. 33 of the reasoning.

[76] Off. Gaz. RS, No. 63/01, Treaties, No. 20/01.

[77] Rm-1/00, paras. 8 and 26 of the reasoning.

[78] The opinion in Rm-1/00 was issued by the Constitutional Court by six votes in favour to three against. Four judges gave their concurring opinions and two judges their dissenting opinions.

Agreement, the existing legal position of the Catholic Church in the Republic of Slovenia is confirmed. In order eventually to review the constitutionality of the preamble, the Constitutional Court considered the significance of a preamble in the law of treaties. It established that, regarding the contents of a preamble, there are no rules in international practice which would determine that it must contain more than the determination of the treaty parties and their plenipotentiaries and the statement regarding an agreement which follows from the text of the treaty. The scope of a preamble depends on the will of treaty parties. Furthermore, it established that:

> [...]parties are not bound by any rule that would determine that all the essential aspects of a concluded treaty must be emphasised in the preamble of such. Thus, from the legal character of a preamble it follows that it is not possible to challenge something that it does not contain, unless the elements that are mandatory constitutive parts of the preamble of every treaty would be missing. However, the Agreement contains such provisions.[79]

Consequently, the Constitutional Court dismissed the proposal to review the preamble as the review of the Agreement's preamble as proposed was by the nature of things impossible.[80]

In the interpretation of the challenged provisions of the Treaty on the Krško NPP, the Constitutional Court considered the contents of the preamble indirectly. The preamble of the Treaty, *inter alia*, referred to the Convention on Nuclear Safety and the Joint Convention on the Safety of Spent Fuel Management and on the Safety of Radioactive Waste Management. In the review of the constitutionality of the Treaty, the Constitutional Court had to take a position concerning the mutual relation between both international conventions and the challenged Treaty. Concerning this the Constitutional Court relied on the international law of treaties, according to which there is generally no hierarchy between treaties, which does not prevent treaty parties from establishing such a hierarchy themselves.[81] Otherwise mutual inconsistencies between treaties are resolved by applying the *lex posterior* and *lex specialis* rules. However, according to the Constitutional Court, the general

---

[79] Rm-1/02, para. 11 of the reasoning.
[80] Ibid.
[81] Rm-2/02, para. 34 of the reasoning.

lex posterior rule does not exclude a different possible interpretation.[82] The Constitutional Court (on the basis of the abovementioned positions regarding interpretation) decided that referring to both Conventions listed in the preamble had to be understood in such a manner that these two conventions supplement the Treaty on the NPP. In the event of inconsistency between them and the Treaty, the two listed international Conventions had priority. If a provision of the Treaty is more specific such provision has priority.

Another important development in the interpretation of a treaty is the interpretation of Article 1 of the Vatican Agreement, in which the Constitutional Court took into account both of the authentic texts, the Italian and the Slovene, in which the Agreement was concluded. For reasons of clarity of its significance it gave the Italian original a greater value than the Slovene original. Consequently, the Constitutional Court faced two possible interpretations; one which was inconsistent with the Constitution, and a second which was not inconsistent with the Constitution.[83] In determining the interpretation which was in conformity with the Constitution, the Constitutional Court took the position that it was possible to interpret the text of Article 1 of the Agreement also in a manner such that 'it allows the Catholic Church to operate in conformity with canon law in so-called mixed areas, as long as this operation does not conflict with the legal system of the Republic of Slovenia.'[84] In that part of review the Constitutional Court relied on the Italian original of the Agreement and thereby referred to Article 33 of the VCLT, and to its rule on the interpretation of treaties authenticated in two or more languages.

As the Constitutional Court has not reviewed an act on ratification of a treaty in terms of substance, except in the case of the review of the government decree on the ratification of military pensions, it has not so far taken a position concerning the interpretation of a treaty which it examines in the posterior review procedure. In theory, a treaty should in every case be interpreted by the rules of international law, i.e., according to the rules contained in the VCLT.[85] It seems important to support such a position. Such a view is grounded on the fact that an act on ratification of a treaty represents only the

[82] Ibid.

[83] *Sous réserve* interpretation. See *supra* n. 45.

[84] Rm-1/02, para. 32 of the reasoning.

[85] M. Pogačnik, *Veljavnost mednarodnih pogodb v Republiki Sloveniji* (Validity of Treaties in the Republic of Slovenia), Pravnik, Ljubljana, 51 (1996), Nos. 6-8, p. 370.

formal framework of a regulation while its substance is embraced in a treaty framed by such an act. A special feature of a treaty is that its substance was created by the parties. The interpretative principles of the VCLT are adjusted to that. This is the reason why the Constitutional Court should interpret a treaty according to the interpretative rules of that convention also in the posterior (indirect) review procedure.

5.3 Interpretation of a Treaty in the light of its performance by the Parties

In one of the cases that have arisen in Slovenia as a result of de-nationalisation, the petitioners lodged a constitutional complaint against decisions of the Supreme Court and the Administrative Court that denied de-nationalisation to the petitioners whose predecessors, the previous owners of property which had been confiscated on the basis of Yugoslav regulations passed in the period 1944–1946. The Courts argued that the petitioners, although legal heirs, were not entitled to request the recovery of their ancestors' property on the basis of the Law on Denationalisation. The reason for the denial was based on the fact that the petitioners' ancestors were Austrian citizens and as such were entitled to receive compensation from the government of Austria for their property, although it was confiscated in the former Yugoslavia, on the basis of Article 27 paragraph 2 of the Austrian State Treaty.[86] The decisive argument for the denial of the claim by the Courts was that the petitioners' ancestors were Austrian citizens at the time when the Austrian State Treaty was concluded. Therefore, Austria was liable to compensate them for the property confiscated in the former Yugoslavia. However, the petitioners further claimed that their ancestors had been Yugoslav citizens at the time of the confiscation of their property and as such they were entitled to denationalisation. They argued that the Courts violated their constitutional right to equality before the law (Article 14 of the Constitution), equal protection of rights (Article 22) and their right to private property and inheritance (Article 33).

---

[86] State Treaty for the Re-Establishment of an Independent and Democratic Austria, signed at Vienna on 15 May 1955, UNTS, Vol. 217 (1955). Article 27, para. 2 provides: 'Nothwithstanding the foregoing provisions, the Federal People's Republic of Yugoslavia shall have the right to seize, retain or liquidate Austrian property, rights and interests within Yugoslav territory on the coming into force of the present Treaty. The Government of Austria undertakes to compensate Austrian nationals whose property is taken under this paragraph.'

In order to establish whether there was a violation of the petitioners' rights, the Constitutional Court had to explore whether the petitioners' ancestors, as Austrian citizens at the time of the conclusion of the Austrian State Treaty, were indeed entitled to receive compensation for their confiscated property from Austria. The Constitutional Court found to the contrary.[87] It interpreted Article 27 paragraph 2 of the Austrian State Treaty (and pertaining to the notion of the Austrian citizen) in such a manner as this provision was interpreted and applied by the former Yugoslavia and Austria as its contracting parties. Austria recognised the right to compensation of those individuals (natural and legal persons) who were its citizens on 15 May 1945 and on 28 November 1955.[88] This practice was recognised by the former Yugoslav authorities that were submitting data on the confiscated property to the Austrian authorities. Thus the Constitutional Court interpreted the said Treaty in the same spirit as it was interpreted and implemented by the former Yugoslavia and Austria as its parties.[89] It established that the Courts' interpretation of Article 27 paragraph 2 of the Austrian State Treaty violated the petitioners' right to equality before the law, reversed the Courts' decisions and remanded the case for further proceedings.

5.4 Performance of a Treaty in good faith as a measure of the constitutionality of a Treaty

One-third of the deputies of the National Assembly who proposed the preventive review of the constitutionality of the Treaty on the Krško NPP, *inter alia*, alleged that the challenged provisions concerning the decommissioning of the NPP and the disposal of nuclear waste (Article 10) were deficient. The challenged provision allegedly only envisaged the adoption of a joint programme, however, the de-commissioning and disposal of nuclear waste was left for a future agreement to be reached between the parties – the Republic of Slovenia and the Republic of Croatia. A similar allegation referred to Article 11 of the Treaty (The Financing of Decommissioning and Disposal).[90] The deputies proposing this asserted the inconsistency of the chal-

[87] Decision No. Up-547/02 of 8 October 2003, Off. Gaz. RS, No. 108/2003.

[88] Ibid., para. 26 of the reasoning.

[89] In para. 19 of the reasoning it is stated that despite the succession of states to treaties no obligations arise for Slovenia from, Article 27 para. 2 of the Austrian State Treaty.

[90] The second item of the opinion that referred to the finding that Article 11 of the Treaty on the NPP was not inconsistent with the Constitution was adopted by seven votes in favour and two against. Judges Ribičič and Škrk voted against.

lenged provisions with Article 72 of the Constitution (Healthy Living Environment).

The Constitutional Court refused the allegations. It explained that in the review of the conformity of the Treaty it followed from the assumption that in its implementation the parties would act in good faith in conformity with the *pacta sunt servanda* principle (Article 6 VCLT). Thus, in the review of the challenged Treaty provisions, the Constitutional Court derived from the assumption that the parties would fulfil the obligations from the Treaty. Concerning this, it warned that in the event of possible non-observance of the Treaty, the parties could use the procedure for a peaceful settlement of disputes, which was envisaged in the Treaty (Article 20), or they could resort to measures according to international law that are provided in the case of a breach of the treaty.[91]

6. *Trias Politica* in the Field of International Affairs – Self-Restraint of the Constitutional Court?

In one aspect the jurisdiction of the Constitutional Court to review treaties requires more tentative scrutiny than its competence to review laws and other national regulations. Each treaty, duly concluded by the state, obliges that state to perform it in good faith. Keeping this in mind the legislature must thus bear its share of responsibility during the process of ratification while the executive branch is responsible for the performance of the treaty commitments on the international level. In other words, the review of the constitutionality of international commitments raises the issue of the separation of powers which is enshrined in Article 3 paragraph 2 of the Constitution.

When, in the procedure of a preventive review, the Constitutional Court issues the opinion that a treaty is not inconsistent with the Constitution, it emphasises that the decision on the adoption of a law on ratification falls within the political discretion of the National Assembly.[92] Furthermore, it emphasises that in such event the weight of possible unfavourable political consequences due to ratification of a treaty must be borne by the National Assembly in deciding on the ratification. In the review of the Transboundary Cooperation Agreement, *inter alia*, the question was raised whether the Agree-

[91] Rm-2/02, para. 35 of the reasoning.

[92] Rm-1/97, para. 38 of the reasoning.

ment coming into force could impair the position of Slovenia in any future determination of the border with neighbouring Croatia. Concerning this the Court stated:

> The question whether the implementation of the Agreement will in practice in fact result in the determination of the borderline in certain parts of the land border, although only for the purpose of implementing the Agreement, or whether such enforcement of actual authority might worsen the position of Slovenia in possible subsequent negotiations, is not a constitutional but a political matter that must be answered by the National Assembly when deciding on the ratification of the Agreement.[93]

The present case law of the Constitutional Court demonstrates that its review was restrained when the matter concerned the review of international obligations assumed by the executive branch of government. We have already mentioned the case of the (posterior) review of the Israeli Agreement.[94] This concerned the review of an unpublished secret military agreement signed by the Ministries of Defence of Slovenia and Israel. The Slovenian government argued that in this case the matter did not concern a treaty at all. The Constitutional Court decided the case by the so-called 'rejection [on procedural grounds] and decision on the merits of a case.' It refused the government's assertion that there was no treaty at issue, and confirmed the requirement that in accordance with international law and the legal order of Slovenia, a treaty must be published and, according to Slovene national law, also ratified by a competent authority. It grounded the requirement concerning the publication of a treaty on Article 154 paragraph 1 of the Constitution, which determines that regulations must be published prior to their coming into force.[95] The Constitutional Court rejected the petition since, apart from Article 160 paragraph 2 of the Constitution, it is empowered to review only those regulations which form a part of the legal order of the Republic of Slovenia. A treaty acquires this status only by virtue of a law or decree on ratification, which did not occur in the case of the Israeli Agreement.[96] For the same reasons the Constitutional Court rejected a petition to review the constitu-

---

[93] Rm-1/00, para. 30 of the reasoning.

[94] See *supra* n. 60.

[95] Order No. U-I-128/98, para. 10 of the reasoning.

[96] Ibid., para. 15 of the reasoning.

tionality and legality of the Agreement on Security and Intelligence Cooperation between the Intelligence and Security Service of the Ministry of Defence of the Republic of Slovenia and the Sector for Security and Intelligence Activities within the Ministry of Defence of the Republic of Macedonia (the Macedonian Agreement).[97]

The Constitutional Court used a similar technique in the review of the constitutionality (and legality) of an unpublished order of the government by which the air-space of the Republic of Slovenia was allowed to be used by military aircraft participating in NATO operations over the territory of the Former Republic of Yugoslavia due to the Kosovo conflict. The petitioner referred to the violation of the right to a healthy living environment (Article 72 of the Constitution) by reason of the noise made by the supersonic aircraft. The Constitutional Court dismissed the petition due to the lack of a legal interest by the petitioner.[98] However, in its reasoning the Constitutional Court clearly stated that the decision of the government allowing NATO military aircraft to use the Slovene air-space (apart from the government's response to NATO) would also require an appropriate normative act to be adopted by the legislature. The Constitutional Court explained that the current legislation prohibited over- flights by foreign armed aircraft over Slovene territory. In the case of the NATO aircrafts, the issue concerned precisely the type of the over flights. Therefore, the government should have proposed a suitable amendment to the current legislation, or the adoption of a special statute, or concluded a treaty subsequently ratified by the National Assembly.[99]

7. Some Concluding Remarks

The survey of the case law of the Constitutional Court in the area of the review of treaties demonstrates that the drafters of the Constitution acted wisely by introducing the institution of preventive review of treaties in the Slovene Constitution. The Constitutional Court can, in a less strained manner and more comprehensively, carry out the review of a treaty which has not yet become part of the domestic legal order, and has not yet begun to oblige

[97] Order No. U-I-265/98, OdlUS X, 41.
[98] Order No. U-I-87/99, Off. Gazette of the RS, No. 60/99.
[99] Ibid., para. 28 of the reasoning.

the state to fulfil its international obligations. The executive and legislative branches of government expect that, as regards preventive review of a treaty, the Constitutional Court would review it in a 'friendly' manner since the executive power has already stated internationally the willingness of the state to enter into such obligations. Nevertheless, it is necessary to be aware of the fact that the internal approval (ratification) of a treaty falls within the exclusive domain of the sovereignty of every state and is the subject of an independent political (and judicial) decision of its competent authorities. The case law of the preventive review of the constitutionality of treaties demonstrates that the Constitutional Court has in all its cases substantively reviewed the challenged provisions of a treaty and thereby followed international law and its own case law, developed in the framework of its jurisdiction to review regulations.

Concerning the posterior (indirect) review of treaties through the review of an act on ratification of a treaty, I would draw a conclusion that the case law of the Constitutional Court so far has been restrained despite the fact that it confirmed its jurisdiction to conduct such reviews. Such restraint is understandable. On the one hand, the Constitutional Court as the guardian of constitutionality and legality is aware of its responsibility not to allow the existence of an unconstitutional provision of a treaty in the internal legal order. On the other hand, it is also aware of the fact that an interference with the unconstitutionality of a treaty cannot be without consequences for the state in fulfilling international obligations for which it is responsible according to international law.

Notwithstanding the fact that the Constitutional Court has, in all cases of treaties unduly concluded by the executive branch of government, formally declined its review by passing so-called 'substantive rejections', it has importantly contributed to the introduction and clarification of certain international and constitutional principles and rules concerning the adoption of treaties in the internal legal order.

The case law of the Constitutional Court in the area of cases with elements of international law, including the review of treaties, also points to the problems regarding international law which Slovenia as a relatively new state has faced. In this regard I should especially emphasise its relations with neighbouring states, the regulation of relations with the Holy See, and the process regulating Slovenia's membership in the international and regional organisations of an intergovernmental and supranational character.

THE EUROPEAN CONVENTION ON HUMAN RIGHTS (ECHR) AND THE POSITION OF THE NATIONAL JUDGE

W.M.E. Thomassen*

Article 1 of the European Convention on Human Rights (ECHR) reads as follows:

> The High Contracting Parties shall secure to everyone within its jurisdiction the rights and freedoms defined in Section 1 of this Convention.

The binding force of the Convention is underlined by the Vienna Convention rule *pacta sunt servanda*. A typical feature of the Dutch legal system is that it is monistic, as is also the case in France. Article 94 of the Dutch Constitution obliges the judge to set aside national rules if their application is in conflict with international law. This means that judges in the Netherlands apply the ECHR as national law. The difference between monistic systems and non-monistic systems and the scope of Article 94 of the Dutch Constitution may have lost some of its impact as in most cases and in most European states compliance with rules of international law can be achieved by interpreting a rule of national law in the light of the particular treaty. Courts will normally try to avoid concluding that any conflict between national law and the ECHR exists, and it is rarely necessary to conclude that a national rule should be set aside in order to achieve compliance with the ECHR.

* H.E. Judge Thomassen is Judge of the Supreme Court of the Netherlands and a former Judge of the European Court of Human Rights (1998–2004).

A.S. Muller and M.A. Loth (eds.), Highest Courts and the Internationalisation of Law

1. Legal Security

The role of supreme courts has become complicated under international law more than it has essentially changed. If ever there was a time when law was simple and a rule was a rule, that was long ago. National supreme courts are confronted with multiple sources of law and with different decision-making bodies like the European Court of Human Rights (ECtHR) and the European Court of Justice (ECJ) which interpret international law on the European level. It is the classical task of supreme courts to bring order out of the chaos of rules and regulations in order to ensure legal security.

In order to fulfil this task judges of a supreme court must have a thorough knowledge of international law, including knowledge of its interpretation by other courts, both national and international. Furthermore, judges of supreme courts should be active in implementing international law in the national legal order. If judges fail to assess correctly and in due time the justified claims of an individual or a company under international law, the latter will be forced to start expensive and time-consuming proceedings elsewhere.

I shall give you the example of M. Poirrez.[1] M. Poirrez, who lived in France, was a national of the Ivory Coast and had been adopted by a French national without becoming a French national himself. He was refused social security by reason of his nationality. M. Poirrez challenged this decision before a national court claiming to be discriminated against on the basis of nationality. The national judge asked for a preliminary ruling by the European Court of Justice in Luxembourg on the question of whether the French law was in compliance with Community law. The Court ruled that the anti-discrimination rules applied to immigrant workers and their children but not to nationals and their children. It was only in Strasbourg that the ECtHR recognised that Mr. Poirrez was discriminated against because of his nationality, in violation of Article 14 ECHR in conjunction with Article 1 of the First Protocol to the Convention. If the national judge had applied the notion of discrimination correctly, the case would have been solved some twelve years before, or, at least, seven years earlier, as the case could have gone to the highest national court without a preliminary ruling from the ECJ.

Knowledge of international law implies knowledge of the interpretation of international law by international courts. As far as the ECHR is concerned

[1] *Koua Poirrez* v. *France*, ECtHR, 30 September 2003, Application No. 40892/98.

judgments of the ECtHR have binding force. Article 46 (1) of the ECHR reads:

> The High Contracting Parties undertake to abide by the final judgment of the Court in any case to which they are parties.

In the interest of legal security, national courts should also apply case law pertaining to other Member States as far as the interpretation of legal notions is concerned. For instance, if an unmarried couple can claim protection of their family life under the Court's case law of Article 8 of the ECHR, should this protection be refused by any Member State which is bound by the Convention? The ECtHR itself takes for granted that its judgments are followed also by states that are not parties to the proceedings. The case of a British national before the ECtHR was declared inadmissible for failure to exhaust domestic remedies because he had not filed a correct appeal to the domestic courts.[2] Although his claim was clearly in conflict with domestic case law, the Court ruled that he should have addressed the British Court of Appeal and given it the opportunity to decide whether the domestic case law could be upheld in the light of a recent ECtHR decision answering broadly the same question.[3]

Knowledge of international law also implies mutual consultation, not only between highest courts in Europe but also between higher courts within the national system, in order to avoid differing interpretations of the same legal rules. The Dutch Supreme Court and the Council of State – the latter being one of three supreme administrative courts in the Netherlands – are organised following the traditional divisions of civil law, criminal law and administrative law. These divisions hold their deliberations separately while running the risk that international legal notions such as freedom of expression or family life are interpreted differently by the civil section of the Supreme Court than by its criminal section or by the Council of State. Because of their role of ensuring the coherence of law, judges of supreme courts need to have a thorough knowledge of international law and need to explore forms of consultation between themselves on international legal issues, including the exchange of case law within this field.

---

[2] *Timothy Upton* v. *United Kingdom*, ECtHR, 11 April 2006, Application No. 29800/04.
[3] *Pla and Puncherneau* v. *Andorra*, ECtHR 13 July 2004, Application No. 69498/01.

2. Human Rights Protection

Aside from ensuring legal security, there is a second role that suits national supreme courts with regard to the Convention. Article 1 in conjunction with Article 13 of the ECHR and the subsidiarity principle of the Strasbourg protection system require Member States to provide an effective remedy for individuals who have an arguable claim that their fundamental rights have been violated. This obligation raises the question whether a supreme court is willing to change certain traditional policies if this is necessary to answer an applicant's claim that his rights under the ECHR have been violated.

An example of a case in which such an attempt was made is the judgment of 31 May 2005 of the Dutch Supreme Court.[4] A woman had been living together with the father of her two children for fifteen years when he was accused of murder. When the woman was summoned as a witness she invoked the legal right of spouses and registered partners not to testify. The court refused her request as she was not married nor was her partnership registered. She was taken into custody for two weeks because she refused to deliver her testimony. In her appeal in cassation she argued that the deprivation of liberty had been discriminatory and in violation of Article 14 ECHR (in conjunction with Article 8 ECHR), the prohibition of discrimination. The Dutch Supreme Court, following its traditional policy, rejected the appeal because the woman, who had been released in the meantime, no longer had any legal interest. However, the Court, departing from its usual approach, did address the legal question raised and explained that the distinction made between a spouse and a registered partner on the one hand and the applicant on the other was justified and proportionate and did not violate Article 14 ECHR. At least her claim was answered on the national level. If the Supreme Court had concluded that Article 14 had indeed been violated, she would have been able to ask for damages in civil proceedings and would not have been a victim in the sense of Article 34 of the Convention. Such an active attitude of a supreme court towards human rights is a contribution to the debate on fundamental values on the national level and to the further interpretation of the ECHR. It can prevent individuals from feeling obliged to address an international court to go beyond the domestic judicial system.

[4] Hoge Raad, 31 May 2005, LJN: AS 2748, 02047/04.

3. Conclusion

The role of national supreme courts towards the ECHR is twofold. Firstly, courts should ensure that the law within their jurisdiction is interpreted and applied in a consistent manner and in compliance with the Convention. Montesquieu in *L'Esprit des Lois* wrote:

> La liberté est le droit de faire tout ce que les lois permettent [...][5]

Individuals and society as a whole need to know which legal boundaries are in force. This knowledge enables them to use the free room which is left to them. By playing an active role in the interpretation of national law in light of the ECHR, supreme courts can contribute to the realisation of this freedom.

The second role of supreme courts is protecting the Convention's human rights and freedoms. Moreover, if possible, a national supreme court should provide for an effective remedy in proceedings pending before it. Applicants should not be obliged to file a complaint in Strasbourg because there is no remedy in the domestic arena.

[5] 'Freedom is the right to do what the laws permit us to do.' Book XI, Chapter 3.

DOMESTIC COURTS AND INTERNATIONAL COURTS: AN ILLUSTRATION AND A CONCLUSION

D. Grimm*

Germany, with its quite elaborate fundamental rights doctrine and jurisprudence, has not often been found in violation of the European Convention on Human Rights (ECHR). Cases in which the European Court of Human Rights (ECtHR) has declared a decision of the Federal Constitutional Court incompatible with the Convention are extremely rare. Recently, however, this indeed happened.[1] The controversy gained wide attention, not only in professional circles but in the general public as well. It caused some irritation for the judiciary as to the consequences of decisions of the ECtHR in domestic law and gave rise to a debate that is still continuing.

The case emerged from a private law litigation. It concerned a conflict between the right to privacy and the freedom of the press. The plaintiff was Princess Caroline of Monaco. The dispute was over some photographs showing Princess Caroline in public places in everyday situations, such as walking on a street and shopping in a market place. Princess Caroline objected to the publication of these photographs in several German magazines. Her objection was not because the photographs were false or because they had an incriminating or disparaging character. Rather, she was of the opinion that the magazines had a right to publish photographs of her without her consent only when she appeared in public in her official function as Princess of Monaco, whereas all other occurrences were part of her private life.

According to German law, photographs of public figures may be published without the consent of a person unless the publication violates a legiti-

* Dieter Grimm is Professor of Public Law, Humboldt University, Germany, and a former Judge of the Constitutional Court of Germany.

[1] *Von Hannover* v. *Germany*, ECtHR, 24 June 2004, Application No. 59320/00.

A.S. Muller and M.A. Loth (eds.), Highest Courts and the Internationalisation of Law

mate interest of that person. This is particularly the case when the private sphere is concerned. The crucial question, therefore, was how to define the private sphere. Differing from the lower courts, which had limited the private sphere to a person's home, the Constitutional Court determined that a legitimate interest of being left alone does not only exist within a person's home. Consequently, the Court extended the private sphere to those places where persons, on account of the particular situation, could reasonably and ascertainably expect to be left alone by others.

At the same time this meant that the right to privacy of public figures ended as soon as they appeared in public places and acted under the eyes of many people. The Constitutional Court concluded that in the public sphere the constitutionally protected interest of the press to publish photographs of public figures prevailed over the interests of such persons not to become the target of photographers. The Constitutional Court understood the freedom of the press as a right to report on all matters for which one assumes there is, or wants to stimulate, public interest. This right exists independently of the quality of the newspaper or the importance of the object. Freedom of the press finds its limits only in the legally protected interests of others, not in a predetermined notion of what ought or ought not to be of public interest.

In cases of conflict between fundamental rights, such as the right to privacy and the freedom of the press, the Constitutional Court routinely applies the principle of proportionality. This means that it strikes a balance between the weight the conflicting rights have in the case at hand and that it weighs the loss that each party would suffer if the other's right prevailed. In the *Caroline* case the Court rated the public interest in public figures, not only when they act in their official capacity, higher than these persons' interest not to become the target of photographers. In addition, the prevalence of freedom of the press was justified because of the danger that otherwise critical reporting on public figures would be severely hampered.

The ECtHR, in its attempt to define the private sphere, also started from the question of defining the conditions under which a person has a reasonable expectation to be left alone. However, differently from the German Constitutional Court, the Strasbourg court rejected any spatial definition of the private sphere. Instead it chose a functional criterion. The ECtHR limited the public sphere to appearances of public figures in their official function whereas all other situations, regardless of where they occur, belong to the private sphere and thus enjoy the protection of Article 8 of the Convention.

Similarly to the Constitutional Court, the ECtHR then raised the question whether the freedom of the press outweighed the privacy interests of Princess Caroline. The answer was that a legitimate interest of the public to be informed about public figures exists only in matters of serious public concern. Only insofar does the press have a right to serve the public interest. Concerning photographs of public figures, the ECtHR ruled that they could be published only when the respective figures appeared in their official function. An exception was made with regard to politicians in a democratic society. All else was found to be mere curiosity or sensation seeking that did not deserve the protection of Article 10 of the Convention. Thus, the tension between the two conflicting fundamental rights was solved by simply eliminating the freedom of the press.

It would not be worthwhile spending many words on the decision if its result were but a shift in the balance between personal privacy and freedom of the press. Yet, the ECtHR did not even arrive at a balance. The two concurring opinions make this clear. The Court denied the photographs the protection of Article 10, and it did so in a paternalistic spirit that seems difficult to reconcile with the meaning of freedom. Moreover, it showed a rather limited understanding of the nature and function of the public discourse and the importance of public figures in social life. As a matter of fact, the ECtHR's reasoning is so far away from the Basic Law and the way it is understood by the Federal Constitutional Court that German courts cannot follow the ECtHR without sacrificing some long established principles of domestic constitutional law.

A year later, a completely different controversy provided the Federal Constitutional Court with an opportunity to develop its opinion as to the consequences of ECtHR rulings in domestic law. This time it was a family law case concerning custody.[2] The mother of an illegitimate child had agreed to the adoption of her child by its foster family. The biological father, Mr Görgülü, had not been asked for his consent. He in fact opposed the adoption and claimed the right to meet his child regularly. He lost his case in the German courts and the Constitutional Court would not entertain a constitutional complaint from him. The ECtHR found that the German civil courts had violated the father's right to family life prescribed by Article 8 of the Convention. Again concerned about the matter, the German civil courts subsequently ignored the judgment of the ECtHR and confirmed their prior decisions.

---

[2] *Görgülü* v. *Germany*, ECtHR, 26 February 2004, Application No. 74969/01.

Once more, the father submitted a complaint to the Constitutional Court. In order to understand the Court's reaction it is important to know that in Germany the ECHR takes the rank of ordinary law, i.e., it ranks below constitutional law. Hence, the Constitutional Court, specialised in adjudicating constitutional law issues, is not entitled to apply the Convention. The Constitutional Court nevertheless found a way to reverse the judgment of the civil court. It decided that ignoring a judgment of the ECtHR not only violates the Convention but also German Basic Law, more precisely the rule of law according to which all state agencies including the judiciary are bound by law. 'Law' includes the ECHR which, by way of ratification, has become a part of domestic law.

The decision could have ended here and Strasbourg would have been satisfied. The impact of the Convention on the national level was strengthened. Respect for the decisions of the ECtHR now has its basis not only in the international treaty, but in the German Constitution as well. Yet, the Constitutional Court used the opportunity to develop some guidelines as to the binding force of ECtHR judgments in Germany and as to the way they should be integrated into domestic law. It is not entirely unlikely that these considerations were prompted by the *Caroline* decision of the ECtHR.

In short, the result of the Constitutional Court's decision was that domestic courts are obliged to take judgments of the ECtHR into account (*berücksichtigen*), but they are not obliged to follow them under any and all circumstances. Since the ECHR and ordinary domestic law operate on the same hierarchical level, courts have to bring ECtHR decisions into harmony with German law according to accepted standards of interpretation and to the extent that the European decisions are compatible with German higher law. If following a ECtHR decision entails a violation of the German Constitution, German courts would be prohibited from adopting the Strasbourg ruling. They are bound by the Basic Law as understood by the Federal Constitutional Court because it ranks higher than the ECHR.

I do not want to discuss here what are the consequences for German courts, the Constitutional Court, and the German legislature and constitution-makers. I pursue this question elsewhere. Rather, I would like to offer some considerations on whether the Strasbourg Court in the *Caroline* case adequately fulfilled its function as an international court in matters of human rights. In addition, I would like to raise the question of whether differences exist between domestic courts and international courts that should lead to different judicial behaviour and role-perception.

The ECtHR rules on alleged violations of the ECHR in 46 states. These states' legal systems differ enormously, and certainly to a larger extent than the legal systems of the 27 Member States of the European Union. They differ in their legal traditions and legal methods. They differ in their legal culture in general. They differ in the way they solve conflicts between certain protected interests, and quite often these solutions are deeply rooted in the countries' traditions. The ECtHR has no mandate to harmonise the law of the Member States of the Council of Europe. It is the guardian of the limits which the European Convention draws to state action in favour of individual freedom. In accordance with this, the ECtHR incessantly emphasises the margin of appreciation that the Member States enjoy.

When it comes to tensions between the freedom of the press and the right to privacy, the differences between the various states are particularly great. For example, in France freedom of the media is quite limited when it collides with personality and privacy rights. Privacy is mostly on the winning side, freedom of the press on the losing side. There is, on the opposite end of the spectrum, the United Kingdom, where persons who have become public figures enjoy little protection against media coverage. There, freedom of the press routinely prevails. Germany finds itself somewhere in between. The Constitutional Court does not recognise a hierarchy among these rights and solves the conflict by balancing the competing interests.

What the ECtHR did when it decided the *Caroline* case was to impose one extreme position of the European spectrum to the whole of Europe. It did so in spite of the great variety of national solutions of the conflict and in spite of Germany's middle position in this spectrum. The margin of appreciation, confirmed on the abstract level, was neglected in the concrete case. Is this understanding of the Court's role, which finds expression in judgements like *Caroline*, appropriate for an international court? I would like to mention three disadvantages of the European Court compared with domestic courts, and, in addition, point to one fundamental difference between international and domestic courts.

The first observation is that, in spite of the considerable differences of opinions, convictions, education and experiences among the 46 judges of the ECtHR, there is no organisational precaution for a consistent jurisprudence. The same subject matter may be handled by different chambers of the Court without any guarantee that they know of each other's pending cases. Hence, the composition of the deciding Chamber matters more than it usually does within the highest domestic courts. The *Caroline* solution could have looked quite different to a differently composed chamber. The possibility to appeal to the Grand Chamber exists, but is an exceptional remedy.

The second feature is more important. Judges of the ECtHR do not have the full range of information about the case they are expected to decide. The files of the domestic courts are not submitted to the judges nor are the domestic judgments translated into the languages used in the court. Rather, a jurist of the Registrar's office who knows the language of the country where the case originated submits a summary report of the case to the judges. In this procedure it is almost inevitable that aspects of the case or of the domestic court's decisions which the rapporteur regards as less relevant do not come to the attention of judges. The fact that the national judge is always involved constitutes no sufficient compensation.

The third observation played an important role in the reasoning of the German Constitutional Court in *Görgülü*. The ECtHR is not necessarily aware of the full range of the interests concerned and the arguments raised in the litigation. The parties to the law suit in Strasbourg are the complainant and the state whose act is challenged by the complainant. They can present their viewpoints and legal opinions. This seems sufficient in bipolar controversies between a citizen and his or her government. This is the type of conflict that states had in mind when they concluded the European Convention in 1950 and established the ECtHR.

In the meantime a different type of controversies has become more and more important, namely treble or multipolar controversies. This is certainly so in every case that arises out of private law litigation, as in *Caroline* and *Görgülü*, but can also occur in administrative law cases when third parties are immediately affected by an administrative act. The losing party in the national court system is represented in Strasbourg, the winning party is not. Its position may be defended by the government, but not necessarily to the extent it could be. The Convention entitles but does not oblige the President of the ECtHR to invite the losing party in the national courts to submit a brief or to argue in the hearing. Attempts to transform the President's discretion into an obligation have failed.

Three- or multi-party litigation differs from bipolar litigation in that not only the complainant enjoys the protection of fundamental rights whereas the government is bound by fundamental rights. Usually both parties of the original private law litigation are holders of different fundamental rights, and the government, whether in its capacity as legislature or as judiciary, is in a mediating role and tries to find a balance between competing fundamental rights. Since the Strasbourg procedure does not reflect this situation it will often create situations in which the national balance is distorted and the result cannot be adopted in the national system without disturbing a well calibrated balance or even without violations of the national constitution, as the *Caroline* case shows.

Moreover, caught in its bipolar view, the ECtHR does not notice that may fall foul of Article 53 of the ECHR. Article 53 prohibits interpretations of the Convention that would curtail or impair fundamental rights guaranteed in the laws of the Convention's Member States. In three-polar conflicts, where both parties have constitutionally protected interests, enhancing one right means curtailing the other. The *Caroline* decision of the ECtHR severely curtailed the freedom of the press which is guaranteed in the German Basic Law. This dilemma calls for a deeper reflection on the standards of review when it comes to reconciling competing rights, especially where national solutions differ greatly.

Finally, I come to the fundamental difference. National courts operate not only on the basis of a national legal order and a shared method of interpretation. They also act within the context of a legal culture which is composed of many more features than simply positive law and doctrine. Furthermore, they act within the context of a continuous legal and public discourse. This context determines judicial behaviour, the role-perception of judges, the borderline between accepted and unaccepted arguments, the degree of deference or activism *vis-à-vis* the legislature, etc. It does so often in a subconscious way, but all the more effectively.

Such a context is largely missing on the international level. International courts are not embedded in a shared legal culture and the international legal discourse is much weaker than the national one. An international public discourse in these matters is almost absent. Taken together this means that the international judge is much freer than the national judge, not in terms of judicial independence, but in terms of extralegal constraints. These extralegal constraints constitute a large part of the legitimacy and acceptance of court decisions on the national level. There has to be compensation on the international level, and it can only be more judicial self-restraint and more respect for national solutions. The margin of appreciation is of vital importance when it comes to international adjudication. It should not remain a matter of merely paying lip service to this principle.

MODERN CHALLENGES FOR THE JUDICIARY AND THE ROLE OF SUPREME COURTS

P. Koskelo*

1. Introductory Remarks

When considering the role of supreme courts in the judicial systems of modern societies, it is useful to start by recalling some general developments that affect the judicial system. Firstly, the tasks of courts are becoming more and more demanding. There are several reasons for this. Cases arise in a multitude of fields, and the subject matter may often be difficult and complicated. The facts to be examined may be intricate and hard to assess. The evidence produced may be sophisticated, involving new technical or scientific methods by which evidence is acquired. The applicable law may be complicated, or it may be either imprecise or inconclusive, leaving plenty of room for interpretation or judicial discretion. There are new issues on which the courts are called upon to rule even if there is no guidance, or no adequate guidance, to be found in legislation. The relevant sources of law are often multi-layered and may include supranational and/or international norms and legal materials, the impact of which is becoming both wider and deeper. Cases may involve important systemic issues or questions of principle, or matters where conflicting interests or values are at stake. Procedural issues and procedural rights are increasingly important, largely as a result of a growing awareness of human rights and fundamental rights. Individual as well as public expectations are higher when it comes to the manner in which proceedings are conducted, judgments made and reasons given.

---

* H.E. Judge Koskelo is President of the Supreme Court of Finland.

A.S. Muller and M.A. Loth (eds.), Highest Courts and the Internationalisation of Law

Thus, while the large mass of cases may be fairly routine ones, other cases may involve difficult issues of fact, of evidence, of procedure, of law, of fundamental rights, of constitutional and other basic principles. The standards of competence that need to be met by the judiciary are increasingly high. At the same time, resources are limited, and the pressures for expedient and efficient handling of cases are ever increasing. In other words, judges and courts are expected to meet more and more demanding professional standards, to deliver justice effectively and efficiently, yet with high quality, and to cope with heavy workloads.

2. Implications for Supreme Courts in the Context of National Law

Given this general background, one can look at the implications for the role of supreme courts. Obviously, the increasing demands apply also to supreme courts themselves. As last instance courts, supreme courts should meet even higher standards than lower instance courts. What is more, the pivotal role of supreme courts in providing guidance to the lower courts is increasingly important. As the latter are hard pressed to manage their case-loads, they should be well-served by a supreme court that can hand down case law to assist the lower courts in their work. There is a patent need for pedagogical, well-structured and adequately reasoned precedents that settle questions of interpretation, highlight or clarify principles, give substance to vague norms, promote uniformity, foster systematic coherence, and advance a proper analytical approach to legal issues.

In Finland, a filtering system at the level of the Supreme Court has been in place since 1980. This means that access to the Supreme Court depends on the granting of leave to appeal.[1] The purpose of this system is to enable the Supreme Court to concentrate on cases that raise issues of more general importance, and thus to serve the abovementioned needs better. This has been a very important development.

In the course of this period, a major change has also taken place in the manner in which judgments are drafted. Today, the reasoning is generally fuller, more open and more 'discursive' than in the past. Thus, the judgments

[1] For further details see the Annex.

give a more informative and transparent account of the grounds and arguments on which the outcome is based. The same is true for concurring or dissenting opinions, as the case may be. The greater openness in the style of reasoning is not only for the benefit of the judicial system but also for the benefit of the legal community as a whole, not to forget the general public.

Indeed, the judiciary in general and highest courts in particular could hardly meet the needs and legitimate expectations of contemporary society by announcing outcomes and providing only succinct, formalistic reasons. While the institutional role of the judiciary is firmly based on the requirements that flow from constitutional rules on the division of powers and from fundamental rights of access to justice for individuals, both accountability and legitimacy ultimately rest on the fair conduct of the process and on the transparency and quality of the reasoning.

3. Implications for the Role of Supreme Courts in the Context of International Law

In today's world, non-domestic legal sources play a very important role. Key areas in this context are human rights law and European Union law, which cover very broad fields of activity and are relevant for a wide range of case law. There are also more specific international instruments such as WTO treaties and other multilateral conventions on matters of intellectual property law, transportation law, family law, and private international law. In all these domains, the role of supreme courts as 'intermediaries' between complex non-domestic sources of law and domestic administration of justice is often quite crucial.

The scope as well as the intensity of the impact of supranational and international law is one of the major changes that have taken place in European legal systems in recent times. In more and more areas, non-domestic law penetrates into the domestic sphere, which has traditionally been governed mainly by norms of internal origin. What has taken place is, at least in part, a constitutional revolution in terms of sources of law and the hierarchy of norms. Another important feature is that the new sources of law, particularly in the fields of human rights law and European Union law, are largely based on the case law of international courts, i.e., the European Court of Human Rights and the European Court of Justice.

These developments entail new tasks and new challenges for national judges. These changes are so important that one may even say that they entail a new role for national judges because they are increasingly called upon to keep an eye on the domestic legal system and to ensure that supranational and international law are respected in the administration of justice. This is a highly demanding role for the judiciary.

While the domestic, 'internal' role of supreme courts is pivotal in order to help the judicial system manage the complexities of contemporary law and modern realities, a similar role is of growing importance when it comes to ensuring the enforcement of relevant international law at the national level. Managing international sources of law is an even greater challenge for national judges than the difficulties raised by domestic law. The vigilance and guidance of supreme courts in this field is therefore essential – as a matter of principle as well as for practical reasons.

At the level of principle, supreme courts as courts of last instance have a special responsibility in ensuring the proper application of supranational and international law. In the field of European Union law, this special responsibility is even formally laid down through Article 234 of the EC Treaty, which imposes an obligation for national courts of last instance to refer questions concerning the interpretation or validity of Community law to the European Court of Justice for preliminary rulings.[2] In other areas the special responsibility is a corollary of the general institutional role of supreme courts at the top of the judicial system. As a practical matter, the pivotal role of the supreme courts as intermediaries between supranational or international law and national enforcement is underscored by the fact that the professional know-how at the lower levels of the judicial system may not be sufficient, especially in an environment where most judges are generalists rather than being highly specialised. Coping with supranational and international sources of law tends to be a slow and difficult learning process in which interventions and guidance from supreme courts are necessary in order to 'ring the bell' and 'spread the message'.

Furthermore, legal and judicial cultures tend to be rather inward-looking, even parochial, whereas the growing importance of non-domestic legal sources demands more outward-oriented professional horizons. As the system of legal sources to which we are subject becomes more diverse and

[2] This obligation applies within the so-called first pillar, whereas Article 35 of the TEU lays down a separate regime for the so-called third pillar.

eclectic, a similar opening and evolution must take place in judicial mentalities and legal cultures.

4. Transnational Interaction

From the observations made above the conclusion follows naturally that transnational interaction between professionals of the judicial system is not only useful, but a necessity. This applies both to interaction between national judges across boundaries and to interaction between judges of courts at the national level and judges of courts at the international level. In this sense, one could use the term horizontal interaction to describe cross-boundary interaction between national judges, and vertical interaction to describe interaction between judges at the national level and those at the international level (in this context, the term vertical does not refer to hierarchy, because it would not be right to describe the relationship between these courts as a hierarchical one).

As our sources of law are increasingly shared, horizontal interaction between judges grows in importance. Likewise, it goes without saying that vertical interaction is crucial where courts at the international level produce case law that must be observed at the national level. Both kinds of professional exchanges serve essential needs by contributing towards enhanced learning and uniform application of common norms. As judges have the same or similar problems to crack, it is helpful and valuable to share information and discuss approaches. Constructive dialogue as well as critical dialogue serve the interests of all those involved at the various levels. At best, transnational interaction can help us to improve professionally.

Furthermore, transnational interaction is also likely to help in bringing about the cultural changes that were referred to above. Judges who are parochially minded are not fit to cope well with the demands of law that is transnationally shaped and shared. Horizontal and vertical interaction across borders is needed in order for judges to understand their role and to help them adopt a professional identity and a mental approach that is in line with the demands and responsibilities that follow from the current, increasingly internationalised and multilayered system of legal sources.

Annex

The Supreme Court of Finland

1. Basic Information

In Finland, the Supreme Court has jurisdiction in civil, commercial and criminal cases. It is not a cassation court: the Supreme Court may examine questions of fact as well as questions of law, and it renders final judgment in the cases that it decides to take up (unless there are particular grounds for remitting the case back to a lower court). Below the Supreme Court, there are two instances, i.e., the district courts and the appeal courts, both of which have full jurisdiction in questions of law and fact. Access to the Supreme Court depends on the granting of leave to appeal. There are only very limited exceptions to this: in certain narrowly defined categories of cases direct appeals are allowed.[3]

The decision on whether or not to grant leave to appeal is always taken by the Supreme Court itself. These decisions are taken by a court composed of two or three justices, whereas judgments in cases decided on their merits require a court composed of five justices. On certain grounds, the President may refer a case, or a given issue in a case, to a grand chamber of 11 justices, or to plenary session. At present there are a total of 18 justices plus the President, some 35 referendaries and some 35 other staff.

2. Grounds for Leave to Appeal

The law provides for three grounds on which leave to appeal may be granted. The first and most important of these grounds relates to reasons of precedent. In other words, leave to appeal may be granted if the case involves an issue or issues where there is a need for guidance in the interpretation of the law or uniformity in its application. Thus, leave to appeal on these grounds is associated with a general interest, namely the interest in elaborating or clarifying a legal situation through case law. The other two grounds are primarily linked with the legal protection of the rights and interests of parties to the individual case. Thus, leave to appeal may be granted if it appears that there has been a procedural error or other error of such

[3] E.g., matters concerning the return of abducted children under the Hague Convention of 1980, where a court of appeal functions as first instance and direct appeal to the Supreme Court is provided for, as well as matters concerning the European Arrest Warrant, where because of the strict time limits there is a regime of direct appeal against decisions of a district court straight to the Supreme Court.

gravity that the lower court's decision would be subject to extraordinary results if it became *res judicata*. Finally, leave to appeal may be granted for other weighty reasons, in particular where important interests are at stake from the applicant's point of view and the case appears to be wrongly decided by the lower court. Leave to appeal may be partial so that it is limited to cover a certain part of the lower court's judgment, or to a certain issue or point of law, whereby the Supreme Court can in other respects rely on the findings (in particular, findings of fact) as established by the lower court.

3. Practice

Statistically, the application for leave to appeal is rejected in more than 90 per cent of cases. An essential feature of the system is that when leave to appeal is refused, no reasons are given for such a decision. The judgment of the lower court (i.e., normally the Court of Appeal) becomes *res judicata* but is neither examined on the merits nor 'confirmed' by the Supreme Court. Reasons of precedent are the most common ground for granting leave to appeal. Judgments in these cases are published on the Supreme Court's website, in a public database as well as in the Court's yearbooks. The number of such judgments is usually in the range of 110–140 each year. The two other grounds for leave to appeal are more in the nature of 'safeguard clauses' that allow the Supreme Court to exercise a supervisory control over the lower courts where necessary. Normally, there are a few dozen of such cases annually.

4. Decisions and Voting

As mentioned above, judgments on the merits are usually taken in a court composed of five justices. In case a unanimous decision on the outcome or on the reasoning cannot be reached, voting takes place, and the dissenting or concurring opinions are published together with the court's judgment.

Part III
Judicial Dialogue: The relation between the Coherency of Law and Judicial Interaction

GLOBALISATION OF THE JUDICIARY: WAYS OF INTERACTION

A. Ušacka*

Globalisation is the increasing interdependence, integration, and interaction among people in disparate locations around the world. While this umbrella term generally refers to a complex of economic, trade, social, technological and political interrelationships, during the past decade judges have been globalising as well, in ways that have important implications for the development of national, international and comparative law. In dealing with the topic of the globalisation of the judiciary, I will draw on my experience as a judge of the Constitutional Court in Latvia (1996 to 2003) and of the International Criminal Court (2003 to the present), and as a professor of public law, with particular focus on Constitutional and Comparative Law.

When one looks at the interaction between courts and judges from all over the world, a number of different types of interactions emerge. In the first place, there is interaction between courts on a national level. This type of interaction is essential to share judicial expertise and to harmonise the jurisprudence within a closed legal system. In the second place, with the establishment of the first international tribunals, interaction between national and international courts came into being. International courts benefit from the experience of national courts and reflect the legal and procedural principles of many national systems. The opposite also applies – national courts seek guidance from the jurisprudence of international courts, especially in

---

* H.E. Judge Ušacka is Judge of the International Criminal Court and former Judge of the Constitutional Court of Latvia. The views expressed in this article are the personal views of the author and do not necessarily represent the official positions of the International Criminal Court.

A.S. Muller and M.A. Loth (eds.), Highest Courts and the Internationalisation of Law

the area of human rights law. In the third place, and most recently, increasing interaction between the different international courts can be observed. This does not only apply to the various international criminal courts, but also to other international judicial institutions dealing with public international law, international human rights law, or other areas of international law. While the first and the third type of interaction between courts may be referred to as horizontal interaction, the second type may be referred to as vertical interaction.

By way of vertical interaction between courts, international law has an impact on national courts, while at the same time domestic law and practice influence the making of the jurisprudence and the practice of international courts. Personally, I strongly advocate in favour of a vivid exchange between national and international courts and agree with the universalist interpretation by Professor Sujit Choudhry to the effect that the law is best understood as a body of principles which transcend national boundaries.[1]

On the other hand, however, an anti-universalist argument may be made favouring the view that nation states and domestic courts should operate in splendid isolation. Opponents to the universalist approach in the United States are of the view that a national Constitution is a unique document, designed specifically for the governance of the people or the nation to which it applies, and only to them.[2] I would argue against this, using the example of my country, Latvia. Our Constitution was initially adopted in 1922 and the architects of that Constitution used the constitutional law and the experience of other democratic countries at that time, such as Great Britain, France, Switzerland and the United States, as a model and source of inspiration. The Constitution of Latvia was renewed in 1990. In 1998, after Latvia had ratified the European Convention on Human Rights, the text of the Latvian Constitution was supplemented accordingly. Similarly, the constitutions of other former socialist states in Eastern Europe were drafted by experts in constitutional law following general principles of law.

Another prominent argument against the universalist interpretation is that international law is used selectively to support the opinion of the judge referring to it. Judge Posner, judge of the United States Court of Appeals of the Seventh Circuit, has argued that free citation of international law would mean

[1] Sujit Choudhry, 'Globalisation in search of justification: Towards a theory of Comparative Constitutional Interpretation', *Indiana Law Journal* (Summer 1999), p. 846.

[2] Seventh Annual Grotius Lecture delivered by Justice Kirby, p. 10.

that any judge wanting a supporting citation has only to trawl deeply enough in the world's *corpus juris* to find it.[3] But then again, we have the example of the constitutional courts coming to different conclusions, using the same precedents or case law from the European Court of Human Rights with both the majority and the dissenters citing the same decision.

A protectionist argument against interaction between national and international courts is that it leads to a loss of national sovereignty. Justice Scalia of the United States Supreme Court stated that in his view the US Supreme Court should not be governed by the views of foreigners.[4] The US Supreme Court, however, ruled differently in *Hamdan* v. *Rumsfield*, illustrating that the cooperative effect for the international rule of law extends to national as well as international courts.

A related argument is that reference to international law is undemocratic in that in many countries there is no or little involvement of the legislative authority in the process of law-making, but that it is in the hands of the executive branch. I do not share this concern as I believe that, today, the separation of powers doctrine among the legislative, executive and judicial power has changed to a certain extent. Institutions are emerging that do not fall within the strict boundaries of the *trias politica* principle. For instance, this applies to the Latvian institutions of the Regulator of Public Utilities, the State Bank and the Human Rights Office and to similar institutions in other countries. To some extent, a deviation from the original thought of the division of powers also applies to the judicial branch, both at the national and the international level. For instance, the International Criminal Court (ICC) and the International Criminal Tribunal for the former Yugoslavia (ICTY), apart from adjudicating on criminal cases, also enter into cooperation agreements with states. Moreover, ICTY judges have the power to adopt the tribunal's rules of procedure and evidence.

Some also argue that international law and jurisprudence are ambiguous and therefore not helpful in adjudicating on a matter before a national court. Personally, I do not agree with such a view. On the contrary, I find that the judgments of the European Court of Human Rights, the Inter-American Court of Human Rights, the International Court of Justice, as well as the UN *ad hoc* Criminal Tribunals are detailed, transparent and well reasoned.

---

[3] Ibid., p. 10, fn. 82.

[4] Ibid., p. 10, fn. 86.

Finally, an argument based on the lack of knowledge of international law among the national judiciary is misplaced, as any such gap may be filled by continuing judicial education in the areas of international law and comparative law.

As a next step, I would like to analyse briefly how national law and practice are influencing the international legal order and the practice of international courts. Article 38 paragraph 1 of the Statute of the International Court of Justice defines the sources of law on the basis of which the court shall adjudicate, and at the same time it creates a hierarchical system of applicable legal sources. This provision states that:

> The Court [...] shall apply:
> (a) international conventions, whether general or particular, establishing rules expressly recognised by the contesting states;
> (b) international custom, as evidence of a general practice accepted as law;
> (c) the general principles of law recognised by civilized nations;
> (d) subject to the provisions of Article 59, judicial decisions and the teachings of the most highly qualified publicists of the various nations, as subsidiary means for the determination of rules of law.

As far as Article 38 paragraph 1(c) is concerned, the International Court of Justice has clarified the role of the international judges in deriving general principles from the national laws of the legal systems of the world. The Court stated that judges are to apply not the concrete rules of law found in national legal systems, but rather the principles underlying these rules.[5]

Similarly, Article 21 paragraph 1 of the Statute of the International Criminal Court sets out the law applicable before the ICC. It states that

> The Court shall apply:
> (a) In the first place, this Statute, Elements of Crimes and its Rules of Procedure and Evidence;
> (b) In the second place, where appropriate, applicable treaties and the principles and rules of international law, including the established principles of the international law of armed conflict;
> (c) Failing that, general principles of law derived by the Court from national laws of legal systems of the world including, as appropriate, the national laws of

[5] Otto Triffterer (ed.), *Commentary on the Rome Statute* (Baden-Baden, Nomos 1999), Article 21, marginal number 16, p. 442.

> States that would normally exercise jurisdiction over the crime, provided that those principles are not inconsistent with this Statute and with international law and internationally recognised norms and standards.

The language of Article 21 leaves a great deal of discretion to the judges in determining which national laws to consider in deriving 'general principles'. In various submissions in the *Lubanga* case, the Prosecutor of the ICC has referred to national systems of law. He submitted that Article 21(1)(c) does not require an exhaustive inquiry into every legal system of the world and specified that it is sufficient to ensure by 'polling' that the norms in question are effectively found in the principal legal systems of the world. In so doing, the Prosecutor offered an analysis of a particular principle of law in various civil law, common law and Islamic law jurisdictions.[6]

The UN *ad hoc* Tribunals rely on domestic law and jurisprudence even more than the ICC. Other than the Rome Statute, the Statutes of the International Criminal Tribunals for the former Yugoslavia and for Rwanda provide that customary international law is a primary source of law. With a view to identifying customary international law, the competent chambers conduct studies with regards to state practice which is supported by the states' *opinio juris*. It did so, for example, in the *Kunarac* case, where the Trial Chamber based parts of its judgement on national legislation and judicial practice in the area of rape and sexual violence.[7]

The interrelationship between the various international courts is another issue which I would like to point out. With the creation of numerous international criminal courts and tribunals that have jurisdiction over the same or similar crimes, it is obvious that each of these courts look at the work of the other courts as a source of inspiration for their own decisions. For example, the ICC, which is the latest creation among these courts, is relying to a considerable extent on the jurisprudence of the ICTY, the ICTR or the Special Court for Sierra Leone. It ought to be pointed out that the ICC is not only relying on the practice of these courts in the area of substantive criminal law, but also with respect to procedural law and general court practice, as far as the judicial discretion allows the chambers to do so. For instance, the Pre-

---

[6] See, for example, Prosecutor's Application for Extraordinary Review of Pre-Trial Chamber I's 31 March 2006 Decision Denying Leave to Appeal, 24 April 2006: <http://www.icc-cpi.int/library/cases/ICC-01-04-141_English.pdf>.

[7] <http://www.un.org/icty/kunarac/trialc2/judgement/kun-tj010222e.pdf>.

Trial Chamber in the *Lubanga* case, when seised with a motion with respect to the proofing of witnesses, analysed the witness proofing practices at the ICTY.[8] Moreover, international criminal courts are also relying on the jurisprudence of other international tribunals, such as the European or other regional Courts of Human Rights (for instance, for the determination of the rights to a fair trial)[9] or the International Court of Justice (for instance, to determine matters of jurisdiction).[10]

Before concluding my presentation, I would like to emphasise that both the vertical and the horizontal dialogue between national courts and international courts have a number of advantages. These methods of interaction allow judges to share expertise and to improve the quality of the jurisprudence. Moreover, they allow for the creation and implementation of common values, which are shared among societies worldwide and are not limited to a particular legal system. The creation and universal proliferation of social values protected by the judiciary constitute a progressive deviation from the original thought of the *trias politica* coined by Montesquieu. Moreover, by globally enforcing general principles of law, both international courts and domestic courts foster the coherency of the law, both on the domestic level and on the international level.

---

[8] <http://www.icc-cpi.int/library/cases/ICC-01-04-01-06-679_English.pdf>.

[9] See for example the decision of the Appeals Chamber in the *Lubanga* case of 12 September 2006: <http://www.icc-cpi.int/library/cases/ICC-01-04-01-06-424_English.pdf>.

[10] See for example the decision of the Appeals Chamber in the *Tadic* case of 2 October 1995: <http://www.un.org/icty/tadic/appeal/decision-e/51002.htm>.

NEW METHODS FOR THE INTERNATIONAL COHERENCY OF LAW

G. Canivet*

1. Introductory Remarks

'Supreme courts in an internationalised world: challenges for the *trias politica* and the coherency of law': it is difficult to mention all the questions raised by these few words. The traditional conceptions of the separation of powers are troubled by the new role which supreme courts have to play. They now are the keepers of fundamental rights, they ensure the respect of the hierarchy of norms. In the European framework, these are the supremacy of Community law and the European Convention of Human Rights. Supreme courts can quash national law and therefore operate in a system of subversion of national law which can result in tensions with the representative organs and governments. During this process they acquire a new political legitimacy. Courts become the place of an organised dialogue where everyone can represent his or her arguments, get to know his or her rights and make the law evolve. This evolution may seem like a form of competition in respect of politics which answers these questions by creating laws and deciding budgets. Increasingly, supreme courts do not stop at applying the hierarchy of norms in order to conform to the case law of international courts. By risking the interpretation of international law, they commit creative acts; they nourish a dialogue with international courts, though also amongst themselves. To that effect, the example of same-sex marriages, or more generally speaking of homo-parental families, is quite topical. Faced with the helplessness

* H.E. Judge Canivet is a Member of the Constitutional Council of France and former President of the *Cour de Cassation* of France.

A.S. Muller and M.A. Loth (eds.), Highest Courts and the Internationalisation of Law

of politicians, judges have often opened the way through fundamental rights, comparative law, inspiration found with other supreme courts, interaction with the European courts, private international law, etc.

After this introductory remark, it is important to summarise briefly the aim of national supreme courts towards coherency of law. In the context of globalisation, the role of supreme courts in respect of the coherency of law is confirmed. In their more traditional task of unifying national law, they have to ensure the reconciliation of the internal judicial order and the international judicial order. To begin with, the risks of making law coherent should be kept in mind. Secondly, the methods put in place by the French Court of Cassation to face these challenges are explained.

2. The challenges of Supreme Courts in making law coherent

Firstly, if one considers the European framework, the reconciliation of the internal order and the international order is a heavy responsibility for supreme courts. The damage done by an incorrect interpretation of Community law will involve claims for compensation, and a violation of the European Convention on Human Rights may give rise to compensation or even a retrial of the case. Supreme courts have to work concurrently to ensure the conformity of the internal law to the European law and to instil this dynamic into the application of the European law among all other judges within the jurisdiction. This adaptation is sometimes perceived as more or less a subversion of the national law, however, it also engages in a dialogue with the European courts. The European courts have recourse to comparative law in order to interpret European law to abstract communal principles. Indirectly, national supreme courts participate across their jurisprudential creation of making European law itself more coherent, by offering indications to the European courts.

Another challenge is the competition of legal systems. There is now a competition between laws in the global sphere and international organisations use the best performing legal system to further economic growth. The case law of supreme courts may play a determinative role in that respect, not only at the base but also and especially by the predictability of their judgments. Effectively, merchants are especially worried about judicial security. In the outset, the perspective of unifying law globally is not realistic; though the competition of the systems stimulates supreme courts to examine the best rule to adopt, not only in the context of globalisation, but also with regard to economic, national, social, and cultural circumstances.

In addition, due to the economic and social development increased by globalisation, new challenges arise simultaneously in most, particularly Western, countries. One may exemplify this, besides the same-sex couple or same-sex parent family already mentioned, by; the responsibility of companies which have exposed their employees to asbestos, the responsibility of health systems in respect of the origin of a blood transfusion contaminated with the Aids virus, the commercial and criminal activities developed on the internet, or the responsibility of cigarette manufacturers to smokers who became ill with a disease linked to smoking. Today, jurists perceive without difficulty that very different solutions are made for similar problems.

Lastly, harmonisation of the European legal systems in view of the ever tighter union is an important task for national supreme courts. This harmonisation seems more than merely desirable if it concerns harmonizing the creation of Community law. The environmental sector offers a significant example of this. The work of the last annual conference of the European Forum of Judges for environmental law has demonstrated that the notion of waste had received very different interpretations from one country to another. As a consequence, the proposed solutions to difficult cases in the application of the relevant European directive were very heterogeneous.

3. New Methods of the French Court of Cassation

3.1 Monitoring European Jurisprudence

Before focusing our attention on the comparative method and the access to foreign laws, it is important to underline that the French Court of Cassation accords great attention to European jurisprudence. For this reason, a watchdog was put in place with the Service for Documentation and Study. A junior judge and a *greffier en chef* are responsible for observing European law. Every day they follow the news of the courts of Strasbourg and Luxembourg. As soon as a relevant judgment is made they inform all the judges of the Court by e-mail. This daily observation, which makes the knowledge of European law instantaneously effective, is made even more useful by a bimonthly review. This review consists of a brief presentation of the major judgments of the two European Courts. It also mentions the studies, comments and works that have appeared in European law, as well as legislative texts. Major decisions of national supreme courts of the European Union are obtained to develop on account of the Network of Supreme Court Presidents of the EU which will be presented below.

3.2 Comparative Law

The judgments of the Court of Cassation have certain characteristics of conciseness and the development of deductive reasoning which prohibits any explanation of motives by direct reference to case law or academic research. The decisions of the Court of Cassation, like the decisions of other French courts, do not include a single trace of comparative law. Even though comparative law cannot be used as a direct source of French law, it has become a secondary source of law. In effect, it is and has been for a number of years a source of inspiration for the judges of the Court of Cassation. In the report of the members of the Court, which presents collegiality and establishes the process of decision, traces of comparative law may be found. Such a report illustrates the complexities of the case and analyses objectively the multitude of different possible solutions. Amongst these solutions those elaborated by foreign systems may appear. This means that parties receiving the report may formulate contradictory observations.

To ensure that the references to foreign law are clear and rigorous, the Court of Cassation commissions a team of researchers to study unresolved questions in comparative law. For example, a study has been conducted on the very controversial question of whether one can claim damages from the doctor who is at fault when a child is born with a disability or health problem following a mistake in the prenatal diagnosis. A similar study is carried out when the Court has to declare *force majeure*. Recently, a study has been requested on the subject of the expansion of the *res judicata*. The outcome is based on the laws of Germany, England, Spain and Italy. A free translation into English illustrates the interest in the question: authority of what has been judged, *res judicata*. As we are creating a European judicial area and decisions of justice are circulating, the resort to comparative law in finding solutions for such types of questions seems indispensable in ensuring the coherency of law.

3.3 International Databases

A communal jurisprudential database seems to be one of the essential tools for many supreme courts to know of other judicial systems, to use in the methods of reasoning of judges, or at least as a basis of their decisions. A communal compilation is indispensable in building such a tool. Regarding the francophone database, JURICAF, it is the communal language as well as a communal judicial tradition that forms the origin of the compilation. It was created by the communal effort and will of the high courts of cassation that have in common the use of the French language, united in a society of French law, AHJUCAF. Established in 2006, within six months of its launch JURICAF counted nearly 41,000 decisions produced by 25 supreme courts; predominantly from Canada, France, Morocco and the Benin.

For certain countries, like Madagascar or the Benin, this communal base is the medium to dispose of a first basic national foundation. For others, where French is not the official language, it demands a lot of effort to translate the decisions into French. At the end of its first year, JURICAF was predicted to contain at least 50,000 decisions and it will continue to grow. Access to the database may be limited to authorised users, as decisions are not made anonymous, however, it is not exclusive to judges of supreme courts. Legal professionals and academics equally have the opportunity to use it free of charge.

The database has as a mission to record the work of the judges of the courts of cassation in the francophone judicial community and to develop the jurisprudential exchanges, with the common law system as a model, at the heart of the judicial cultural community where the French doctrine and the case law of the Court of Cassation have been dominant up to the beginning of the twenty-first century. Non-francophone jurists who wish to access French case law may consult the *Jurisprudence Française en Langue Anglaise*, a database that was created in 2003 on the initiative of Professor Sir Basil Markensinis and the Institute of Global Law.

In the framework of the European Union, supreme courts have equally expressed an interest in the ability to access each other's case law. The creation of a database seemed too complex as regards technology and language. Therefore it was decided to create a communal 'Portal of European Jurisprudence' with the financial assistance of the European Commission. This project is part of the political development of information technology in the judicial system led by the European institutions. The Portal is envisaged to become a tool of comparative law for European judges, with the aim of harmonizing the laws of nations and creating a Union of communal thought and values. In two or three years, it will allow consultation of the entirety of the jurisprudential base of supreme courts in the official languages of the European Union. The user will be able to formulate a question in his or her own language. This request will then be translated into the languages of the Union and a meta research engine will search the connected databases. At the beginning the results will come up in the original language. Later, automatic translation means may be installed when these are more reliable. One of our system prototypes is *Systran*, already in use by the European institutions. Recently, a project supervisor has been employed by the Network of EU Supreme Court Presidents to put in place the technical requirements of the Portal.

3.4 The Network of Supreme Court Presidents

A number of networks of judges have been created, some specialise, for example, in commercial or environmental law, others are on a more general footing. On 10 March 2004, the Presidents of Supreme Courts of the European Union created a type of network modelled on the French Law Society. This network has, so far successfully, undertaken a number of objectives, such as providing a discussion forum between the European Supreme Court Presidents; reinforcing relations between the supreme courts; working on communal topics; aiding their insertion into the judicial architecture of Europe and initiating relations with the institutions of the European Union; comparing and approximating methods of judgment; and, creating a community of thought and values between the different legal orders of the EU Member States. Thus, new working methods emerge on the European stage: they reflect the basic law as well as the methods of administration and organisation of the judiciary and the collaboration with other powers.

The creation of the network itself was an opportunity for the supreme court judges to develop personal ties with one another, which previously existed as either bilateral relationships or in the framework of the Council of Europe, of which the Judicial Cooperation Service had been organizing conferences for supreme court presidents for more than a decade. The dialogue between the members is animated by an Administration Council. One of the beneficial tools is the intranet of the network's internet site, created in 2005.

Besides the dialogue undertaken by the Presidents, the personal exchanges at the network are reinforced by secondments: fifteen exchanges were thus organised in 2005. In 2006, some twenty other judges arranged to participate individually in the work of their colleagues of another supreme court linked with the European Network of Judicial Training, which is in charge of coordinating the European Judicial Exchange Programme for all judges and crown prosecutors of the EU.

The exchange of information and jurisprudence, transferred by the designated correspondents in each of the supreme courts, creates a community of thought and values between the different jurisdictions of the Member States and favours the development of the comparative method. Decisions rendered by national courts on questions of European law as well as major decisions of the Courts of Luxembourg and Strasbourg can be found recapitulated in the *Review of the Observatory of European Law*, the European version of the *Lettre bimestrielle of the Observatoire of the Service de Documentation et d'Etudes de la Cour de Cassation*. This review is accessible on the website of the Network.

Since the opening conference on 10 March 2004, the network has begun to work on the subject: 'The representation and defence of parties, especially in criminal law, before the European Union supreme courts.' The debate held during the conference as well as national reports are available on the internet site of the network, open to the public since December 2005.[1] The conference held in Warsaw in June 2006 was entitled, 'The relationship between the Supreme Court and the Executive,' and especially concerned the appointment of judges to supreme courts and matters of discipline as well as budgetary matters.

Relations with the European institutions have been developed since the creation of the network and are continued through visits by the President of the network to Brussels, the Commission, the European Parliament and the Council of Europe. The members of the network were invited to participate in a presentation seminar of the European Institute in Brussels in November 2005. At this seminar, Mr Franko Frattini, Vice-President of the European Commission, and Mr Jean-Marie Cavada, President of the Civil Liberties Commission of Justice and Internal Affairs, especially expressed their interest in the activities of the network and the dialogue with its members in respect of the construction of a European judicial space.

As a result, the network has been involved in engaged consultations with the Head Office of Justice, Liberty and Security in the field of training judi-

---

[1] <www.rpcsjue.org>.

cial officers and with regard to green papers which link to the principle of *ne bis in idem*. The network has equally offered to participate in the pursuit of efforts taken in relation to the communal referential basis administered by the Head Office of Health and Consumer Protection and to reflect internally on the proposition of a directive on the subject of mediation as well as a directive on the liberalisation of services.

The network is consulted in law-making processes. It may create awareness of certain difficulties and raise questions from a technical viewpoint. State representatives have a political mandate and may, at times, experience the powerful influence of lobbyists. The dialogue with the European judiciaries builds true collaboration with the other powers, the European executive and the legislative. We therefore return to the heart of the posed challenge, to know the interactions between the principle of the separation of powers and the coherency of law.

The work of the network seems to be a step towards putting in place a veritable European judicial architecture of a real European judicial power. If the law demands harmonisation, judicial institutions that are appointed to this task have to be equally permanent.

4. Conclusion

In conclusion, it seems that new working methods call for new interaction, favourable to the harmonisation of law. The vocation of the Hague Institute for the Internationalisation of Law and the subject itself of 'supreme courts in an internationalised world: challenges for the *trias politica* and the coherency of law' naturally suggest that European and international networks of professors, of researchers and of judges create a veritable cooperation. The study of comparative law, hence facilitated, can enrich the work of judges, as well as that of researchers.

Part IV
Case Studies

THE ROLE OF THE ISRAELI SUPREME COURT IN THE FIGHT AGAINST TERRORISM

D. Beinisch*

1. Introduction

There is no doubt that international law has developed immensely over the last decade. Part of this development is the growth, in numbers as well as in functions, of international tribunals which have become important players in the different realms of international law. However, national courts which apply international law still afford the best means for the enforcement of international law. In this regard, most nations share similar concerns, as the plague of terrorism is spreading throughout the world. Still, as is well-known, the Israeli Supreme Court, unfortunately, has more experience in this subject than any other court in the world. The harsh reality of the situation in Israel has, over the years, brought before us many opportunities to apply and interpret international norms.

In September 2000, a wave of terrorist attacks and gun battles of ever-increasing violence forced Israel into a period of armed conflict. The government took steps to fight terrorism and, as a result, the Supreme Court was flooded with petitions requiring us to adjudicate the proper balance between the need to protect the public and preserve security on the one hand, and the need to preserve basic human rights on the other.

We live in a period of constant tension and contradiction. The public demands security and the government is under pressure to protect the public and ensure that they can lead peaceful and safe lives. The Court acknowl-

---

* H.E. Judge Beinish is a Judge of the Supreme Court of Israel.

A.S. Muller and M.A. Loth (eds.), Highest Courts and the Internationalisation of Law

edges the duty of the executive to protect its citizens and preserve their right to life against the threat of terrorism. The Court also recognises, however, that it is the duty of the judiciary to guarantee that a nation fighting for its survival will not sacrifice those very values that make the fight worthwhile. Indeed, the level of protection of human rights in times of peace differs from their protection in times of war and armed conflict, when, naturally, the balance between security and human rights shifts. But if the State does not protect human rights in times of emergency, it may lose its democratic character in times of peace. Therefore, the Court exercises judicial review both in times of peace and in times of emergency.

In times of emergency it is the difficult role of the judiciary to guard against disproportional infringements of the basic human rights of every individual, including terrorists. In today's reality, our Court confronts the challenge of balancing these dual values of security and human rights on a daily basis. No other court in the world faces so many cases involving issues of safeguarding human rights and humanitarian considerations while fighting terrorism in such a complicated reality. We as judges never know if we have done enough to achieve the best results in finding the proper balance between protecting human rights and security needs. We do know, however, that we are making our best efforts to strike this balance as we are faced with hundreds of cases per year during the very painful and complicated emergency period in which we find ourselves today. Ultimately, our guiding principle is that the battle against terrorism must be fought within the law, and that no war may take place outside the boundaries prescribed by the law.

Four aspects of our judicial review make the Supreme Court particularly responsive to the needs of our time: (1) broad access to the court facilitated by the practical elimination of any standing requirement; (2) judicial review exercised in real time, rather than retrospectively; (3) the status of our Court as the highest court of the land; and (4) the use of international law as substantive law and as an interpretive guide. I shall now examine each of these important tools.

2. Aspects of Judicial Review

2.1 Access to Justice

When basic human rights are at stake, the doors of the Supreme Court are open to anyone seeking a remedy against any activity of the executive branch or public authority, including the military. Anyone – Israelis, Palestinians from the West Bank and, until recently, the Gaza strip, and foreigners – has direct access to the Court, irrespective of citizenship. In fact, Palestinian residents of the territories who are not even subject to Israeli law have the same rights to approach the Court as do Israeli citizens. Moreover, there is no standing requirement and thus civil rights groups and NGOs may challenge activities taken against Palestinians in the territories, and they often do.

Furthermore, it is very rare for the Court to determine that an issue is non-justiciable. The Court does, of course, recognise that the political nature of some issues renders them outside the appropriate purview of the Courts, but these cases are the exception, not the rule. Typically, where a case raises a legal issue affecting human rights or a question regarding the legality of government activity, we will not hesitate to exercise judicial review. Naturally, due to this position, the Court has often attracted criticism from politicians.

2.2 Real Time

Virtually every day, the justices of the Supreme Court consider all sorts of requests for injunctions against the use of different measures taken in the name of security. In most cases, as in any other judicial proceeding, the Court grants injunctions immediately before deciding on the legality of the acts themselves. Since 2002, our Court has heard numerous petitions against the Israeli Defense Force's actions (hereinafter: IDF) in its military operations against the terrorist infrastructure in the territories. In contrast to most petitions, which require *ex post facto* judicial review of an action that has already been taken, some of these petitions required *ex ante* judicial review, while military operations were still underway.

2.3 The Status of the Court

The status of the Supreme Court as the highest court in the country, and the public trust and deference which accompanies such status, gives the Court its power to make unpopular decisions. As a result, the executive branch is well aware of the need to abide by the Court's decisions, no matter how unpopular. Indeed, the status of the Israeli High Court of Justice has played a significant role in the enforcement of its decisions which ruled against the

State on highly controversial issues, such as in decisions concerning the interrogation methods of the General Security Service, the construction of the security fence between Israel and the territories, and the disengagement plan. The very existence of the High Court of Justice and its willingness to review almost any governmental or military act when basic human rights are at stake serves in and of itself as an important check on the executive's decision making.

2.4 International Law

At the heart of our discussion is the implementation of international (and also comparative) law by the Israeli Supreme Court. When the Court reviews actions taken against those suspected of terrorist activity, the extent of our application of international law differs depending on whether the suspects are Israeli citizens or Palestinian residents of the West Bank. Israeli citizens are subject to domestic Israeli law. Therefore, when dealing with Israeli citizens who are involved in terrorist activity, the Court generally applies domestic criminal law, using international law mainly as a source of interpretive guidance. In the West Bank, however, international law, namely the laws of belligerent occupation, is the basic norm. In addition, in reviewing the actions of the Israeli army in the territories in recent years, the Court has shown a growing readiness to apply principles from human rights conventions, such as the International Covenant on Civil and Political Rights, and fundamental principles of Israeli law, alongside with the international humanitarian law and the laws of belligerent occupation.

One example of the Court's use of international law is the *Marab* case,[1] concerning the legality of administrative detentions of large numbers of suspected terrorists for the purpose of interrogation. In this case, the Court held that the order issued by the commander of military forces in the West Bank, which authorised the detention of a person for 18 days (or, as was later amended, for 12 days) without bringing him or her before a judicial authority, contradicts fundamental principles of international and Israeli law. This conclusion was based, *inter alia*, on an analysis of the relevant articles of various human rights conventions, as well as European Court of Human Rights' decisions and other sources of international and comparative law.

---

[1] *Marab* v. *The Commander of IDF Forces in the Judea and Samaria Area*, HCJ 3239/02, 5 May 2002.

Following this, the army regulations were changed and the period between the detention and the first instance of judicial review of the detention order was considerably shortened.

In rulings on other petitions, the Court has set out detailed standards of shelter, hygiene, and medical treatment that the Fourth Geneva Convention requires of the detaining power. This demonstrates that when international humanitarian law does not have the tools to deal with certain situations, we find solutions in other areas of law, such as in international human rights law.

3. Recent Examples

In order to demonstrate how these four characteristics mentioned above function *de facto*, I will now turn to elaborate on two recent decisions. The first case deals with the 'early warning' procedure employed by the IDF to arrest Palestinians suspected of terrorist activity. According to this procedure, arrest operations may be aided by a local Palestinian resident whose assistance is engaged to issue an early warning to the residents of the house in order to allow the innocent individuals to leave the building and the wanted persons to turn themselves in before it becomes necessary to use force in a manner liable to endanger human life. Several human rights organisations filed a petition claiming that this procedure was illegal as it amounted, in fact, to the use of a protected civilian as a 'human shield' and put protected civilians in real and tangible danger. The respondent emphasised important precautionary conditions contained in the procedure – mainly, assessment of low risk – and noted the reality in which the IDF is obliged to combat terrorists hiding among the civilian population, whom this procedure was intended to protect.

In our judgment, we determined that the considerations in favour of banning the army from using local residents in this way should prevail, for several reasons: first, the existence of a general prohibition against using protected residents as a part of the war effort of the occupying army; second, the distinction between the civilian population and military targets in principle mandates that local residents would not to be brought, even with their consent, into the zone in which combat activity is taking place; and third, the inability to know in advance whether the relaying of a warning involves danger to the local resident who relays it.

These considerations led the Court to the conclusion that the 'early warning' procedure contradicted international law and was, therefore, illegal. The

Court emphasised that there was no relevance to the question whether the assisting civilian gives his consent to relay the warning, since he is not permitted to waive his rights pursuant to international humanitarian law and also since it is difficult to judge when his consent is being freely given.

By prohibiting the use of the 'early warning' procedure, the Court deprived the IDF of an efficient military procedure. The novelty of this decision is in the adoption of what seems to be a higher standard than the one required by the existing norms of international law. The Court based its decision not on the positive rules of international humanitarian law, but rather on its fundamental principles and their rationales.

The second example on which I want to elaborate is the security fence, which is a well-known issue throughout the world. Many petitions were filed in an attempt to attack the legality of orders issued by the IDF Commander in the West Bank to take possession of land for the purpose of erecting the security fence. The most renowned petition was the one concerning the route of the fence in the Beit Sourik area (approximately 40 kilometres west and northwest of Jerusalem).[2] The petitioners pointed to their resulting harm in the form of loss of and damage to land, limited access to farming, and limitation of their freedom of movement. The respondent argued that the security fence was a necessary and legitimate barrier against potential terrorist attacks.

In an opinion written by President Barak, the Court accepted the respondent's claim that the fence was built for reasons of national security and that, according to principles of international law, the taking of land for that purpose could be justified. In this regard, the Court determined the proper balance between the security considerations and the rights of the local residents, by applying the proportionality test, which is found in both Israeli administrative law and international humanitarian law. Within this framework the Court ruled that the IDF Commander did not exercise his discretion proportionately in this case, and therefore should reduce the infringement upon the local inhabitants' rights and interests by altering the route of the fence in the areas complained of in the petition.

After this judgment was given, the International Court of Justice (ICJ) submitted its advisory opinion regarding the legal consequences of the con-

---

[2] *Beit Sourik Village Council* v. *The Government of Israel*, Commander of the IDF Forces in the West Bank, HCJ 2056/04, 30 June 2004.

struction of the separation fence (the 'wall' in its terminology).[3] It declared that it could not be persuaded that the fence was necessary to achieve security objectives, and found that in fact, it was 'tantamount to *de facto* annexation.'

After the advisory opinion was given, petitioners asked the Court to review its previous decisions regarding the security fence in the light of the ICJ's opinion. In the judgment concerning the legality of the separation fence in the area of Alfei-Menashe,[4] the Court attempted to reconcile the two allegedly contradicting judgments. The Court found that the main difference between the decisions was mainly with the different factual bases upon which each tribunal decided. The ICJ based its judgment upon the factual basis regarding the injury to the rights of the Palestinian residents alone. In contrast, in the *Beit Sourik* case, an extensive factual basis was laid before the Court regarding both the infringement upon the human rights of the local residents and the security-military needs. This comprehensive factual basis allowed the Court to determine that the decision to erect the fence arose out of security-military considerations and that, although certain segments of the barrier violated rules of international law, others did not. Another difference between the decisions related to the ways in which each court conducted proceedings. The case before the ICJ regarded the entire route of the fence. Therefore, a particular and separate analysis of the various segments of the fence could not have been performed. In contrast, in the *Beit Sourik* case, the Court dealt with one segment of the fence (40 km long), and similarly, in other petitions pending before us, additional segments are being examined. This enables the Court to examine closely the delicate balancing undertaken between human rights and security needs with respect to each segment of the fence.

Regarding the specific route of the fence at Alfei-Menashe, the Court was not convinced that it met the requirement of proportionality. In this case, the Court determined that the necessary effort had not been made and the details of an alternative route had not been sufficiently explored, in order to ensure security while keeping injury to the residents of the relevant villages to a minimum. Therefore, the Court ruled that the respondents must examine the

---

[3] Advisory Opinion on the Legal Consequences of the Construction of a Wall in the Occupied Palestinian Territory, ICJ, 9 July 2004.

[4] International Legality of the Security Fence and Sections near Alfei Menashe, HCJ 7957/04, 15 September 2005.

possibility of removing the villages from the enclave to the western side of the fence.

Regarding the ICJ's advisory opinion, we stated that the Court shall grant full weight to the rules of international law as developed and interpreted by the ICJ, which is the highest judicial body in international law. However, with regard to the ICJ's final conclusions concerning the security fence, which were based upon a different factual basis, the Court held that they were not *res judicata* and therefore did not obligate the Court to determine that all segments of the fence violated international law.

While formally the ICJ's advisory opinion does not have a binding effect on the relevant parties, the Court acknowledged the important role of the ICJ in interpreting and implementing questions of international law. The Court emphasised its respect for the ICJ's normative statements and stated that it will follow them in its judgments. Despite the fact that ultimately the Court reached a different substantive conclusion, it did not ignore the ICJ's decision. On the contrary, the Court explained carefully the reasons for the differences. In the end, the Court accepted the petitions and ordered the respondent to change the route of the security fence. This willingness to apply international standards, as interpreted by the ICJ, in an effective manner and over such a delicate and sensitive issue, is indicative of the Court's commitment to international law, its underlying principles, and its central judicial bodies.

Finally, I would like to mention a recent judgment concerning the rights of the Palestinians in the West Bank to property and to freedom of movement. The IDF military commander in the West Bank is expected to protect the lives and the well being of the Israeli settlers and the local Palestinians residents living in the West Bank. In order to achieve these goals, the military commander decided to restrict access to certain agricultural areas that belong to Palestinians, reasoning that the restriction was necessary in order to protect Israeli settlers from terrorist attacks by Palestinians, as well as to protect Palestinian farmers from attacks against them carried out by extremist Israelis.

In our judgment, we affirmed that the military commander has the authority to restrict access to certain areas in order to protect the lives and well-being of all residents of the West Bank. Nevertheless, we determined that the military commander was not authorised to restrict the access to areas that belong to Palestinians in order to protect them from attacks directed against them in these areas. The primary reason for this conclusion was that the use of the military commander's authority must be performed according to the principle of proportionality, which requires a rational connection between the desired purpose and the means taken. We held that setting restrictions on access to areas that belong to Palestinians is not a rational means for the purpose of protecting them. Therefore, we ruled that the military commander was obliged to take other measures in order to protect the security of the Palestinian farmers who desire to enter their fields.

4. Conclusion

The government of Israel and the Knesset, as elected bodies, may respond to public opinion in deciding how they will cope with terrorism. However, the professionalism and independence of the judicial system obliges us, as judges, to exercise objective judgment that is not affected by public pressure, despite the fact that we all live in the heart of this terrifying reality. In exercising judicial review, the Court's basic premise is that the law is not silent before the guns of war.

It should not be understood that the Court decides which methods are appropriate for fighting terrorism. Choosing such methods is the responsibility of the government and the military commanders. Nevertheless, the Court does consider it to be its role to ensure that both domestic law and international humanitarian law are observed while implementing such security measures.

Our conviction is that the Court fulfils its role when it exercises judicial review in times of war as in times of peace. A democracy that ignores basic principles of human rights is liable to give terrorism the victory it seeks. Let us hope that the difficult times that we are experiencing will soon pass, and that we will all be able to advance the values of law and justice in times of peace.

CONFRONTING COMPARATIVE METHODS: APPROACHES TO USING EXTRA-SYSTEMIC PARAMETERS BY THE CANADIAN SUPREME COURT AND THE SOUTH AFRICAN CONSTITUTIONAL COURT

A. Lollini*

1. INTRODUCTION

With increasing interest in the last decade, scholars in comparative constitutional law have begun to look at the phenomenon generally defined as 'dialogue between courts.'[1] Looking at superior jurisdictions (national, international, supra-national, etc.), in this article we will deal with the idea of 'communication' between judges of supreme courts and judges of constitutional courts. This form of 'legal' dialogue between judges is articulated in the following way; when interpreting constitutional provisions, judges consider extraneous legal elements, those defined as extra-systemic to their domestic legal systems. Hence, this article intends to proceed with an initial analysis of how these parameters are concretely metabolised into legal reasoning and consequently, what the patterns of legal argumentation here discovered are. In other words, which language does syntax use for communication.

Public law doctrine has been working on a broad and detailed classification of the phenomenon. The following models have been mentioned from

* Dr Andrea Lollini is a member of the Department of Politics of the University of Bologna, Italy.

[1] See B. Markesinis, *Comparative Law in the Courtroom and Classroom: the Story of the Last Thirty-Five Years* (Oxford, Hart 2003) and B. Markesinis and J. Fedtke, 'The Judge as Comparatist', 80 *Tulane University Law Review* (2005) p. 11.

A.S. Muller and M.A. Loth (eds.), Highest Courts and the Internationalisation of Law

time to time: (a) *cross-judicial influence*;[2] (b) *cross-constitutional influence* or *cross-constitutional fertilisation*;[3] (c) *judicial transplant*;[4] (d) *trans-judicial communication* or *judicial dialogue*;[5] and, (e) *trans-judicial borrowing* or *precedent borrowing*.[6] This last definition explicitly connects the entire phenomenon with Anglo-American law, which follows the principle of the binding precedent (in its various declensions). Thus, modern borrowing of precedents between constitutional judges would be an expansion of a typical source of Common Law, which evolved from the historically widespread practice of judges of the British Commonwealth. At the beginning of the twentieth century, British judges, in particular the Privy Council, frequently used precedents from foreign judges. This was mainly practised by the Court of Final Appeal for Colonies and Dominions, a practice that, still today, is being applied concerning a small group of Caribbean countries. Its function, of ensuring the exact observation and interpretation of the law, deeply influenced the development of law in countries such as New Zealand, Australia, India, South Africa (along with other countries in the British colonial area of east and southern Africa), Hong Kong, Canada and countries in the Caribbean.[7]

---

[2] Cf., A.K. Thiruvengadam, *Legal Transplants through Judiciaries: Cross-judicial Influences on Constitutional Adjudication in the Post-World War II Era. A study in comparative constitutional law focusing on theoretical and empirical issues*, Paper on the Issue of Transjudicial Borrowings (New York University 2001).

[3] Cf., S. Choudhry, 'Globalisation in search of justification: Towards a theory of comparative constitutional interpretation', 74 *Indiana Law Journal* (1999) p. 821.

[4] Cf., B. Ackerman, 'The Rise of World Constitutionalism', 83 *Val. L. Rev.* (1997) p. 821.

[5] Cf., A.-M. Slaughter, 'A typology of transjudicial communication', 29 *University of Richmond Law Review* (1994) p. 99; eadem, 'A Global Community of Courts', 44 *Harvard International Law Journal* (2003) p. 191. It should be noted that Anne-Marie Slaughter was one of the first to start the debate on this practice.

[6] Cf., K.L. Scheppele, 'Aspirational and aversive constitutionalism: The case for studying cross-constitutional influence through negative models', 1 *International Journal of Constitutional Law* (2003) p. 296.

[7] See P. Nevill, 'New Zealand: The Privy Council is replaced with a domestic Supreme Court', 3 *International Journal of Constitutional Law* (2005) p. 115. In some Commonwealth and former Commonwealth countries, the appeal to the Privy Council was only recently annulled formally. In others, as in the case of South Africa, it was abolished a long time ago. The case of Australia is worth noting: only in the 1980s did it eliminate this mechanism that put the national legal system in direct communication with the British Courts, which, as stressed by Australian doctrine, produced a strong legal influence. The mechanism of the Privy Coun-

As we shall see below, the phenomenon of 'borrowing' precedents and interpretive solutions or argument models currently goes well beyond the legal rationale and the geo-cultural borders that defined the relationship between the British Empire's *centre* and its *peripheries*. The analysis of constitutional court rulings in legal systems that have adopted new constitutional texts (for example, Canada in 1982 or South Africa in 1996) or in legal systems such as Israel, shows that judges increasingly resort to practices of comparing constitutional law, specifically referring to and citing rulings and interpretive solutions of foreign constitutional courts, including solutions from the Romano-Germanic legal tradition. Interpretative solutions are now being actively sought and borrowed by courts from different legal traditions, a practice that no longer arises out of subordination.

Subsuming this phenomenon under the function of interpretation allows us to refer to various theories and procedures of legal reasoning, making it possible to verify whether we are dealing with a legally acceptable form of legal argumentation.[8] It is no longer a question of verifying the existence of this phenomenon as fact: the evidence is simply irrefutable. The question is, rather, to analyse how these extra-systemic

---

cil is analysed also by P.K. Tripathi, 'Foreign Precedents and Constitutional Law', 57 *Columbian. Law Review* (1957) p. 319. See also the study of S. Gardbaum, 'Japanese Law Symposium: The New Commonwealth Model of Constitutionalism', 49 *American Journal of Comparative Law* (2001), p. 707.

[8] Here reference is made to Robert Alexy's reconstruction of argumentative theories and techniques. In his famous study Alexy carefully examines the 'canons of interpretation' according to the models of Von Savigny (grammatical, logical, historical and systematic elements), Larenz (literal meaning, contextual meaning, the regulatory purposes, aims and normative intentions of the historical legislator, objective-teleological criteria, and conformity of interpretation to the constitution), and Wolff (philological, logical, systematic, historical, comparative, genetic, and teleological interpretations), all before dealing with his theory of rational legal argumentation. See R. Alexy, *A Theory of Legal Argumentation: The theory of rational discourse as theory of legal justification*, translated by R. Adler and N. MacCormick (Oxford, Clarendon Press 1989) p. 3. See also, for example, the triad: 'cognitive interpretation, decisional interpretation, creative interpretation' defined by the Italian scholar R. Guastini in *L'interpretazione dei documenti normativi* (Milan, Giuffré 2004), and reasserted by the same author in *Ancora sull'interpretazione costituzionale* (Diritto pubblico, n° 2, 2005) p. 459. See also the argumentation theories classification by E. Diciotti, *Interpretazione della legge e discorso razionale* (Turin, Giappicchelli 1999). A comprehensive analysis is also in M. Rosenfeld, *Just Interpretations. Law Between Ethics and Politics* (Berkeley CA, University of California Press 1998).

parameters are integrated in the interpretative phase and how the comparative method is actually used.[9]

The positions of legal scholars are polarised between celebration of the phenomenon and radical scepticism about it.[10] This study proposes to evaluate if, and to what extent, the comparative method can be a resource for constitutional judges,[11] in particular assessing the risk that its use could give judges an uncontrollable and arbitrary freedom to manipulate the interpretation and application of the law.

What we intend to do here is to compare different 'patterns' of legal argumentation based on extra-systemic parameters used by different supreme and constitutional courts. In particular, we will comparatively analyse judgments of the Canadian Supreme Court and the South African Constitutional Court in order to look at how judges of different courts use concretely extraneous legal parameters.

2. Why Canada and South Africa?

The decision to select Canada and South Africa as examples of how judges communicate with other foreign jurisdictions is based on empirical and 'structural' considerations. In this perspective, the first choice is motivated by the empirical observation which shows that the Canadian Supreme Court, in its judgments, very often uses foreign law or extra-systemic parameters. From this angle, this practice seems to be an interpretative modality with which the Canadian judges are comfortable.[12]

---

[9] See A. Lollini, 'La circolazione degli argomenti: metodo comparato e parametri interpretative extra-sistemici nella giurisprudenza costituzionale sudafricana', 1 *Rivista di diritto pubblico comparato ed europeo* (2007) p. 479.

[10] The ambivalence of the positions and the opposing views are evident cf., W. Osiatynski, 'Paradoxes of constitutional borrowing', 1 *International Journal of Constitutional Law* (2003) p. 244; W. Ewald, 'Comparative Jurisprudence (II): The Logic of Legal Transplant', 43 *American Journal of Comparative Law* (1995) p. 489; H. Klug, 'The Dignity clause of the Montana Constitution: May foreign jurisprudence lead the way to an expanded interpretation?', 64 *Montana Law Review* (2003) p. 133; D.E. Childress, 'Using comparative Constitutional Law to resolve federal questions', 53 *Duke Law Journal* (2003) p. 193.

[11] See the extensive analysis in J. Fedtke and B. Markesinis, *Judicial Recourse to Foreign Law: A New Source of Inspiration?* (New York, Routledge-Cavendish 2006).

[12] Choudhry, op. cit. n. 3; C. L'Heureaux-Dube, 'The Importance of Dialogue: Globalisation and the international impact of the Rehnquist Court', 34 *Tulsa Law Journal* (1998) p. 15;

The justification of the second choice, South Africa, is slightly more complicated. It is based not only on empirical and quantitative considerations, but more specifically on key structural characters of the constitutional legal order. The Constitution of post-apartheid South Africa is, actually, the only constitution that has an express provision allowing judges to use *extra*-systemic parameters for its interpretation.[13] Therefore, in this phase it is the South African 'model' itself which must be examined because it is a constitutional system endowed with a norm that has allowed the Constitutional Court to become a pioneer in developing a practice of interpretation.

Nonetheless, it should be clarified that the South African Court is not the first to work in a dialogue with foreign bodies of law; some examples include the established jurisprudence of the Supreme Courts of Canada[14] and Israel, the frequent references that constitutional judges in Latin-American countries such as Argentina make to the Supreme Court of the United States, or the unexpected comparative references made by the French *Cour de Cassation* (under the current Chief Justice Guy Canivet[15]), or those made in some important judgments of the British House of Lords. The South African Court, however, was the first one to do so based on a positive norm. The judges in these examples had to tackle the problem of systematically setting up the criteria and limits of this practice.

Section 39 of the 1996 Constitution of South Africa (indexed as 'Interpretation of the Bill of Rights') states that the Constitutional Court, when interpreting the Bill of Rights, must promote the 'values that underlie an open and democratic society,' *must* consider international public law, and *may* take foreign law into consideration.[16] South African constitutionalist doctrine

---

H. Webb, 'The Constitutional Court of South Africa: Rights Interpretation and Comparative Constitutional Law', *University of Pennsylvania Journal of Constitutional Law* (1998) p. 205; K. Greenwalt, 'Free Speech in United States and Canada', *Law & Contemporary Problems* (1992) p. 5.

[13] One of the first studies on this subject is Webb, op. cit. n. 12.

[14] See the study of the former Canadian Supreme Court Judge C. L'Heureaux-Dube, op. cit. n. 12.

[15] On this matter see the study on the use of comparative law by the *Cour de Cassation* by G. Canivet, 'The Practice of Comparative Law by the Supreme Courts: Brief reflexions on the dialogue between the judges in French and European experience', 80 *Tulane Law Review* (2006) p. 1377.

[16] Cf., section 39: '(1) When interpreting the Bill of Rights, (a) a court, tribunal or forum must promote the values that underlie an open and democratic society based on human dignity, equality and freedom; (b) must consider international law; and; (c) may consider foreign

agrees on three main reasons for this provision.[17] First, the necessity of international legitimacy, required after decades of isolation by the apartheid regime, which had ignored international standards on fundamental rights. Second, the search for international *repères*, capable of aiding the interpretive work of an entirely new constitutional text. In this context, the drafters of the Constitution became increasingly aware of not being able to find points of reference with the previous regime which was based on a segregationist rationale (established with the Republic of South Africa in 1961). This led to the Constitutional Court having to formulate a particular form of historical interpretation of the Constitution aimed at recuperating the common law of the 1910 South African Union (which partially recognised the rights and guarantees of 'non-white' people). The third and final reason for this provision is the fact that introducing judicial review in South Africa requires a period of legal and cultural 'learning.' If the transformation of the entire legal system did not already require a major effort from all participants in the South African legal system, the introduction of constitutional justice, on the other hand, brought with it the need for developing a pedagogical approach to using this instrument for members of the ordinary judiciary, the components of the legal system, and the constitutional judges themselves.[18]

---

law. (2) When interpreting any legislation, and when developing the common law or customary law, every court, tribunal or forum must promote the spirit, purport and objects of the Bill of Rights. (3) The Bill of Rights does not deny the existence of any other rights or freedoms that are recognised or conferred by common law, customary law or legislation, to the extent that they are consistent with the Bill'. It is worth noting that these same provisions are also in the text of the Interim Constitution of 1993. Section 351 Constitution 1993 nevertheless has slightly different provisions: 'In interpreting the provisions of this Chapter a court of law shall promote the values which underlie an open and democratic society based on freedom and equality and shall, where applicable, have regard to public international law applicable to the protection of the rights entrenched in this Chapter, and may have regard to comparable foreign case law.' In the transition from the interim text to the definitive one, the phrase 'where applicable' was removed. Constitutionalist doctrine and the Constitutional Court did profound interpretive work on the matter. Section 39 of the 1996 Constitution, in fact, seems to reinforce the openness of the South African constitutional system towards extra-systemic sources by eliminating the criteria of evaluating the applicability ('where applicable') of international public law or foreign law.

[17] See J. Dugard, 'International Law and the Final Constitution', 11 *South African Journal of Human Rights* (1995) p. 241; G. Carpenter, 'The South African Constitutional Court: Taking stock of the early decisions', 1 *Human Rights & Constitutional Law Journal of South Africa* (1996) p. 24; and Webb, op. cit. n.12, at p. 219.

[18] In the beginning, the constitutional judges made pedagogical and explanatory efforts to illustrate in detail *constitutional procedural law*. This attitude appears to have been toned

For these reasons, post-apartheid South Africa has had to make virtue of necessity. It tried to make up for its decades-long cultural and legal setbacks by acting as a listener, referring to interpretive models of other constitutional judges, calling upon a widespread legal institutional culture, and breathing life into a courageous constitutional compromise. Hence, it is evident why we consider the jurisprudence of the Canadian Supreme Court and of the South African Constitutional Court as very interesting 'laboratories' for the study of cross-judicial communication.

3. A Hypothesis

The hypothesis we would like to demonstrate here is based on patterns of legal argumentation developed by jurisprudence. Amongst the numerous different patterns of legal argumentation based on extra-systemic parameters developed by courts, it is possible to detect one that is recurring: we will define it as the 'setting two extremes' technique.[19]

---

down in more recent decisions. This is all comprehensible in light of the fact that judicial review, which was previously unknown to the South African system, needed grounding and consensus amongst the various legal players. The Court, thus, attempted to facilitate transparency through argumentative and syntactical clarity of the court decisions, drafting long explanations of the new constitutional context. For example, the Court frequently 'illustrates' what should be the roles of the different institutional and private players. The Court's concern is to minimize the perception of constitutional justice as an infringement on the separation of powers (a comprehensive example is *Phillips and Others* v. *Director of Public Prosecutions and Others*, CCT 20/02, § 12).

[19] We have analysed yet another recurring pattern of legal argumentation based on extra-systemic parameters from the case law of the jurisprudence of the South African Constitutional Court which we have defined as 'probative importation.' In this technique, foreign interpretations or 'extraneous legal elements' are cited as 'proof' *against* (when a judge in a dissenting opinion provides a different interpretation to that of the main judgment to disapprove of its result) or *for* (when a judge, even in a concurring opinion, provides converging foreign case studies in support of his or her hypothesis). This first pattern is grounded in the assertion: 'They also think this way abroad.' In order to buttress a certain interpretation, judges assert that it corresponds, falls in line or coincides with the interpretation of a foreign judge. The interpretation precedes the citation of foreign cases. The use of extra-systemic parameters in this case has the function of adding rhetorical and evidentiary force to the interpretation. A second pattern falls under probative importation; it is similar to the first, but corresponds with the assertion: 'Considering that they think this way abroad…' (that is, if this constitutional utterance shares this meaning with other *pre-selected* systems), then '… we also assign to it this same meaning.' This formula differs from the previous one because it proceeds first

In accordance with this pattern, the judges seem to construct two extremes in which the interpretation oscillates: the two extremes consists of foreign constitutional interpretations of similar cases and principles. Here, comparative law helps to determine the two opposing extremes of interpretation (as if they were embankments) derived from foreign constitutional courts. Setting two extremes limits the interpretation's oscillation, which is subsequently chosen by the judge in the case in question. The judge may converge on one of those or, on the contrary, he or she may decide to reject both cases, collocating their interpretation somewhere in between the two. As previously mentioned, the 'setting of two extremes' mode is not the only pattern of legal argumentation based on *extra*-systemic parameters; many other types exist. However, the empirical observations of the jurisprudence of the two selected courts show a certain degree of recurrence of the 'setting two extremes' mode.

In the following paragraphs we will analyse some examples from case law of the Canadian Supreme Court and the South African Constitutional Court in which this pattern of legal argumentation has been developed.

4. An Example from Case Law of the Jurisprudence of the Canadian Supreme Court

The first case is the Canadian Supreme Court decisions in *R.* v. *Advance Cutting & Coring Ltd.*[20] In this case the judges had to decide whether Sec-

with identifying the foreign interpretive model to which it subsequently links the interpretation. In this case the phenomenon has even more problematic consequences. Potentially infinite foreign interpretations or argumentations can contain parameters that can be used to distil the 'meaning' of a national constitutional norm or to derive argumentative models. If assigning meaning to a statement usually hides a 'limited creative procedure' that sometimes relies on data outside of positive law, here 'creation' goes further. In fact, deriving directly and automatically the meaning of national normative utterances from extra-systemic parameters, indirectly means incorporating a *pseudo-source*. In this case, having the judge's point of view preceded by the assertion: 'considering that they think this way abroad…' produces a *consequential dimension*. The interpretation of a specific constitutional utterance is automatically derived from a foreign parameter by means of a procedure whereby an extra-systemic precedent *subsumes* a particular case. For a comprehensive jurisprudential analysis of this pattern of legal argumentation see A. Lollini, 'Legal argumentation based on extra-systemic parameters. An example from case law of the South African Constitutional Court jurisprudence', 2 *Utrecht Law Review* (2007) p. 66.

[20] See *R.* v. *Advance Cutting & Coring Ltd* [2001] 3 SCR 209, 2001 SCC 70.

tion 2(d) of the Canadian Charter of Rights and Freedom, protecting the freedom of association, also guarantees the 'right not to be associated' (or right of negative association). The relevant issue was:

> The appellants, who are contractors, real estate promoters and construction workers, were charged with hiring employees who did not have the required competency certificates to work on a construction project or with working in the industry without the proper competency certificates, contrary to s. 119.1 of the Quebec Act Respecting Labour Relations, Vocational Training and Manpower Management in the Construction Industry (the 'Construction Act'). The appellants asserted that workers could not obtain the proper competency certificates without becoming members of one of the union groups listed in s. 28 of the Construction Act. They claimed that this obligation was unconstitutional because it breached the right not to associate which, in their opinion, was a component of the guarantee of freedom of association in s. 2(d) of the Canadian Charter of Rights and Freedoms.[21]

What the Court had to decide was the constitutionality of a legal provision which, the applicants asserted, compelled them to be associated mandatory to the union groups listed in Section 28 of the Construction Act. The Court ruled five to four that the impugned legislation is constitutional, in other terms that Section 2(d) of the Canadian Charter of Rights and Freedoms does not contain any binding constitutional 'right of negative association' and, consequently, that Section 28 of the Construction Act is not directly unconstitutional. As we shall see, the judges of the majority opinion did not exclude *a priori* the possibility of recognizing forms of negative rights of association. Instead, it had to be determined case by case taking into consideration several factors.

The 'borrowing' of *extra*-systemic parameters is detectable in both the majority and dissenting opinions; extraneous legal elements became part of the legal reasoning and of the 'dialectical disagreement' between judges of the majority and those of the minority. Therefore, before we look at how *extra*-systemic parameters are concretely used, it is important to illustrate the different interpretative positions, *vis-à-vis* the existence of a right not to be associated under the Canadian Charter.

In the majority opinion, delivered by Justice LeBel, some forms of 'compelling association' may be compatible with the values and the guarantee of

[21] See *R.* v. *Advance Cutting & Coring Ltd*, p. 3.

freedom of association under Section 1 of the Charter. Indeed, the right not to be associated would come up when there are evidences of *ideological coercion* or *imposed conformity* by forced association. The majority decision took into consideration the number and types of obligations the appellants had to comply with in associating themselves with groups listed under Section 28 of the Construction Act. It also took into consideration the troubled history of labour relations in the Quebec construction industry, which the impugned Construction Act deals with, and how the limited form of compelling association required by the law respects fundamental democratic values. For this reason, the impugned provision was considered constitutional.[22]

On the contrary, in the dissenting opinion delivered by Justice Bastarache, and in agreement with the judges of the majority, in some cases a negative right of association may be read into Section 2 of the Canadian Charter. However, the two sides disagreed with the test to determine whether the freedom of association has been violated and a negative right to association is awarded. In the present case, the mandatory association to a trade union implies, by the intrinsically ideological nature of a trade union, a form of *ideological coercion* or *imposed conformity*.[23]

The existence of a constitutional right not to be associated has been widely discussed in several domestic constitutional systems and in supra-national legislation such as in the European Convention for the Protection of Human Rights and Fundamental Freedoms (ECHR). Certainly, the Canadian Supreme Court does not limit its comparative inquiry to European systems, enlarging its reasoning to the US modality of recognition of the freedom of association (and consequently of the right not to be compulsorily associated).

In doing this, the majority in *R.* v. *Advance Cutting & Coring Ltd* seems to make use of the 'setting of two extremes' mode by fixing two opposite poles in order to delimit the range of interpretation of the Canadian Charter. In this case, the two poles are, on the one hand, the principle of freedom of association as interpreted by the US Supreme Court, and on the other hand, the jurisprudence of the European Court of Human Rights.

In a paragraph entitled 'Comparative Law Aspects' in the majority opinion, the Canadian judges articulate the reference to *extra*-systemic parameters entering into a virtual 'dialogue' with foreign judges.[24] According to

---

[22] Ibid., pp. 72 et seq.
[23] Ibid., pp. 23-72.
[24] Ibid., p. 146.

Justice LeBel, the first pole fixed is the US approach to the freedom of association in the following terms:

> The United States Supreme Court has also cited the liberty and due process clauses of the Fifth and the Fourteenth Amendments and even the Ninth Amendment in generating a constitutional freedom to associate. Nevertheless, the source of the right to associate was usually to be found in the First Amendment, as a corollary of freedom of speech.
>
> While the United States Supreme Court has been willing to recognise a right not to associate, also based on the rights of free speech and belief, the history of its jurisprudence shows that the Court has not invalidated every form of compelled association. It has attempted to draw a distinction between traditional union functions and political activities and has sought to protect the right of individual members to restrict the use of their dues in respect of causes they disapprove of. A more exhaustive review of this jurisprudence would not be useful, and I will only outline its most important features.
>
> The Supreme Court refused to invalidate the provisions of a state constitution that restrained or prohibited some forms of closed shop or union shop (Lincoln Federal Labor Union v. Northwestern Iron & Metal Co., 335 U.S. 525 (1949); American Federation of Labor v. American Sash & Door Co., 335 U.S. 538 (1949)). On the other hand, the Court found that the provisions of the Railway Labor Act which authorised a form of union shop did not infringe the First Amendment, absent evidence that it deprived employees of their freedom of thought and conscience (Railway Employes' Department v. Hanson, 351 U.S. 225 (1956), at p. 238).
>
> In a later case, it held that the compulsory withholding of union dues from wages was only a device to compel otherwise 'free riders' to share in the cost of negotiating and administering collective agreements. Yet such compulsory dues should not be used to compel employees to support causes that they oppose (International Association of Machinists v. Street, 367 U.S. 740 (1961)). (See also Brotherhood of Railway and Steamship Clerks v. Allen, 373 U.S. 113 (1963).) In Abood v. Detroit Board of Education, 431 U.S. 209 (1977), the Supreme Court revisited the problem of the relationship between compelled union support and the guarantee of freedom of speech and opinion. On this occasion, it examined the validity and effect of an agency-shop clause similar to the Rand formula whereby every employee represented by the union, whether he or she had joined it or not, had to pay it a service fee equal to union dues. A group of employees objected to the enforcement of this provision. In their view, such a provision deprived them of their freedom of association protected by the First Amendment. They asserted that they were opposed to the payment of union dues to unions as well as to collective bargaining in the public sector and objected to various social and po-

> litical activities carried on by their union. A majority of the Supreme Court held that the obligation to join the union was constitutionally justified 'by the legislative assessment of the important contribution of the union shop to the system of labor relations established by Congress' (p. 222, per Stewart J). Union dues could be exacted as long as they were used for collective bargaining, contract administration and grievance-adjustment purposes. Beyond that, the obligation to contribute to causes that members disapproved of violated their freedoms of association, speech and belief protected by the First Amendment.

Without a doubt, as expressed in paragraph 248, Justice LeBel affirms that the Court already chose to diverge from the US approach to the right not to associate. Even if the Canadian judges, in the majority opinion, had chosen the US approach as a sort of extreme, they still seemed to disagree with the US solution which protects the right not to associate in the following manner: in case of compelling association, which is tolerated, the individuals may restrict the use of their dues in respect of causes they disapprove of. In this way, the individual freedom of speech is safeguarded.

Moving on to the opposite extreme, Justice LeBel takes under consideration the ECHR. From this perspective, he affirms that, like the Canadian Charter, the ECHR recognises a broad conception of the right of association 'without expressly acknowledging the presence of a negative mirror component' (Article 17):[25]

> Nevertheless, despite this silence of the Convention, since Young, James and Webster, Eur. Court H.R., judgment of 13 August 1981, Series A No. 44, the European Court has moved towards a recognition of the right not to associate as a necessary component of the guarantee of freedom of association under Article 11(1) of the Convention. In this case, in the opinion of the court, a union shop arrangement which imposed ideological conformity under the threat of dismissal from employment infringed Article 11 of the Convention and was not held to be justifiable. The court, nevertheless, held that not all forms of compelled association were inconsistent with Article 11. For example, a public interest law compelling doctors to join a professional regulatory body did not engage the guarantee of freedom of association (Le Compte, Van Leuven and De Meyere, Eur. Court H.R., judgment of 23 June 1981, Series A No. 43). In Sigurjónsson v. Iceland, Eur. Court H.R., judgment of 30 June 1993, Series A No. 264, the court clearly accepted that a right not to associate should be read into the guarantee of Article

[25] Ibid., p. 149.

11(1). In that case, it found that the legislative obligation to join a taxi-driver's union infringed the guarantee of freedom of association. It viewed this compulsion as a violation of the freedom of opinion of the complainant. On the other hand, the court held that Article 11 did not grant an employer the right to refuse to enter into a collective agreement as required by the relevant national legislation (Gustafsson v. Sweden, Eur. Court H.R., judgment of 25 April 1996, Reports of Judgments and Decisions 1996-II). In a recent judgment, outside the sphere of labor relations, an obligation to join hunter associations under a French law was declared invalid. On this occasion, the court reasserted the existence of the negative component of the guarantee of freedom of association (Chassagnou and Others v. France [GD], Nos. 25088/94, 28331/95 and 28443/95, ECHR 1999-III).'[26]

However, in dissenting from the European Court's approach, LeBel argued that:

It must be understood, as well, that the European Convention is applied in a legal environment that reflects a different history of labour relations than in Canada or Quebec, in particular. The structures and methods of collective bargaining, the patterns of union organisation and their status within the enterprise all differ deeply from the Canadian experience in the development of labour law and the management of labour relations. These labour systems may reject the principle of monopoly representation by a particular union or forms of union security like the union shop and the compulsory check off of union dues. On the other hand, the right to strike may be affirmed by the constitution itself, as in France. (See A. Mazeaud, Droit du travail (2nd ed. 2000), at pp. 204-5.) Many European nations recognise the broad societal role which unions play, and have entrenched union rights to participate in the management of private commercial and industrial enterprises. (See M. Weiss, 'Workers' Participation in the European Union', in P. Davies et al., eds., European Community Labour Law: Principles and Perspectives (1996), p. 213; B. Bercusson, European Labour Law (1997), at pp. 248-61.) The labour laws of a country evidence a social and political compromise about the place of unions in that society and the proper balance between unions and employers. Thus, interesting as it may be, the consideration of European jurisprudence is not determinative, although it confirms an interpretation whereby a limited right to refuse to associate should be read into s. 2(d) of the Charter.'[27]

According to Justice LeBel, in the cases where the European Court recognises a right not to be associated, these are due to different structures and methods

[26] Ibid., p. 150.
[27] Ibid., p. 151.

of collective bargaining, the pattern of union organisations and the history of labour relations. They appear to be much more intrusive to the individual's sphere, allowing the European judges to tolerate forms of a negative right of association which does not operate, for example, in the case of collective bargaining dealt in accordance to national legislations. In conclusion, what the Canadian majority opinion tried to accomplish was to explore an alternative option, located in between the two extremes. This is clarified in the following:

> In the present case, the appellants have not made out a case that the challenged legislation establishes a form of ideological conformity that would trigger the application of s. 2(d). Moreover, the compulsion to join a union in this case is carefully embedded in a democratic process which safeguards each member's right to support or withdraw support from a particular union at regular intervals. Therefore I find no breach of the freedom to associate as protected under s. 2(d) of the Charter. Given this conclusion, it is not necessary to discuss the application of s. 1 of the Charter and the constitutional question should be answered in the negative. Nevertheless, I am willing to assume that an infringement of a constitutional right not to associate occurred in order to further address the justification of the law under s. 1 and to demonstrate that, even if it had infringed the s. 2(d) right not to associate, the law would still pass full constitutional scrutiny.[28]

The US and European approaches are carefully and extensively examined. On the one hand, they seem to allow Canadian judges to delimit a sort of perimeter of the oscillations of their interpretation, and on the other, to allow the peculiarities of the Canadian labour relations to emerge with legal reasoning and argumentation.

5. Examples from Case Law of the Jurisprudence of the South African Constitutional Court

As mentioned, some South African Constitutional Court cases show a very similar technique of legal reasoning to that of the Canadian Supreme Court. From this standpoint, we can find an example in the dissenting opinion of Justice Madala in *Lawyers for Human Rights and Ann Francis Eveleth* v.

---

[28] Ibid., p. 152.

Minister of Home Affairs.[29] The judge goes into depth on a minor issue in terms of the question of illegitimacy dealt within the judgment (the illegitimacy of some provisions on illegal immigration and the possible arrest and temporary detainment of illegal aliens). However, of great general importance is the content of the *right to standing*, that is, the possibility, according to Section 38 of the South African Constitution, to approach a court (including the Constitutional Court) directly when a right guaranteed by the Bill of Rights is infringed.

Madala cites two very different interpretations: the first is from Canada and the second from India. Madala claims that a similar tendency appears in Canadian jurisprudence that recognises a certain 'discretion' in evaluating the right to standing on the basis of the criteria summed up by these three points: (1) the action brought before the court raises a *serious legal question*; (2) the plaintiff has a *genuine interest in the resolution of the question*; and, (3) there is no other way that the issue may be brought to court.[30]

Justice Madala then demonstrates an opposite version of the *right to standing* according to the Indian system; *judicial redress* is allowed only for those who claim a violation of one of their rights by the state, public authorities, or by another person.[31] Between the relatively wide Canadian interpretation of the right to standing and the much more restrictive Indian version, Madala recognises, in the case in question, the right of all applicants to go to the Constitutional Court. Madala argues that the wide interpretation of Section 38 is intended to protect the more vulnerable sections of South Africa's society, who in the past have felt the effects of the apartheid regime, by facilitating access to the judiciary and for a more effective protection of the rights guaranteed by the Constitution.

This technique can be seen in another decision: *State* v. *Russel Mamabolo et al.* of 11 April 2001.[32] The dispute concerns the constitutionality of the criminal offence of 'scandalizing the Court' (part of the broader category of contempt of Court) in relation to Section 16 of the Constitution (freedom of

---

[29] Cf., *Lawyers for Human Rights and Ann Francis Eveleth* v. *Minister of Home Affairs*, 2003 (8) BCLR, 891 (T).

[30] Madala deduces these criteria from *Canada (Minister of Justice)* v. *Borowski* [1981] 2 SCR, 575, 64 CCC (2d), 97, 130, DLR (3d), 588; and from *Canadian Council of Churches* v. *The Queen*, (1992), 88, DLR (4th).

[31] Madala, ibid., § 76-77, citing *S.P. Gupta et al.* v. *Union of India et al.* [1982] 2 SCR, 365, 520.

[32] Cf., CCT 44/00.

expression). The applicant is an important political exponent of the radical right-wing, who was imprisoned for having indirectly criticized a judgment by claiming in a national newspaper the need to introduce the responsibility of judges.

Even though the Court judged these manifestations not to constitute the offence of scandalizing the Court (thus the imprisonment was unlawful), the judges felt compelled to develop a long and complicated argument about the constitutional legitimacy of this offence. The decision set up two poles: on the one hand, numerous common law systems that provide for this offence (the United Kingdom, Canada, India, Australia, New Zealand, Hong Kong, Zimbabwe, Namibia[33]) and on the other, the United States. Even though the US has an offence of contempt of the court, it does not have a legal sanction against 'scandalizing the court', due to the dominating principle of freedom of expression that is based on the interpretation of the First Amendment.[34]

The South African decision is of great interest because we can see the penetration of extra-systemic parameters in the formation of disputes before the Court. In fact, the counsel arguing in favour of the unconstitutionality of the crime of scandalizing the Court, cites, using a positive probative method, the case of *R.* v. *Kopyto* determined by the Ontario Court of Appeal.[35] In that judgment, it also appears that in Canada the judges had discussed the need for introducing the interpretation of the freedom of expression according to the American version. Counsel agreed with the judges of the majority opinion in the Canadian case who were in favour of introducing the famous American test of 'clear and present danger' for evaluating the legitimate cases of limiting freedom of expression.

However, it is at this point that the South African judges, having drawn the boundaries along the field of interpretive oscillation, proceed with an interesting comparison. First, discussing counsel's argument, the judges declare themselves in line with the minority opinion of *Kopyto*. Justice Kriegler states:

---

[33] Cf., ibid., §20 where at note 21 the Court cites the jurisprudence of these countries that would confirm the Court's thesis.

[34] The South African judges delimit the opposite pole using a famous US Supreme Court case: *Bridges* v. *California*, 314, US, 252 (1941).

[35] (1987) 47 DLR (4th), 213 (Ont.CA). Although the Ontario Court of Appeal's website with its jurisprudence archives is available on-line, the database only goes back as far as 1999, which prevented the recovery of this court decision.

> I respectfully share the misgivings expressed by Gubbay and Dubin (in minority) about the suitability of that test in a jurisdiction that does not have to apply the First Amendment nor enjoy the benefit of the extensive and complex jurisprudence so carefully constructed by the United States courts (§35). [...] Before one could subscribe to such importation of a foreign product, one need to be persuaded, not only that it is significantly preferable in principle, but also that its perceived promise is likely to be substantiated in practice in our legal system and society it has been developed to serve. More pertinently, it would have to be established that the clear and present danger test, in the adapted form proposed or in some permutation, was consonant with our South African constitutional values system [...]. I remain very much unpersuaded (§36).

The Court used comparison in its reasoning to diverge from the US interpretation (the opposite pole):

> [...] one should be slow to engraft such a test on to our law: the two [that is, the American system of regarding freedom of expression and the South African one] are inherently incompatible, because they stem from different common law origins and subsist in materially different constitutional regimes. The balance which our common law strikes between protection of an individual's reputation and the right to freedom of expression differs fundamentally from the balance struck in the United States.[36] The difference is even more marked under the two constitutional regimes. The Unites States Constitution stands as a monument to the vision and libertarian aspirations of the Founding Fathers; and the First Amendment in particular to the values endorsed by all who cherish freedom. Our Constitution is a wholly different kind of instrument [...] more explicit, more detailed, more balanced, more carefully phrased and counterpoised, representing a multi- disciplinary effort on the part of hundreds of expert advisors and political negotiators to produce a blueprint for future governance of the country. [...] [Freedom of expression] [f]or us is not a pre-eminent freedom ranking above all others. It is not even an unqualified right. The First Amendment declaims an unequivocal and sweeping commandment; section 161, the corresponding provision in our Constitution, is wholly different in style and significantly different in content. It is carefully worded, enumerating specific instances of the freedom and is immediately followed by a number of limitations. (§ 40).[37]

---

[36] The Court establishes the US model of balancing in *The New York Times Co.* v. *Sullivan*, 376 US, 254 (1964).

[37] Refer to the preceding §40 where the limits of the freedom of expression were analysed in reference to a different case.

Concluding that the South African interpretation of freedom of expression differs from the US model, the judges state:

> The Constitution proclaims three conjoined, reciprocal and covalent values to be foundational to the Republic: human dignity, equality and freedom [...]. What is clear is that freedom of expression does not enjoy superior status in our law (§41).

Using the argumentative technique of setting two extremes, the Court reasserts that it distances itself from the Canadian interpretation:

> It is therefore in my view not wise to choose a re-tooled version of a minimalist test, that was originally crafted for the American system where minimal interferences with a predominant constitutional right under First Amendment was called for, and was then adapted by Canadian provincial courts [...].

Freedom of expression must be balanced in accordance with the limits provided by Section 162 (Election of new provincial governments). In conclusion, the instance in question is not unconstitutional, even if the Court deems the penalty system to be disproportionate.

Part V
Concluding Observations

THE CHANGING ROLE OF HIGHEST COURTS: CONCLUDING OBSERVATIONS

M. Scheltema*

1. Introduction

In today's world of globalisation the position of the highest courts on the national level is changing, and the courts are well aware of this. This is the first conclusion that can be drawn from the colloquium and from the contributions to this book.

This change of position is remarkable. Until recently, the national courts of last instance were the highest courts indeed, each in its own jurisdiction. They gave the final answers to all questions of law that were brought before them. Being on the top of the hierarchy of courts in their country, there was no other authority above them: their interpretation of the law was the final one.

This position was the natural one in a time in which the national legal systems were fully autonomous. Those systems were the result of the historical developments in a particular country and the result of the decisions of national legislators and national courts. Within a national legal system the need for coherence and uniformity in the interpretation of the law demanded the existence of one highest court that could provide the final answer to all disputes regarding the law; developments outside the national legal system were not relevant for their work. Since each court operated within its own system, no reasons existed why the law in one country should not be different from the law in another country.

* M. Scheltema is Honorary Professor, Utrecht School of Law, The Netherlands.

A.S. Muller and M.A. Loth (eds.), Highest Courts and the Internationalisation of Law

In the last fifty years, this situation has changed dramatically. Internationalisation of society has brought the domestic legal systems into close contact with each other. Treaties and other sources of law outside the domestic order have become of greater importance. The highest courts are the courts that have to reconcile the consequences of all this international and transnational law-making with the needs of a clear and dependable domestic legal system.

This change of perspective is felt clearly by the highest courts. Judge Koskelo, president of the Supreme Court of Finland, speaks of a new and highly demanding role for the judiciary. The highest courts have a special responsibility here, since 'legal and judicial cultures tend to be rather inward-looking, even parochial.'

2. Different Positions of Highest Courts

All highest courts are accustomed to their position within their domestic legal order: on the top of the hierarchy of courts. However, their position towards the sources of the law outside their system is less clear and varies from country to country. Constitutional provisions on the position of courts and on the relationship between international law and the domestic legal system are relevant here. Monistic systems assign a greater role to the courts than dualistic systems. Nevertheless new questions arise in both systems as a result of new developments on the international level. At times, dualistic systems exclude the outside world too much in new situations. This can be seen in some of the Member States of the European Union. On the other hand monistic systems might encounter difficulties when they accept international law even if it violates fundamental national principles. But still, even in a monistic system the highest court is autonomous: it is the highest judicial authority that decides on the consequences of international law for the domestic legal order.

In some cases, supranational courts are set up to guarantee a uniform interpretation of instruments of international law. The European Court of Justice and the European Court of Human Rights are impressive examples. To a certain extent, these courts can be seen as being above the highest national courts, although their positions clearly differ from the position of a highest court within a national legal order. Yet, much international law exists without provisions for uniform interpretation. Minister Donner stated in his opening address to the colloquium that he would not be in favour of a broad extension of this form of international court hierarchy to ensure more transnational coherence. Nevertheless, the need for a good connection of the domestic legal system with international law and the law of other countries goes much further than the reach of international courts and of instruments of international law.

How can highest courts react to all these developments? Many speakers at the colloquium and contributors to this book pay a lot of attention to a more horizontal coordination by the highest courts. There is a general feeling that the interpretation of national law should not be done without taking note of the legal developments in other countries and those on the international level. In fact, this seems to be a key transition in the position of national courts: that they should take into account the case law of foreign (and international) courts, although foreign judgments have no legal authority for them. What then could be the reasons for a national court to reflect on judgments of foreign courts?

2.1 The traditional argument

The first argument is that one may learn from the judgments of other jurisdictions. The comparative study of the law may offer interesting ideas for finding solutions for difficult national cases. This argument does not give any kind of authority to the judgment of a foreign court, but considers it as a source of information and inspiration. An academic book or article could provide the same kind of information. This is the traditional comparative approach. It does not render the court less autonomous in deciding its cases, but it widens the range of sources of inspiration for the judges.

Nevertheless, the routine of international orientation by judges can be an important factor in bringing coherence across national borders. Judges who are not acquainted with any other law than their own will go their own way. But if courts compare their work with judgments of other courts, a certain transnational understanding might grow. At the moment, this kind of understanding can more easily be seen among common law countries than in continental Europe. Common law countries have the advantage of using the same language. Also, the practice of most courts in continental Europe of delivering one opinion as the judgment of the court may be a disadvantage.

2.2 The influence of international law-making

As a result of internationalisation, the number of transnational legal issues has grown enormously. Consequently, the need for international law-making has increased. Treaties and regulations by international organisations have become of great importance. Many of those international rules are made with the clear intent to provide for uniform rules across national borders. However, a uniform interpretation is not guaranteed. The most common instrument within national jurisdictions to come to a uniform interpretation – giving that task to the highest court – cannot be used in most cases. It cannot be expected that this situation will change in the near future. Apart from some important exemptions, treaties and international regulations have to be interpreted by the national courts.

Although no legal relationship exists between (highest) national courts, it would be contrary to the professional attitude of the highest courts to ignore the judgments of their colleagues in other countries. Since the very intent of much international law-making is to come to uniform rules in different countries, courts would impede the achievement of that goal if they interpreted the rules each in their own way. And indeed, in the light of the task of the highest courts to foster coherence in the law, it would be hard to understand that they would not see the need for coherent interpretation as soon as international rules are at stake.

Of course, the judgments of foreign courts have no legal authority for them. However, they are relevant as the very goal of the international law-making – uniform rules across borders – is endangered if they come to an interpretation that differs from the judgment of the highest court in another country. So, there is a strong argument for taking into account the judgments of foreign (highest) courts when a court decides on the interpretation of the same rule. In other words, courts should look to foreign precedents, and – although they are legally free to do so – should not decide in another way unless they can state strong arguments for that.

2.3 The influence of internationalisation as such

Perhaps the most important factor for the growing international orientation of courts is the internationalisation of society itself. Borders are much less important than before, and the national society is no longer isolated from the rest of the world. Consequently, it is much less self-evident that the law differs from country to country. On the contrary, it will be seen as a problem that the rules are not the same across borders. This is especially true for rules that regulate subjects having transnational effects, such as rules on commercial or financial transactions, rules on the protection of the environment and on many other subjects. The same is true for rules that are fundamental for our legal systems. The protection of fundamental rights and the access to an independent court should be reflected in the law of every country.

Those developments bring the courts into a difficult position. On the one hand, they have their roots in their own national legal system. Accordingly, they have the task to provide for coherence in the law within that particular system. Since their authority comes from the nation state, courts have to fulfil this task in the interest of that state, and in accordance with the constitutional prescriptions of that state.

On the other hand, courts cannot ignore the fact that the need for coherence in the law does not stop at the national border. Moreover, it would undermine their position if they did not take into account the growing importance of the international context of the law. This international context also has the effect that a greater awareness exists of the way courts in different countries decide their cases. If new questions come up in modern society, the courts in many countries may have to tackle the same issues. If the highest courts of a number of countries come to very different solutions, even if the legal culture of the countries involved provide no arguments for those differences, this might harm the authority of the courts. It could give the impression that the courts do no more than declare their own preferences as the law of the land. However, if a large number of highest courts come to the same solution, it will strengthen the position and the authority of the courts and of the law. Then it becomes clear that the law is more than just the opinion of the court, and that it can offer a basis for deciding new questions. In an internationalised world some kind of transnational consistency is important for the authority of the courts and of the law.

This factor seems to be of growing importance. In all the contributions of the presidents and judges of the highest national courts in this book, the need for some kind of interaction or coordination among highest courts is stressed. Some good examples of transnational interaction can be found in the contribution by Andrea Lollini. In discussing cases in the field of human rights, he shows that the Canadian Supreme Court and the South African Constitutional Court – when interpreting human rights in the national constitution – discuss the case law of foreign courts, like the US Supreme Court and the

European Court of Human Rights. Their approach begins with the idea that the case law at hand is relevant for their own judgment. When the courts come to their own conclusion, they feel the need to put forward the arguments that guide them to adopt or to reject the solutions that are presented by the other courts.

This example shows that the interpretation of national rules on human rights – and even of the national constitution – cannot be done in isolation from the development of the law in other countries. In a globalising society, it will become harder to explain that fundamental human rights change as soon as a national frontier is passed. This does not mean that precedents from other jurisdictions are binding. On the other hand, however, they cannot be ignored altogether. Especially when a general tendency exists in many other countries with the same legal culture, a court should not decide in another way without taking into account the developments elsewhere and stating the reasons for deciding otherwise.

3. Transnational Coherence is not the same as Coherence within a National Legal System

Internationalisation means that the need for coherence in the law is not restricted to coherence within a national legal system. In a global society, transnational coherence is also important. For this reason, many treaties are concluded and harmonisation or unification of rules is sought.

In this respect, the contributions of Dieter Grimm and of Ernst Hirsch Ballin to this book are particularly interesting. It follows from their contributions that bringing coherence in an international context is more difficult than providing for uniform interpretation within a national setting. Accordingly, the solution of creating a highest court to guarantee coherence is not as self-evident on an international level as it is on the national level. In addition, the role of such a court might differ from that of a highest national court.

When questions of interpretation arise, the supranational court has to find answers that, on the one hand, are in conformity with the need for international coherence in the law, as expressed in the treaty subject to interpretation. On the other hand, such a court has to be aware of the fact that its judgment has to have its effects within the legal systems and the legal traditions of many different countries. Consequently, the effects of a certain solution may vary significantly from country to country.

The problem is that the court has the final authority to decide questions of interpretation of an international treaty or other international instruments, yet it has no authority on – and often even no knowledge of – questions of domestic law within the countries where the court's case law is to be transformed into national solutions. This clearly differs from the position of the highest court in a country, which has the authority (and the knowledge) to judge on all questions of law that are involved in a case.

Accordingly, the task of a supranational court is different from the task of a highest national court. A supranational court should attempt to come to solutions that – while bringing uniformity in the interpretation of the international body of law – correspond as much as possible to the different legal systems of the countries under its jurisdiction. This can be done by leaving a margin of interpretation to the national courts and authorities, as the ECHR often does, or by trying to frame its judgments in accordance with the legal principles that are common to the countries under its jurisdiction. As regards questions on which the solutions on the domestic level show important differences, the court should best follow a middle way approach. The arguments Dieter Grimm puts forward in his article are convincing on this point.

It thus becomes clear that uniformity on the international level does not automatically lead to uniformity on the national level. Uniform interpretation of a rule on the international level does not in itself lead to uniform consequences when that rule is applied within the different national legal systems. Transnational coherence is therefore a different kind of coherence. Within a national legal order, coherence means the uniform application of the law, guaranteed by the authority of one highest court. In a transnational setting, coherence does not go that far. Uniformity is not a goal in and of itself, but a transnational society needs transnational consistency in the application of the law. In cases in which uniformity across borders is important, that uniformity should be reached if arguments to the contrary are absent. Uniformity cannot be reached only by the application of uniform rules, but also by coming to the same results in different ways. However, in a globalising world the authority of the law will be endangered by differences in the law for which no convincing arguments exist, especially if those differences impede transnational relations or transactions, or relate to basic questions of justice and human rights.

4. A New Role for Highest National Courts

Highest national courts have a crucial role in the process of attaining more transnational coherence. In some respects, they are in a better position than supranational courts to do so, because they can best reconcile the national perspective with the needs of internationalisation. Moreover, in most cases international courts are absent. So, the highest courts are the only courts to bring some coherence in the law across national borders.

If highest national courts take on that role, they will not only be the highest court within their national jurisdiction. They will also share a responsibility with other highest courts for the transnational coherence of the law. Additionally, they have a role in connecting their own legal system with the outside world. Of course, they are not the only player in the field. National and international legislation is extremely important in connecting the national legal systems with each other. The work of the courts may also gain this international dimension. In constitutional terms this is an important development. It means that the courts have to leave their role as courts with a purely national orientation. Their national position is supplemented by a position as an organ of the transnational legal community. What consequences does this have for their constitutional position?

It is quiet clear that this development does not fit the scheme of the *trias politica* of Montesquieu. The equilibrium between the three powers of the *trias* is based on the presumption of a sovereign nation-state that frames its legal system autonomously. It does not take into account the role of the courts in connecting domestic law with the law outside the state.

The new developments may have as a consequence that the position of the courts becomes stronger *vis-à-vis* the other state powers, especially the legislative power. To a certain extent, this depends on the provisions in the national constitution on the position of the highest court. If the highest court has the power to annul national legislation that violates international rules, the strengthening of its position is clear. But even if this is not the case, its position is changing. The sheer fact that it uses arguments based on the developments in international law or the developments in the national law of other counties, means that factors outside the reach of the national legislature play a role in interpreting domestic law. This does not coincide with the ideas of the *trias politica*. Consequently, new questions arise about the legitimacy of this new role of the courts. How far can they go, and what about the accountability of what they are doing?

Separation of powers is important in the *trias politica*. This kind of separation of powers cannot be found in the transnational setting. In a way, the shared responsibility of the highest national courts means that they can only be successful in shaping transnational coherence if they do that together. They are dependent on each other. Accordingly, they cannot fulfil this transnational role if they stay with their own preferences – they have to share their views and their powers with their colleagues in other countries.

For that reason, it is interesting to note that (some) courts feel the need for a stronger legitimisation of their judgments in the light of internationalisation. Indeed, this is important for the legitimacy of their judgments. Brief judgments, stating just the conclusion of the court without providing many underlying arguments, are less convincing. In cases in which arguments from outside the domestic system are relevant, it is essential that the court offers its arguments for the conclusion it has reached.

Some of the highest courts are changing the form of their judgments. In Finland, since the 1980s, the judgments have become more informative and transparent by including the grounds and arguments of the court (see the contribution by Judge Pauliine Koskelo). In France, important judgments with international aspects also seem to include a more extensive reasoning than before. Another argument for this approach is to make the judgments more accessible for the international world. In the world of the common law, dissenting and concurring opinions are the rule, and in some other countries like Finland this is the case as well. It might be argued that this furthers the use of foreign case law since this can find a place easily in the debate among the judges in the various opinions. The contribution of Andrea Lollini on the courts of Canada and South Africa illustrates this.

A transnational role for national courts means that their position cannot only be based on national constitutional arrangements. The courts share a responsibility that goes beyond the reach of the national constitutions. An important question to be solved is how this new role can gain a sound base of legitimacy.

BIBLIOGRAPHY*

Ackerman, B.,
'The Rise of World Constitutionalism', 83 *Virginia Law Review* (1997) 771

Alen, A., and Renaud, B.,
'The relations between the constitutional courts and the other national courts, including the interference in this area of the action of the European courts: I. The factors determining the relations between the constitutional courts and the other courts', 23 *Human Rights Law Journal* (2002) 304-321

Alexy, R.,
A Theory of Legal Argumentation: The theory of rational discourse as theory of legal justification, translated by R. Adler and N. MacCormick, Oxford, Clarendon Press 1989

Allard, J., and Garapon, A.,
Les Juges dans la Mondialisation. La Nouvelle Revolution du Droit, Paris, Ed. du Seuil 2005

Angulo, M.R., and Reardon, J.D.,
'The apparent political and administrative expediency exception established by the Supreme Court in United States v. Humberto Alvarez-Machain to the rule of law as reflected by recognised principles of international law', 16 *Boston College International and Comparative Law Review* (1993) 245-284

Arnold, R.,
'La Cour constitutionnelle fédérale et les institutions politiques', 55 *Revue internationale de droit comparé* (2003) 965-973

Aust, A.,
Modern Treaty Law and Practice, Cambridge University Press (reprinted) 2002

Benvenuto, O.J.,
'Reevaluating the debate surrounding the Supreme Court's use of foreign precedent', 74 *Fordham Law Review* (2006) 2695-2759

Bethlehem, D.,
'International Law, European Community Law, National Law: Three Systems in Search of a Framework – Systemic Relativity in the Interaction of Law in the European Union', in: M. Koskenniemi, ed., *International Law Aspects of the European Union*, The Hague, Kluwer Law International 1998, 169-196

---

* With many thanks to the Library of the Peace Palace in the Hague

Blackmun, H.A.,
'The Supreme Court and the Law of Nations', 104 *Yale Law Journal* (1994) 39-49

Blagojevic, S.,
'The role of constitutional judiciary in protecting constitutional rights and freedom', in: *International Public Law between desires and reality*, Central European Academy of Science and Art / Académie centrale européenne de Science et Art, 1999, 157-162

Bohr, S.,
'Sanctions by the United Nations Security Council and the European Community', 4 *European Journal of International Law* (1993) 256-268

Bork, R.H.,
Coercing Virtue: The worldwide rule of judges, The AEI Press 2003

Botha, N.,
'Extradition again before the Constitutional Court: *Geuking* v. *President of the Republic of South Africa*, 2003 3 SA 34 (CC), 28', *South African Yearbook of International Law* (2003) 318-330

Boyle, K., Omar Sherif, A. (eds.),
Human rights and democracy: The role of the Supreme Constitutional Court of Egypt, London, Kluwer Law 1996

Brilmayer, L.,
'International law in American courts: a modest proposal', 100 *Yale Law Journal* (1991) 2277-2314

Brownlie, I.,
Principles of Public International Law, Oxford University Press 2003

Brückner, P.,
'The European Community and the United Nations', 1 *European Journal of International Law* (1990) 174-192

Buergenthal, T.,
'Self-executing and non-self executing treaties in national and international law', 235 *Recueil des Cours, Académie de droit international* (1992) IV

Burmeister, F.,
Gutachten des Bundesverfassungsgerichts zu völkerrechtlichen Verträgen, Berlin, Duncker und Humblot 1998

Burnham, M.A.,
'Cultivating a seedling Charter: South Africa's Court grows its Constitution', 3 *Michigan Journal of Race and Law* (1997)

Bybee, J.S., and Samahon, T.N.,
'William Rehnquist, the Separation of Powers, and the Riddle of the Sphinx', 58 *Stanford Law Review* (2006) 1735-1762

Calabresi, S.G.,
'Separation of Powers and the Rehnquist Court: the Centrality of Clinton v. City of New York', 99 *Northwestern University Law Review* (2004) 77-87
Calabresi, S.G. and Zimdahl, S.D.,
'The Supreme Court and foreign sources of law: Two hundred years of practice and the Juvenile Death Penalty decision', 47 *William and Mary Law Review* (2005) 743-909
Canivet, G.,
'The practice of comparative law by the Supreme Courts: Brief reflections on the dialogue between the judges in French and European experience', 80 *Tulane Law Review* (2006) 1377-1400
Canor, I.,
'"Can two walk together, except be agreed?" The relationship between international law and European law: The incorporation of United Nations sanctions against Yugoslavia into European Community law through the perspective of the European Court of Justice', 35 *Common Market Law Review* (1998) 137-187
Carolan, B.,
'Consideration of foreign judgement by the Irish Supreme Court: an extra- constitutional analysis of several select cases', 12 *Irish Journal of European Law* (2005) 115-141
Carpenter, G.,
'The South African Constitutional Court: Taking stock of the early decisions', *Human Rights & Constitutional Law Journal of South Africa* (1996), I
Cassese, A.,
'Remarks on Scelle's Theory of "Role Splitting" (dédoublement fonctionnel) in international law', 1 *European Journal of International Law* (1990) 210-231
Chapman, K.D.,
'Separation of powers and unilateral executive action: the constitutionality of President Clinton's Mexican loan initiative', 26 *Georgia Journal of International and Comparative Law* (1996) 163-185
Chaskalson, A.,
'Judging Human Rights in South Africa', 3 *European Human Rights Law Review* (1998) 181-190
Childress, D.E.,
'Using comparative Constitutional Law to resolve federal questions', 53 *Duke Law Journal* (2003)
Choudhry, S.,
'Globalisation in search of justification: Towards a theory of Comparative Constitutional Interpretation', *Indiana Law Journal* (1999) Summer
Collofong, D.,
'Das Verfassungsgericht der Republik Benin als Beispiel für die Durchsetzung von Rechtsstaatlichkeit und Gewaltenteilung im frankophonen Afrika', 1 *Recht in Afrika* (1998) 169-205

Costello, C.,
'European Community judicial review in the Irish courts: scope, standards and separation of powers', in M.C. Lucey and C. Keville, eds., *Irish Perspectives on EC Law*, Dublin, Round Hall 2003, 17-49
Czaplínski, W.,
'International law and Polish municipal law: recent jurisprudence of the Polish supreme judicial organs', 53 *Zeitschrift für ausländisches Öffentliches Recht und Völkerrecht* (1993) 871-881
Daniele, L.,
'Aprés l'arrèt Granital: droit communautaire et droit national dans la jurisprudence recente de la Cour constitutionnelle italienne', 28 *Cahiers de droit européen* (1992) 3-21
Davis, M.,
'International Human Rights and United States Law, Predictions of a Court-watcher', 64 *Albany Law Review* (2000) 417-436
De Wet, E.,
'The "Friendly but Cautious" reception of international law in the jurisprudence of the South African Constitutional Court: Some critical remarks', 28 *Fordham International Law Journal* (2006) 1529-1565
De Wet, E.,
'The International Constitutional Order', 55 *International and Comparative Law Quarterly* (2005) 51-76
De Wet, E.,
'The place of public international law in the New South African Constitutional Order: with special reference to international human rights and humanitarian law', 1 *Recht in Afrika* (1998) 207-234
Deleanu, I.,
'Separation of Powers: Constitutional Regulation and Practice of the Constitutional Court', 3 *Journal of Constitutional Law in Eastern and Central Europe* (1996) 57-73
Deleanu, I., and Boc, E.,
'The control of the constitutionality of laws in Romania', 2 *Journal of Constitutional Law in Eastern and Central Europe* (1995) 119-129
Delmas-Marty, M.,
La Refondation des Pouvoirs. Les Forces Imaginantes du Droit (III), Paris, Ed. du Seuil 2007
Diciotti, E.,
Interpretazione della legge e discorso razionale, Turin, Giappicchelli 1999
Di Manno, T.,
Le juge constitutionnel et la technique des décisions 'interpretatives' en France et en Italie, Economica 1997

Diagne, M.,
'La mutation de la justice constitutionnelle en Afrique: l'exemple du Conseil Constitutionnel Sénégalais', 12 *Annuaire internationale de justice constitutionnelle* (1996) 99-122

Dickson, B.,
'Protecting human rights through a Constitutional Court : the case of South Africa' Symposium: Human Rights on the Eve of the Next Century: Aspects of Human Rights Implementation', 66 *Fordham Law Review* (1997) 531-566

Doldur, C.,
'Consequences of the decisions of the Constitutional Court and the State governed by the rule of law in Romania', 9 *Journal of Constitutional Law in Eastern and Central Europe* (2002) 97-114

Doldur, C.,
'La suprématie de la constitution et la défense des droits de l'homme reflétées dans la jurisprudence de la Cour constitutionnelle', in S. Milacic, ed., *La réinvention de l'état*, 2003, 285-303

Dugard, J.,
'International Law and the Final Constitution', 11 *South African Journal of Human Rights* (1995) part 2, 241-251

Dugard, J.,
'Is the Truth and Reconciliation process compatible with international law? An unanswered question?', 13 *South African Journal of Human Rights* (1997) 258-268

Dupré, C.,
Importing the law in post-communist transitions: the Hungarian Constitutional Court and the right to human dignity, Oxford, Hart Publishing, 2003

Dupré, C.,
'The importation of law: a new comparative perspective and the Hungarian Constitutional Court', in A. Harding and E. Örücü, eds., *Comparative law in the 21st century*, London, Kluwer Academic Publishers 2002, 267-279

Dworkin, R.,
Taking Rights Seriously, London, Duckworth 1977

Eeckhout, P.,
Does Europe's Constitution Stop at the Water's Edge: Law and Policy in the EU's External Relations, Fifth Walter van Gerven Lecture, Leuven 2005

Eeckhout, P., 'The domestic legal status of the WTO Agreement: Interconnecting legal system', 37 *Common Market Law Review* (1997)

Eeckhout, P.,
'Judicial Enforcement of WTO Law in the European Union: Some further reflections', 5 *Journal of International Economic Law* (2002) 91-110

Eeckhout, P.,
External Relations of the European Union. Legal and constitutional foundations, Oxford University Press 2004
El-Morr, A.M., El-Rahman Nossier, A. and Sherif, A.O.,
'The Supreme Constitutional Court and its role in the Egyptian judicial system 1998', in *The Review – International Commission of Jurists* 60 (1998) 113-134
Epiney, A.,
'Zur Stellung des Völkerrechts in der EU', 10 *Europäische Zeitschrift für Wirtschaftsrecht* (1999) 5-11
Ewald, W.,
'Comparative Jurisprudence (II): the Logic of Legal Transplant', 43 *American Journal of Comparative Law* (1995) 489-510
Fain, N.,
'Human rights within the United States: The erosion of confidence 2003', 21 *Berkeley Journal of International Law* (2003) 607-630
Fedtke, J., and Markesinis, B.,
Judicial Recourse to Foreign Law: A New Source of Inspiration? New York, Routledge-Cavendish 2006
Fenwick, S.,
'The Rule of Law in Mongolia: Constitutional Court and Conspiratorial Parliament', 3 *The Australian Journal of Asian Law* (2001) 213-235
Fields, S.E.,
'Constitutional Comparativism and the Eighth Amendment: How a flawed proportionality requirement can benefit from foreign law', 86 *Boston University Law Review* (2006) 963-999
Fombad, C.M.,
'Challenges to constitutionalism and constitutional rights in Africa and the enabling role of political parties: Lessons and perspectives from Southern Africa', 55 *American Journal of Comparative Law* (2007) 1-45
Franck, T.M.,
Political Questions/Judicial Answers, Princeton University Press 1992
Friedmann, W.G.,
The changing structure of International Law, London, Stevens 1964
Frowein, J.A., and Marauhn, T.,
Grundfragen der Verfassungsgerichtsbarkeit in Mittel- und Osteuropa, SpringerLink 1998
Gabr, H.A.L.,
'The role of the Supreme Constitutional Court of Egypt in upholding democracy and the rule of law', in E. Cotran and A.O. Sherif (Eds.), *Democracy, the rule of law and Islam*, Kluwer Law International, 1999, 273-283

Gardbaum, S.,
'Japanese Law Symposium: the New Commonwealth Model of Constitutionalism', 49 *American Journal of Comparative Law* (2001) 707-760
Garry, P.M.,
'The Unannounced Revolution: how the Court has indirectly effected a shift in the Separation of Powers', 57 *Alabama Law Review* (2006) 689-723
Gillis, M.,
'Constitutionalism in the Czech Republic: An investigaton of two major aspects; the infusion of constitutional principles into the remainder of the legal order and the generally binding nature of Constitutional Court decisions', 5 *Journal of Constitutional Law in Eastern and Central Europe* (1998) 105-245
Ginsburg, R.B., and Jones Merritt, D.,
'Affirmative action an international human rights dialogue', 21 *Cardozo Law Review* (1999) 253-282
Ginsburg, R.B.,
'"A decent respect to the opinions of (Human)Kind": The value of a comparative perspective in constitutional adjudication', 99 *Proceedings of the ASIL Annual Meeting* (2005) 351-359
Ginsburg, T.,
Judical review in new democracies: constitutional courts in Asian cases, Cambridge University Press 2003
Glensy, R.D.,
'Which Countries Count?: Lawrence v. Texas and the selection of foreign persuasive authority', 45 *Virginia Journal of International Law* (2005) 357-449
Goerlich, H.,
'The role of Constitutional Court in resolution of constitutional disputes: a critical outline guided by the German example', 44 *Journal of the Indian Law Institute* (2002) 3-36
Graseli, A.,
In: Šturm (ed.), *Komentar Ustave Republike Slovenije* [Commentary on the Constitution of the Republic of Slovenia], Ljubljana, Fakulteta za podiplomske državne in evropske študije 2002
Grau, N.,
Der Tribunal Constitucional und die Kontrolle des Gesetzgebers: eine Analyse unter besonderer Berücksichtigung der Rechtsprechung des spanischen Verfassungsgerichts, Resensburg, 2002
Greenwalt, K.,
'Free Speech in United States and Canada', 55,1 *Law & Contemporary Problems* (1992) 5-33
Griller, S.,
'Judicial Enforceability of WTO Law in the European Union: Annotation to Case C-149/96, Portugal v. Council', 3 *Journal of International Economic Law* (2000) 441-472

Guastini, R.,
'Ancora sull'interpretazione costituzionale', *Diritto pubblico* n° 2, 2005
Guastini, R.,
L'interpretazione dei documenti normativi, Milan, Giuffré 2004
Halmai, G. (Ed.).,
'Free Speech in United States and Canada', 55,1 *Law & Contemporary Problems* (1992) 5-33
Hartwig, M.,
'The institutionalization of the rule of law: The establishment of constitutional courts in the Eastern European countries', 7 *The American University Journal of International Law and Policy* (1992) 449-470
Harutunian, G.,
'Democratic processes and present-day tasks of the Constitutional Court of the Republic of Armenia', 26 *Review of Central and East European Law* (2000) 259-266
Henkin, L.,
'A decent respect to the opinions of Mankind', 25 *John Marshall Law Review* (1992) 215-233
Henrad, K.,
'Het Grondwettelijk Hof van Zuid-Afrika : samenstelling, procedure en belangrijke ontwikkelingen in de jurisprudentie', 53 *Tijdschrift voor bestuurswetenschappen en publiekrecht* (1998) 853-863
Hoffmeister, F.,
'Das Völkerrecht als Maßstab verfassungsgerichtlicher Entscheidungen' und 'Die verfassungsgerichtliche Kontrolle der auswärtigen Gewalt': *Diskussionsbericht*, in J.A. Frowein and T. Marauhn, eds., *Grundfragen der Verfassungsgerichtsbarkeit in Mittel- und Osteuropa*, Springer 1998, 547-550
Holle, L.,
Das Verfassungsgericht der Republik Südafrika: Entstehung, Aufbau, Zuständigkeit nach der Übergangsverfassung vom 27. April 1994, Baden-Baden, Nomos, 1997
Hsu, J.,
'Looking beyond the boundaries: Incorporating international norms into the Supreme Court's constitutional jurisprudence', 36 *New Mexico Law Review* (2006) 75-98
Iwanicki, J.,
'The Universal Declaration of Human Rights in the Supreme Court of Canada', in W. Sweet, ed., *Philosophical theory and the Universal Declaration of Human Rights*, University of Ottawa Press 2003, 127-142
Iwasawa, Y.,
'The Doctrine of Self-Executing Treaties in the United States: A Critical Analysis', 26 *Virginia Journal of International Law* (1985) 627–692

Jackson, V.C.,
'Constitutional comparisons: Convergence, resistance, engagement', 119 *Harvard Law Review* (2005) 109-128
Jackson, V.C.,
'Constitutions as "Living Tree"?: Comparative constitutional law and interpretive metaphors', 75 *Fordham Law Review* (2006) 921-960
Jacobs, F.G.,
European Community Law and Public International Law – Two Different Legal Orders?, Vortrag am Institut für Internationales Recht an der Universität Kiel, 20 April 1983
Jain, M.P.,
'The Supreme Court and Fundamental Rights', in S.K. Verma and K. Kusum, eds., *Fifty Years of the Supreme Court of India: its Grasp and Reach*, Delhi, Oxford University Press 2003, 1-100
Klabbers, J.,
'International law in Community law: The law and politics of direct effect', 21 *Yearbook of European Law* (2001) 263-298
Klug, H.,
'Introducing the devil: An institutional analysis of the power of constitutional review', 13 *South African Journal of Human Rights* (1997) 185-207
Klug, H.,
'The Dignity clause of the Montana Constitution: May foreign jurisprudence lead the way to an expanded interpretation?', 64 *Montana Law Review* (2003)
Kochan, D.J.,
'Sovereignty and the American Courts at the cocktail party of International Law: The dangers of domestic judicial invocations of foreign and international law', 29 *Fordham International Law Journal* (2006) 507-551
Koh, H.H.,
'Paying "decent respect" to world opinion on the death penalty', 35 *U.C. Davis Law Review* (2002) 1085-1131
Koh, H.H.,
'Paying decent respect to international tribunal rulings', 96 *Proceedings of the ASIL annual meeting* (2002) 45-53
Koja, F.,
'Parlament gegen Verfassungsgerichtshof?: Sind Verfassungsgesetze zur Ausschaltung von Gesetzaufhebungen durch den VFGH zulässig?', 44 *Österreichische Zeitschrift für Öffentliches Recht und Völkerrecht* (1992) 55-61
Koutrakos, P.,
'Is Article 297 EC a "Reserve of Sovereignty"?', 37 *Common Market Law Review* (2000) 1339-1362

Koutrakos, P.,
Trade, foreign policy and defence in EU constitutional law: The legal regulation of sanctions, exports of dual-use goods and armaments, Oxford, Hart 2001

Koutrakos, P.,
EU International Relations Law, Oxford, Hart 2006

Kriegler, J.,
'The Constitutional Court of South Africa', 36 *Cornell International Law Journal* (2003) 361-379

Krug, P.,
'Assessing legislative restrictions on constitutional rights: the Russian constitutional court and Article 55(3)', 56 *Oklahoma Law Review* (2003) 677-696

Kumm, C.M.,
'Who is the final arbiter of constitutionality in Europe? Three conceptions of the relationship between the German Federal Constitutional Court and the European Court of Justice', 36 *Common Market Law Review* (1999) 351-386

Kuyper, P.J.,
'Sanctions against Rhodesia: The EEC and the implementation of general international legal rules', *Common Market Law Review* (1975) 231-244

Langa, P.N.,
'The role of the Constitutional Court in the enforcement and protection of human rights in South Africa', 41 *Saint Louis University Law Journal* (1997) 1259-1277

Larsen, J.L.,
'Importing constitutional norms from a "Wider Civilization": Lawrence and the Rehnquist Court's use of foreign and international law in domestic constitutional interpretation', 65 *Ohio State Law Journal* (2004) 1283-1327

Lasser, M. de S.O.L'E.,
Judicial Deliberations, A Comparative Analysis of Judicial Transparency and Legitimacy, Oxford University Press 2004

Lavranos, N.,
Legal interaction between decisions of international organizations and European law, Groningen, Europa Law 2004

Lenaerts, K., and de Smijter, E.,
'The United Nations and the European Union: Living Apart Together', in: K. Wellens, ed., *International Law: Theory and Practice. Essays in Honour of Eric Suy*, The Hague, Nijhoff 1998, 439-458

Lenaerts, K., and de Smijter, E.,
'The European Union as an Actor under International law', 19 *Yearbook of European Law* (1999) 95-138

L'Heureux-Dubé, C.,
'The importance of dialogue: Globalisation and the international impact of the Rehnquist Court', 34 *Tulsa Law Journal* (1998) 15-40

Lollini, A.,
'La circolazione degli argomenti: metodo comparato e parametri interpretative extra-sistemici nella giurisprudenza costituzionale sudafricana', *Rivista di diritto pubblico comparato ed europeo* (2007) n°1, 479-523
Lollini, A.,
'Legal argumentation based on extra-systemic parameters. An example from case law of the South African Constitutional Court jurisprudence', 3,2 *Utrecht Law Review* (2007)
Lutz, C.,
Kompetenzkonflikte und Aufgabenverteilung zwischen nationalen und internationalen Gerichten : erste Bausteine einer Weltgerichtsordnung, Berlin, Duncker & Humblot 2003
MacBride, J.,
'The Necessity Test in the jurisprudence of the Hungarian Constitutional Court and the European Court of Human Rights', 8 *Journal of Constitutional Law in Eastern and Central Europe* (2001) 205-227
Mahoney, P.,
'Separation of Powers in the Council of Europe: The status of the European Court of Human Rights vis-á-vis the Authorities of the Council of Europe', 24 *Human Rights Law Journal* (2003) 152-161
Markesinis, B.,
Comparative Law in the Courtroom and Classroom: The Story of the Last Thirty-Five Years, Oxford, Hart 2003
Markesinis, B., Fedtke, J.,
'The Judge as Comparatist', 80 *Tulane University Law Review* (2005) 11-167
Markesinis, B.S., Auby, J.B., Coester-Waltjes, D., Deakin, S.,
The Tortious Liability of Statutory Bodies. A Comparative and Economic Analysis of Five English Cases, Oxford, Hart 1999
McGoldrick, D.,
International Relations Law of the European Union, London, Longman 1997
Melchior, M.,
'Les cours constitutionnelles et l'épuisement des voies de recours interne au regard de la Convention européenne des droits de l'homme', in *Mélanges offerts à Silvio Marcus Helmons: Avancées et confins actuels des droits de l'homme aux niveaux international, européen et national* (2003) 231-241
Messitte, P.J.,
'Citing Foreign Law in U.S. Courts: is our sovereignty really at stake?', 35 *University of Baltimore Law Review* (2006) 171-184
Morshchakova, T.G.,
'The competence of the Constitutional Court in relation to that of other Courts in the Russian Federation', 42 *Saint Louis University Law Journal* (1998) 733-742

Nevill, P.,
'New Zealand: The Privy Council is replaced with a domestic Supreme Court', 3 *International Journal of Constitutional Law* (2005)

Novak, R.,
'Die Verfassungsgerichtshof im Dialog mit dem Europäischen Gerichtshof', in B.-Ch. Funk et al., eds., *Der Rechtsstaat vor neuen Herausforderungen: Festschrift für Ludwig Adamovich zum 70. Geburtstag*, 2002, 539-551

O'Regan, K.,
'Human rights and democracy: a new global debate: Reflections on the first ten years of South Africa's Constitutional Court', 32 *International Journal of Legal Information* (2004) 200-216

Osiatynski, W.,
'Paradoxes of constitutional borrowing', 1 *International Journal of Constitutional Law* (2003) 244-268

Pescatore, P.,
'The doctrine of "direct effect": an infant disease of Community law', 8 *European Law Review* (1983) 155-177

Peters, A.,
'The position of international law within the European Community legal order', 40 *German Yearbook of International Law* (1997) 9-78

Petersmann, E.U.,
'Artikel 234 EEC rn.8', in: H. von der Groeben, H. von Boeckh & J. Zhiesing, eds., *Kommentar zum EWG-Vertrag*, Baden-Baden, Nomos 1974

Pogačnik, M.,
Veljavnost mednarodnih pogodb v Republiki Sloveniji (Validity of Treaties in the Republic of Slovenia), Ljubljana, Pravnik, 51, 1996

Puissochet, J.P.,
'La place du droit international dans la jurisprudence de la Cour de Justice des Communautés Européennes', in: *Scritti in onore di Giuseppe Federico Mancini*, Milan, Giuffrè 1998, 781-788

Puissochet, J.P.,
'The Court of Justice and international action by the European Community: The example of the embargo against the Former Yugoslavia', 20 *Fordham International Law Journal* (1996) 1557-1576

Rakate, P.,
'A note on the certification of the Constitution of the Republic of South Africa, 1996 by the Constitutional Court', 9 *African Journal of International and Comparative Law* (1997) 934-942

Rappaport, A.J.,
'The Court of International Trade's political party diversity requirement: unconstitutional under any separation of powers theory', 68 *University of Chicago Law Review* (2001) 1429-1458

Resnik, J.,
'Constricting remedies: the Rehnquist judiciary, Congress, and federal power', 78 *Indiana Law Journal* (2003) 223-310

Rodin, S.,
'Judicial Review and Separation of Powers in Croatia in light of the German Experience', 4 *Journal of Constitutional Law in Eastern and Central Europe* (1997) 75-107

Rogowski, R., and Gawron, T.,
Constitutional courts in comparison: The U.S. Supreme Court and the German Federal Constitutional Court, New York, Berghahn Books 2002

Rosenfeld, M.,
Just Interpretations. Law between Ethics and Politics, Berkeley CA, University of California Press 1998

Rossatanga-Rignault, G.,
'*La Cour Constitutionnelle: Pierre angulaire de l'état de droit au Gabon?*', Annual conference of the African Society of International and Comparative Law (1997) 260-281

Rousseau, D.,
La justice constitutionnelle en Europe, Montchrestien 1998

Sachs, A.,
'War, violence, human rights and the overlap between national and international law: Four cases before the South Africa Constitutional Court', 28 *Fordham International Law Journal* (2005) 432-476

Sadurski, W.,
Constitutional courts in the process of articulating constitutional rights in the post-Communist states of Central and Eastern Europe, European University Institute, 2002

Sadurski, W.,
'Transnational Constitutionalism: Simplistic and fancy theories', in A. Czarnota, M. Krygier and W. Sadurski, eds., *Rethinking the Rule of Law after Communism*, Budapest, Central European University Press 2005, 9-24

Scheppele, K.L.,
'Aspirational and aversive constitutionalism: The case for studying cross-constitutional influence through negative models', 1 *International Journal of Constitutional Law* (2003)

Schütze, R.,
'Parallel external powers in the European Community: From "Cubist" perspectives towards "naturalist" constitutional principles?', 23 *Yearbook of European Law* (2004) 225-274

Schütze, R.,
'EC Law and International Agreements of the Member States – An Ambivalent Relationship?', 9 *Cambridge Yearbook of European Legal Studies* (2006) 387-440

Schütze, R.,
'Dual federalism constitutionalised: The emergence of exclusive competences in the EC legal order', 32 *European Law Review* (2007) 3-28
Schütze, R.,
'The morphology of legislative power in the European Community: Legal instruments and the federal Division of Powers', 25 *Yearbook of European Law* (2007) 91-151
Schwartz, H.,
'The new East European constitutional courts', 13 *Michigan Journal of International Law* (1992) 741-785
Schwartz, H.,
The struggle for constitutional justice in post-communist Europe, University of Chicago Press 2000
Shany, Y.,
'How Supreme is the Supreme Law of the Land?: Comparative analysis of the influence of international Human Rights Treaties upon the interpretation of constitutional texts by domestic courts', 31 *Brooklyn Journal of International Law* (2006) 341-404
Sherif, A.O.,
'Separation of powers and judicial independence in constitutional democracies: The Egyptian and American experiences', in E. Cotran and A. Omar Sherif, eds., *Democracy, the rule of law and Islam*, London, Kluwer Law International 1999, 25-44
Shkarich, S.,
'Constitutional Judiciary, Rule of Law and Separation of Powers in the Republic of Macedonia', 9 *Journal of Constitutional Law in Eastern and Central Europe* (2002) 1-50
Silver, J.G.,
'Lobue v. Christopher: Age-old separation of powers debate rages on as court rules extradition statute unconstitutional', 26 *Georgia Journal of International and Comparative Law* (1996) 247-261
Simma, B.,
'Self-Contained Regimes', 16 *Netherlands Yearbook of International Law* (1985) 111-136
Simons, W.B.,
'Russia Constitutional Court and a decade of hard cases: a postscript', 28 *Review of Central and East European Law* (2003) 655-678
Slaughter, A.-M.,
'A typology of transjudicial communication', 29 *University of Richmond Law Review* (1994) 99
Slaughter, A.-M.,
'A global community of courts', 44 *Harvard International Law Journal* (2003) 191-219

Slaughter, A.-M.,
A New World Order, Princeton University Press 2004

Sofio, L.,
'Recent Developments in the debate concerning the use of foreign law in constitutional interpretation', 30 *Hastings International and Comparative Law Review* (2006) 131-150

Sólyom, L., and Brunner, G.,
Constitutional judiciary in a new democracy: the Hungarian Constitutional Court, University of Michigan Press, 2000

Spirovski, I.,
'The Role of Constitutional Court in the building of the Constitutional Democracy', 10 *Journal of Constitutional Law in Eastern and Central Europe* (2003) 183-211

Stein, E.,
'European Political Cooperation (EPC) as a component of the European Foreign Affairs System', 43 *Zeitschrift für ausländisches öffentliches Recht und Völkerrecht* (1983) 49-69

Stone Sweet, A.,
Governing with judges: Constitutional politics in Europe, Oxford University Press 2000

Takács, A.,
'A Constitutionalist Revolutionary: László Sólyom: Scholar, Judge and President of the Constitutional Court', in G. Halmai, ed., *Constitution found?: The first decade of Hungarian Constitutional Review on Fundamental Rights*, 2002, 75-103

Tamanaha, B.Z.,
On the Rule of Law. History, Politics, Theory, Cambridge University Press 2004

Testen. F.,
In: Šturm (ed.), *Komentar Ustave Republike Slovenije* [Commentary on the Constitution of the Republic of Slovenia], Ljubljana, Fakulteta za podiplomske državne in evropske študije 2002

Thiruvengadam, A.K.,
Legal Transplants through Judiciaries: Cross-judicial influences on constitutional adjudication in the Post-World War II era. A study in comparative constitutional law focusing on theoretical and empirical issues, Paper on the Issue of Transjudicial Borrowings, New York University 2001

Timmermans, C.,
'The EU and Public International Law', 4 *European Foreign Affairs Review* (1999) 181-194

Tomuschat, C.,
'Case Note on Yusuf and Kadi', 43 *Common Market Law Review* (2006) 537-551

Triepel, H.,
Völkerrecht und Landesrecht. Hirschfeldt, 1899

Tripathi, P.K.,
'Foreign Precedents and Constitutional Law', 57 *Columbia Law Review* (1957)

Tushnett, M.,
'Referring to foreign law in constitutional interpretation: An episode in the Culture Wars', 35 *University of Baltimore Law Review* (2006) 299-312

Uerpmann-Wittzack, R.,
'The Constitutional Role of Multilateral Treaty Systems', in A. von Bogdandy & J. Bast, eds., *Principles of European Constitutional Law*, Oxford, Hart 2006, 145-181

Vallières, A.,
'L'influence des normes internationales et nationales étrangères sur les droits de la personne en Afrique du Sud', 14 *Revue québécoise de droit international* (2001) 137-187

Vedder, C., Folz, H.P.,
'Case Note on *Centro-Com* and *Ebony Maritime*', 35 *Common Market Law Review* (1998) 209-226

Verdussen, M.,
'La justice constitutionnelle en Europe centrale: essai de synthèse', in M. Verdussen, ed., *La justice constitutionnelle en Europe centrale*, Brussels, Bruylant 1997, 229-251

Verdussen, M., Karagiozova-Finkova, M.T. (eds.),
La justice constitutionnelle en Europe centrale, Brussels, Bruylant 1997

Villar-Borda, L.,
'The role of the Constitutional Court in the advance of law in a developing country', in A. Soeteman, ed., *Pluralism and Law: Proceedings of the 20th IVR World Congress Amsterdam, 2001*, Franz Steiner Verlag Wiesbaden GmbH 2003, 106-114

Waggoner, J.,
'Discretion and valor at the Russian Constitutional Court: Adjudicating the Russian Constitutions in the civil-law traditon', 8 *Indiana International & Comparative Law Review* (1997) 189-229

Webb, H.,
'The Constitutional Court of South Africa: Rights Interpretation and Comparative Constitutional Law', *University of Pennsylvania Journal of Constitutional Law* (1998) 205-283

Werhan, K.,
'Checking Congress and balancing federalism: A lesson from separation-of-powers jurisprudence', 57 *Washington and Lee Law Review* (2000) 1213-1284

Wildhaber, L.,
'Eine verfassungsrechtliche Zukunft für den Europäischen Gerichtshof für Menschenrechte?', 29 *Europäische Grundrechte-Zeitschrift* (2002) 569-574
Wouters J., and van Eeckhoutte, D.,
'Giving effect to customary international law through European Community law', in: J.M. Prinssen and A. Schrauwen, eds., *Direct Effect – Rethinking a Classic of EC Legal Doctrine*, Groningen, Europa Law 2002, 183-234
Wyatt, D.,
'New Legal Order, or Old?', 7 *European Law Review* (1982) 147-166
Yang, K.,
'The Constitutional Court in the context of democratization: the case of South Korea', 31 *Verfassung und Recht in Übersee* (1998) 160-170
Yap, P.,
'Transnational Constitutionalism in the United States: Toward a worldwide use of interpretive modes of comparative reasoning', 39 *University of San Francisco Law Review* (2005) 999-1044
Yarbrough, T.E.,
The Rehnquist Court and the Constitution, Oxford University Press 2000
Zakrzewska, J.,
'L'état de droit et Tribunal Constitutionnel en Pologne', 41 *Jahrbuch des Öffentlichen Rechts der Gegenwart* (1993) 15-27
Zifcak, S.,
'Dealing with the past: The constitutional treatment of political laws in Hungary and the Czech Republic', 4 *East European Human Rights Review* (1998) 153-185
Zifcak, S.,
'Hungary's remarkable, radical, Constitutional Court', 3 *Journal of Constitutional Law in Eastern and Central Europe* (1996) 1-56

INDEX

Cases

ARTICLES

National Constitutions

The European Council Regulation

The EC Treaty

European Convention

Vienna Convention

UN Charter

The Statute of the International Court of Justice

International Conventions

MIX
Papier aus verantwortungsvollen Quellen
Paper from responsible sources
FSC® C105338

If you have any concerns about our products,
you can contact us on
ProductSafety@springernature.com

In case Publisher is established outside the EU,
the EU authorized representative is:
Springer Nature Customer Service Center GmbH
Europaplatz 3, 69115 Heidelberg, Germany

Printed by Libri Plureos GmbH
in Hamburg, Germany